CW00546629

First Limited Print Edition
in association with *F1 Racing* Magazine

Author: Maurice Hamilton
3,000 copies

Printed by Butler, Tanner & Dennis, Frome, Somerset
Repro by Haymarket Pre-Press
With thanks to Jon Crampin, Torben Krog, John Lilley,
Sunita Davies, Ewan Buck and Steve Bidmead

Published by *F1 Racing* Magazine, Haymarket Media Group,
Teddington Studios, Broom Road, Teddington, Middlesex TW11 9BE, UK
Tel + 44 (0)20 8267 5382
www.haymarket.com
www.f1racingbooks.co.uk

ISBN 978-0-9575320-2-1
A copy of this title is available from the British Library

012
036
048
024
060
150
174
214
162
202
CIPRIANI

072
113
126
084
138
226
250
262
238
274

From guarded driver to sparky lunch companion, that's Damon Hill

Happy, active retirement Jean Alesi-style: in an Avignon mansion

This Berger enjoys a bit of 'ham', as Maurice was reminded

Österreichring 77: Alan Jones's maiden F1 win was for Shadow

The Author
Maurice Hamilton

"Time without number, I'd sit at the table and quietly reflect on how fortunate I am to chat informally with someone who, in many instances, was a hero back in the day."

Maurice Hamilton, his enthusiasm undimmed, is now enjoying his fifth decade as an F1 journalist

As writing assignments go, this one takes some beating. You have a long and enjoyable lunch with someone you've known and admired for many years, and the publisher picks up the bill. All you have to do is put it in writing. The hardest part is deciding what to leave out.

F1 Racing magazine first mentioned the idea in late 2010. It was suggested that, since I had been covering F1 since 1977, I must have met more than a few interesting people along the way and wouldn't it be a good idea to sit down over lunch and have a chat? It would be at a venue of my guest's choosing to help them feel completely at ease and encourage the flow of conversation. I jumped at the chance.

In the end, it has worked out even better than I expected. One of the many advantages of reaching a certain age is the accumulated store of knowledge and experience I've gathered on each of my interviewees. Whereas in the past, when they were drivers, officials, designers or whomever, they would have been speaking to me in the paddock as a journalist searching out facts and details that they might not necessarily have wished to impart.

Now, across a lunch table on neutral ground, the passage of time has granted us our version of an F1 Freedom of Information act that requires no coercion whatsoever. My guests could feel free to reveal what really happened, or what was thought, but which could not be spelled out at the time because of political or other pressures.

My job specification as a freelance writer and reporter has become deeply ingrained, although I'd like to think the professional sense of purpose did not stifle the passion and enthusiasm that drew me to the sport in the first place. Time without number, I'd sit at the table and quietly reflect on how fortunate I was to chat informally with someone who, in many instances, was a hero back in the day when they wore a crash helmet at work.

To say this has been a privilege is an understatement, and it is a pleasure to share these moments with you in this book. I have chosen a cross-section of 20 interviews to start what I hope will eventually become more than one volume. Each piece has had new passages included from the original interview, but otherwise the narrative has remained more or less untouched rather than being brought up to date in the light of more recent events.

So, come and join us at the table, make yourself comfortable and listen in on some wonderful stories about the sport we all love.

Maurice Hamilton
November 2013

At lunch with **Damon Hill**

"The Michael rivalry created a diversion in my mind. And he just rubbed my nose in it. I took it personally and it got to me. I defeated myself, quite frankly."

Damon Hill was one of the early interviews for this series. The plan had always been to find a lunch venue where the interviewee felt comfortable; a place where we could chat informally.

No surprise, then, that we chose the Barley Mow in Tilford near Farnham; not far from home for either of us. It was the perfect location, overlooking the village cricket green. On the bench table, a pint of lager-shandy with jacket potato, cheese and beans. Just what you'd expect from this most unassuming and thoughtful of British world champions.

Since retiring from the cockpit Damon played a major role in shaping the UK's F1 future through his work with the British Racing Drivers' Club before taking on a pundit role with Sky F1.

Rereading the interview, I'm struck once more by Damon's disarming honesty and easy conversation. He's a very different character from the rather formal and guarded driver I worked with when ghosting his columns and books in the mid-1990s.

I'd gone into this interview not really knowing what to expect and came out of it delighted with the content. Damon must have enjoyed it too: he sent a "thank you" email when the story was published; a rare occurrence in this series but, as you'll discover, very Damon Hill.

Maurice Hamilton I know we're not far from where you live, but it's good of you to take the time out. But then I suppose things have calmed down a bit, certainly as far as BRDC business is concerned. Tell me, firstly, about the feedback you've had from spectators about the revised track?

Damon Hill When you look at how a circuit is designed, you also have to think of the spectators. It's okay having fast corners with lots of run-off, but spectators are so far away that they don't get a feel for it. Monaco has the slowest average speed of all the circuits but, if you're very lucky, you can sit bloody close to the cars. You're not left in any doubt as to how fast and how powerful these cars are.

So, you don't need a fast corner to get the sense of how impressive the cars are and how good the drivers are. That was the reason for the tight section at the beginning of Wellington straight. Luffield is another opportunity for people to get very close to the cars and see their acceleration.

I mean, you can be testing on a cold day at Silverstone and there's nothing. But when the place is full for the British GP, it's a totally different experience. The stadium at Hockenheim is another place. The hair is standing on the back of my neck just thinking about it. On the old circuit, you'd go off into the woods for miles, tanking on at 200mph with not a soul in sight. Then you come into the stadium and they're letting off fireworks, there's stuff landing in the car and the whole place erupts. That's a fantastic experience.

MH How can you be focusing on driving with all that going on?

DH You've got one mind on the driving and another bit is saying: 'I'm really loving this experience'.

MH This is where you differ from we mere mortals because I'd be distracted by that. I can't do two things at once.

DH We can all do two things at once, Maurice! You're thinking now at two levels. You're here doing the interview and the other part of your brain is preparing the next question. In any sport or skill, you develop to such a high level that, after a while, it becomes automatic. You actually become a spectator of the experience.

The extreme example is what Ayrton Senna talked about when he went round Monaco, feeling he was outside his car because he had so much faith in his ability. He didn't have to consciously do it anymore. That was a very scary disconnect - but that's the thrill of it. When you do a quick lap, you're also enjoying the ride. You're very much in the present, so you're not bothered by whether you've filled in your tax form. Mind you, are we ever bothered about that?

MH Talking of Monaco reminds me that your dad, Graham, won that race five times. When you were a lad, sitting on the floor in your father's office at home and you saw all those BRDC stars and you knew how important the BRDC was, I bet you never thought you might be president one day.

DH No, I was far removed from that. But when I became president, I did think to myself: 'My Dad would be pretty chuffed at this.'

MH He would have been. Did your reflections on your father affect how you worked with Josh when your son was racing? You're a racing dad like your father was to you, and here was your boy coming through. I remember you telling me that, when you were a boy, you'd go into your dad's office and you could listen but you couldn't speak.

DH Well, I felt I couldn't speak. I probably could have done but I didn't feel like I should interrupt. "Don't interrupt," you were told. My dad was... not authoritarian, that's too strong a word, but definitely you were expected to show some respect and that was probably a good idea.

MH Your father died when you were 15. I remember seeing you when Josh was taking part in a kart race, up in the Midlands somewhere. It was cold, it was wet, it was miserable, there was a van selling horrible burgers. Josh then would have been about 15 or 16. I suppose I couldn't imagine your dad doing that sort of thing with you.

DH It was very different back then. In those days, you could make opportunities for yourself if you were younger and you could go out and work as a mechanic in exchange for a drive or something, and end up in GP racing.

That sort of opportunity has gone. I got the tail end of it. I actually got paid for driving in F3 and F3000. I had to drive shitboxes, but I could claw my way up and look for a lucky break. I could go and talk to Ken Tyrrell and say: "How about it Ken?" And he'd say: "You haven't got a hope in Hell. Go away." But at least I could do that.

Drivers today don't speak to the team owners; they don't even know who the team owners are! They've got managers and there's a different structure. Before, drivers could make a living by going from one track to another, hiring out their services.

The professional status of the driver has been shot to pieces. It's gone. In my view, if the sport was run properly there should be respect for the professional status of the driver. You should be able to achieve a certain professional status, in which case you shouldn't be required to bring investment with you.

MH One of your worst periods was during that time in F3000. You were married, and Oliver, your first-born, had arrived. The going was very tough, wasn't it? You had no drive and you were really struggling.

DH It was mad, Maurice. I was 29 or whatever. I had no money, no house and I still wanted to be a racing driver. At which point my dad, had he been around, probably would have said to me: "Listen son, it's about time you got a job." So, yes, I was probably mad. Certifiable. But it was different.

MH You drove that dreadful Footwork thing. Do you remember that F3000 car? It was a real shitbox.

DH A driver got killed in it at the end of the year in Japan. It wasn't safe. The cockpit was horrific, if you think about it now.

Regrets? One was Damon's naive take on F1 politics

MH But it was a drive. Did you think: 'I'll show what I can do in this because everybody knows it's a bad car'?

DH I just had to do better with that car than had ever been done before. That's all I did. It was the same with the F1 Brabham. I managed to get it into two races, Hungary and the British Grand Prix. I hadn't qualified at all up until then.

MH And there you were in the British Grand Prix, trailing round and the leaders would be lapping you five times. How difficult was that, because you were also test driver for Williams at the time, driving the best car on the grid?

DH It goes against all career planning and logic, but you know what? I got experience from it and that experience made me better able to take opportunities when they next came along.

MH You appreciated things more? You appreciated life more?

DH It's not appreciating. It's simply knowing what's involved.

MH A better perspective. Is that a more suitable way of putting it?

DH No, what I'm saying is, why would you put someone in the car? Can they do the job? How do you know? What have they done? It's like going for any job. What have you done before? Nothing. Or what have you done before. Well, I've written an article for a local newspaper. If you haven't written anything, you've got no chance. In my case, if you've done a qualifying session for a Formula 1 race then that's better than nothing at all. And you learn so much, whatever car you're in.

I worked with Tim Densham in the Brabham. He did something to the damping on that car. I still want to know what he did because I said: "Listen, mate, I can't drive this car, and that bump is terrible." The next day, I went over that bump like it wasn't there. It was amazing. He waved his magic wand overnight and it was just fantastic.

MH But it was a dog of a car.

DH It was - but you learn all the time.

MH As we said, you had the test role with Williams, then you were with Alain Prost in 1993. What was your attitude then? He was in it to win the World Championship...

DH Well, my view was, it didn't matter to me what Alain Prost was doing! If you had said to me three years before that I would be driving the best car in F1 and be team mates with Alain Prost, I would have said: "Take this man away. He's obviously deranged."

MH It didn't go to plan in 1994 for all the reasons we know, but it got off to a bad start because the Williams FW16, by Adrian Newey's own admission, didn't work well initially. He remembers going to a test at Nogaro. He went out and watched the car on the circuit and was appalled by what he was seeing, because the car was jumping around all over the place. Do you remember that?

DH I'd forgotten about that test.

MH Maybe it's just as well. That car was difficult to drive.

DH It wasn't very easy. It was on a bit of a knife-edge. Ayrton fell off in every single race he did, which shows it was hard to drive.

MH Putting all that into perspective is what happened at Imola on 1 May 1994. Having had this role where you were understudy, if you like, to Ayrton Senna and Alain Prost, suddenly now you were leading the team.

DH I'm not sure that I was seen as a leader.

MH That's a point actually because you did say that at the time, you felt that they didn't regard you as a leader.

DH Which I can understand because up until then I'd given every indication that I was very happy with my position as team-mate to Alain and Ayrton. Although I clearly wanted to beat them - and I did beat Alain on several occasions - I don't think I thought I was going to overturn Ayrton. I knew it was a benchmark to aim for. But I did feel after the Imola weekend that someone had to carry the load and pull these guys back up again, because everyone was suffering.

MH Monaco was a shocking weekend for you because it was the race after Imola and then you had the incident on the first lap with Mika Häkkinen. You ground to a halt

Adelaide 1994: "Up Schuey's chuff" fighting for the title

with a damaged car in Casino Square. That walk down the hill back to the pits must have been the longest walk of your life.

DH I'd clean forgotten about that. To be honest, Monaco was just a non-event.

MH Everyone was on autopilot, weren't they?

DH Yeah. It was much too soon to come back and it took a while to answer the questions: "What are we doing here? Why are we doing this?" There was a lot of nervousness in the drivers, people talking about whether or not the cars were safe and what could be done about it; press interest in taking a closer look at the ethics and the moral justification for racing and various things. And we had Karl Wendlinger have his shunt at Monaco. It was one thing after another. And then there was Andrea Montermini's shunt during practice at the next race, in Barcelona?

From Imola onwards, it was suddenly like a war zone. I mean, you can't compare it with a real war zone but for us it was going from a relatively secure environment to having the whole thing turned round on you. I think everyone was jittery. I definitely was.

MH Montermini's wrecked car, with his feet exposed, ended up near your pit. I remember seeing you at the back of the garage afterwards. You were shocked and you were very pale.

DH I just thought: "Not again. Not again. I've had enough." I love racing and everything, but I don't like people getting hurt.

MH You, perhaps more than many of your contemporaries, were aware that motor racing can do that, having being through it with your dad and his close friend, Jim Clark, being killed and so on. You knew that motor racing could bite back. Even so, was this becoming too personal? Was it too much?

DH It suddenly seemed like it was raining big accidents with people getting hurt. It was like a long overdue evening of the score. Niki Lauda said something, in that peculiar sort of perceptive way that he has, which was that when Ayrton died, he wondered if God had had his hand on F1 for a long time and had just taken it away. Suddenly, a whole lot of stuff that shouldn't have happened in the last 10 years, suddenly started happening in a flurry. It was a real test for everybody.

MH Having endured all of that up to the Spanish GP, you then went on to win the race, which was a great result for everybody, including yourself.

DH That kick-started things. I wanted to win grands prix anyway, but it was triply important to be doing it at that point. It was a way of saying: "We're not going to give up here just because Ayrton's not around." There was a sense of doing it for Ayrton; a tribute to him, in a way. Meanwhile, in the background, you've got people accusing team personnel of being responsible for Ayrton dying. It was a really, really stressful year.

MH I remember doing your column at the time. You wouldn't say much about it on the record, but you hinted that Renault [*engine partner*] didn't seem to be in favour of you.

DH People were looking round for someone who was a lead driver and the team was used to having mega stars in their team. So, here's Hill Junior. I'm sure they were thinking they needed someone with a bit more depth.

MH Did you want to say: "Oi! Excuse me! I can do the job!"

DH I was trying to say that.

MH They weren't necessarily paying much attention to you.

DH I think this is where my British diffidence, my reserved nature, went against me. I don't like to blow my own trumpet. I thought: 'Hang on a minute. How do I compare? What are my performances saying? Why do I need to say anything?'

I knew I'd never be an Ayrton Senna or an Alain Prost. But, at the time, I was in the hot seat and I felt no one else could do any better. It was slightly frustrating. Still, at the end of the day I won Sports Personality twice over, but mainly thanks to Williams and that situation. I think that happened because I'd kept my head down and kept going.

MH You say that but, at the end of 1994, you had that truly fantastic drive at Suzuka. I'll never forget that.

DH It was the time when I went out further on a limb than I'd done in a racing car for a long period of time. I never went that far again. I wouldn't have done it if it hadn't been so important. You get to certain points in your career where it is important to do

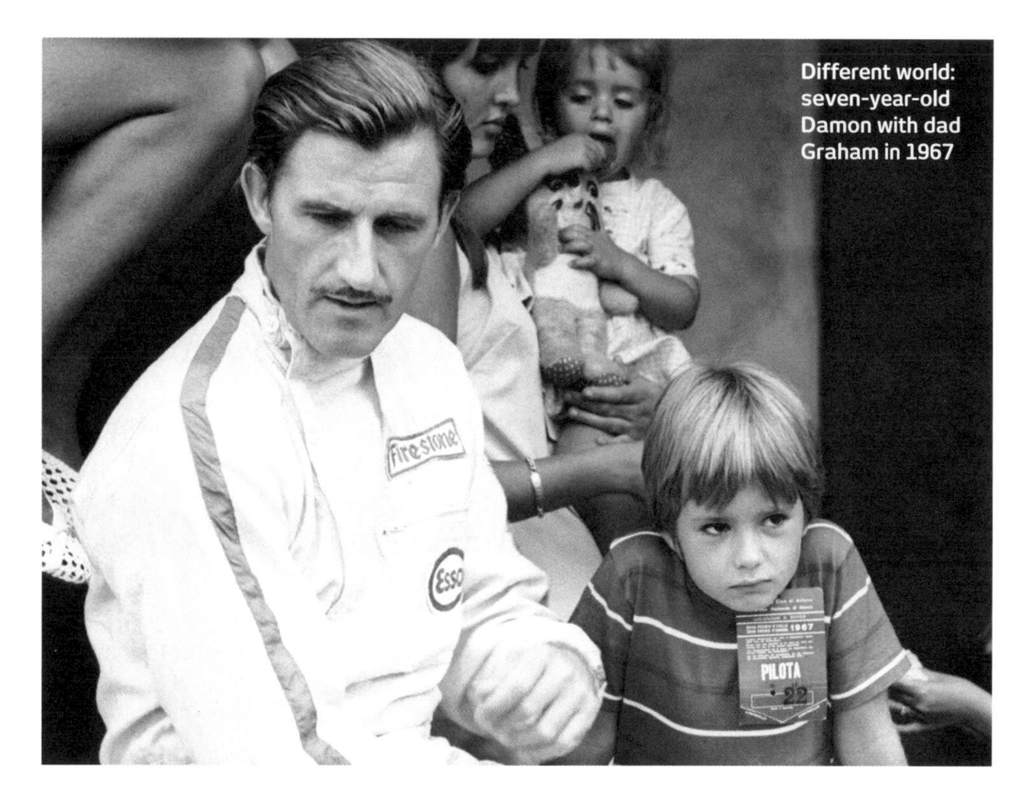

Different world: seven-year-old Damon with dad Graham in 1967

something special. I recognised that at Suzuka. It was a massive showdown and allowed me and the team to show we weren't going to go down without giving absolutely 100 per cent of everything we'd got. I'm glad I did that. But I wouldn't want to do it again!

MH You were fighting against this unseen opponent - Michael Schumacher - which was even more difficult. The race was in two parts and against the clock. You just had to go as hard as you possibly could.

DH Sometimes you're racing against something you can't see and there's only one thing for it; you've got to just drive like you've never driven before. Then we went to Adelaide for the final round - and that was Suzuka, Part Two!

MH That was absolutely brilliant. Those first 34 laps or whatever, you were right up Michael's chuff and you weren't letting him go. It was just amazing. You often get this coming at the crunch of a championship; two contenders who are on a different plane from everybody else.

DH You rise up. That's the great thing. Once you get into that zone, a lot of things happen in your mind. You realise that everything you've ever thought about in your entire life has come to this climax. So you get the best out of it. That's why sport shows such extraordinary feats because it's the crucible; it's a mixture of all of the factors. The world seems to stop in order to watch what's going to happen. You're on the spot; you've really got to perform and this has a multiplying effect.

MH And then it all comes to an end when Schuey has you off. I happened to be with you after the race when Barry Sheene arranged for you to see the video of the incident. You weren't aware that Michael had touched the wall, were you?

DH I had no idea.

MH People question why you went for that gap. But it was because you thought it was the only chance you were going to get. You didn't know he'd hit the wall.

DH That's the point. I'd watched him closely enough at Suzuka to see him nearly go off, then actually go off - but always get back on. The guy seemed to have more than nine lives. So I see he's gone wide without me realising he's damaged his car, and I thought: "I'm never going to get another bite at this one." So I went for it. And the rest, as they say, is history.

MH If you'd arrived at the corner a second earlier, you would have seen it, or a second later, you wouldn't...

DH He'd started to get away from me and I was thinking: 'Bugger!' But the reason he went off was because he was trying too hard. We'd been going hammer and tongs, lap after lap, and then he just got enough of a break on me. But that's the game isn't it? He had to get away - and he overstepped the mark.

MH There's a brilliant picture of the two of you line astern coming into the braking area at the end of the long back straight. You're both lapping someone and you've arrived just before the turn-in point, you're right-front is locked and I'll swear the Benetton and the Williams are joined together.

DH I remember! There were a couple of times I was pretty close. I was almost in his gearbox.

MH But you were braking from 180mph, plus!

DH It's not like that, Maurice. It's like driving in traffic; like around the M25. All that matters is how far the guy in front is and whether or not you can stop more quickly than he can. Saying that, I remember thinking: 'Fucking hell, we're braking late! This is just amazing!'

I think that's what must have been difficult for Michael because if you've got a guy who just will not let go of the gearbox. There's no point in me trying to pretend I'm as good as Michael Schumacher over every single lap of my racing career. But there were times when I could match him and maybe irritate him a bit - and that was one of those days.

MH He wasn't used to that. He didn't like it.

DH No, he didn't like that, because it doesn't compute in his head, does it?

MH He sort of got his own back in 1995. I don't know if disaster is too strong a word to describe that season for you, but it wasn't good, was it?

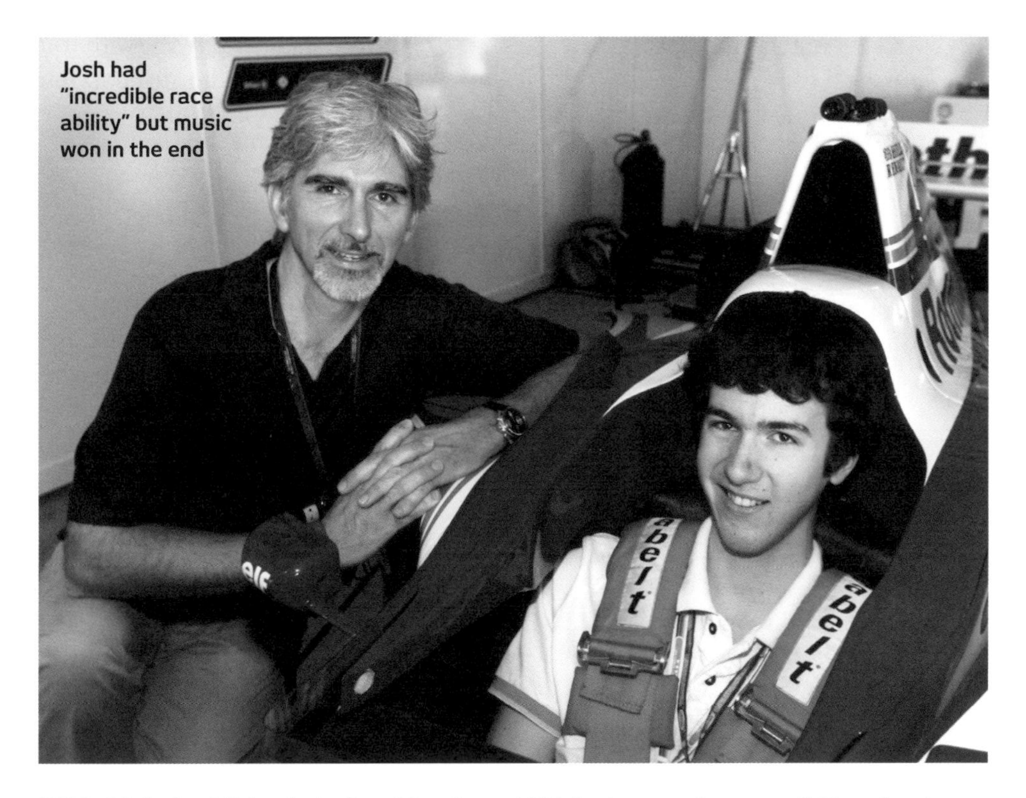
Josh had "incredible race ability" but music won in the end

DH I think the Michael rivalry thing from 1994 had created a sort of diversion in my mind. And he just rubbed my nose in it. Not that he was too bothered about whose nose he rubbed in the dirt, but I tended to take it personally and I think it got to me eventually. I defeated myself, quite frankly. And that, in my view, sowed the seeds for what happened in 1996. Because, in 1995, Frank thought: 'Damon's finished'.

MH So, that's why your contract wasn't renewed at the end of 1996 even though you'd won the championship? Your view seemed to be: 'I've won the title, so everything will be all right.' You were a bit stunned when Frank didn't seem to want to keep you.

DH I didn't understand the position team owners are in at times like that. If I'm honest, my career was a lesson in how not to do it! The fact that I got anything out of it is just a pure... miracle, I suppose.

When Josh was racing and I came across Eddie Jordan, and said to EJ: "Running my own son, I completely understand the frustration." And I could say the same to Patrick Head as well: "I completely understand the frustration that you guys must go through with drivers." There's two sides to every story. Frank told me in 1996: "I've got to do what's right for the team." Now I see that he had his reasons. It wasn't done out of spite; it was because he had to do what he had to do. That's fine. But I needed to learn that.

MH Would part of that lack of understanding account for the way you arrived in Adelaide for the last race in 1994, got off the plane and announced to the media that you weren't being paid enough? I mean, what a story for the media! We loved it. But you were going for the championship, for Heaven's sake! What was that all about?

DH Please don't! I was so naive! I'd sat the whole way on the plane with Barry Sheene and he was saying: "You're not being paid enough. You need to tell Frank he's being a mean b..." And all this stuff. And I'm going: "Yeah, you're right, Barry. That never occurred to me before, Barry." By the time I got off the plane, I was thinking of nothing else. And I know Barry would have gone to Gerhard Berger or someone like that and said: "Watch this!" I fell for it, completely. Like an idiot! I was so pumped up. I was just so inexperienced in those things. I'd no idea. What can you say?

MH Okay, let's get up to date. What's your take on F1 these days, with the tyres. DRS, KERS and so on?

DH It seems to me that there are two distinct reactions. One is: "I'm so confused, I don't know what's going on." And the other one is: "That's exciting, isn't it?" If someone has a real duff start and has the opportunity to fight their way back up to the podium, like we've seen several times, then that's good and adds interest to the race.

I think that the little flappy wing thing on the back is great to watch on TV! People love that. You wait; someone's going to appear soon in a road car with a wing like that on the back! But the tyre degradation means that drivers have to really be thinking. I have to say it looks pretty healthy to me.

MH What about the confusion factor? I've struggled to follow some races

DH There's always the danger that you've got too much artifice in sport. It used to be that drivers were admired, first of all because they were brave enough to do it. They had extraordinary skill. If you look at someone like Jackie Stewart; if he won a race by two minutes it was still an extraordinary feat of daring and skill and he was respected for that. It got to the point where Michael won every race and that was... dull. It was not very interesting. Then you bring in changes like fuel stops to spice it up - and then you ask: "Where's the race gone?" They start and then they get all muddled up and the race finishes and you can't work out what happened. That's a danger.

I think people have been sitting on the edge of their seats and thinking: "What's going to happen?" In some races, you're convinced one driver is toast and another has it made. Then you find that these arguments are flawed in some way because the tyre performance goes sky-rocketing up and then drops like a stone. The drivers are having to juggle these variables - and I think that's good. It's a bit like a wet race; lots of variables that can't be accounted for. Skill and calculation are required.

MH What do you say when people ask what you do these days? You seem very relaxed now; got your life under control.

DH That's because I don't race any more! Racing is an all-consuming thing.

MH True! What about Down's Syndrome Association? You've been playing a big part in that, haven't you?

DH I'm a patron of the Down's Syndrome Association. Also, I'm involved with a local charity called Halow, an acronym made up of the initials of children with learning difficulties. That provides what is called Nurturing Independence which gives people at school leaving age recreational activities and other social activities that will help develop independence. That's local to Guildford. That's going well but, like everything, budgets have been slashed and there is the need to raise money. I think it's important to have things to keep the mind alive. Everyone wants to have recreational or challenging things. And then I was trying to find money for Josh. So, I was back where I started!

MH You went to most of his races. Did you enjoy that? Or could you hardly bear to look?

DH I was right in there! You know what it's like with racing drivers, Maurice. It's a very touchy thing, isn't it? You can never say the right thing, whatever you do! Josh had incredible race ability. He'd done some stunning races and overtakes. Even if I say so myself, he was a good racing driver. But he had a lot to learn because he hadn't done enough karting and he couldn't switch it on immediately when he needed it.

MH When you say he was a good racing driver, what was it you were seeing that made you say that?

DH He wanted to overtake the guy in front! He seemed to be able to work things out; out-fox the other guy. I'm not sure but I think it might be the product of computer games because he's done a lot of that. There seemed to be some sort of skill he'd acquired from somewhere. I mean, how else can you spend that long in your bedroom and not turn out to be a racing driver!

MH If Josh asks how you would sum up your time as an F1 driver, what would you say?

DH I'm not making any great claims for myself. I think I was a very good driver. Put me in a racing car and I wanted to beat whoever I was racing against. I resolutely refused to believe they were any better than me. Saying that, I know where I stand in the pantheon of great drivers. I think I made the best of what I had, and that's really all you can say.

MH That's a perfect point to end on. Good to see you again and thanks for coming over.

DH You're welcome. See you at the next Grand Prix.

At lunch with **Max Mosley**

"All the beautiful people went to Ayrton Senna's funeral, but I went to Roland Ratzenberger's. To his family, it mattered just as much. It was awful. Terribly sad."

I'd had many lunches with Max Mosley, but never before on a one-to-one basis. I approached this one with a mixture of pleasure and apprehension. Max never fails to be exceptionally good company thanks to his eloquence, intellect and a wonderfully waspish sense of humour. But I knew he could also use the occasion to gently raise a few points over which we'd disagreed in the past. The problem would be that Max is always two steps ahead; it's impossible to win.

Not long after our lunch in June 2011, the closure of the *News of the World* would have brought quiet satisfaction to Mosley. The newspaper that had launched a ruthless personal attack had been brought down by allegations of phone hacking, one of the many breaches of privacy that Max subsequently fought against with typically quiet vigour. Max chose Cassis on London's Brompton Road, a French restaurant described as having "a certain Provençale panache".

Panache: a very good word to describe my guest. I was bracing myself, although I knew it would be entertaining, come what may. And so it proved.

Maurice Hamilton Good of you to come. You've been busy recently; popping up a lot in the media...

MM I'm as busy as when I ran the FIA.

MH How much of that has got to do with the *News of the World* and your privacy pursuit through the European Court of Human Rights?

MM Quite a lot, but it's really more about the general privacy campaign going on in the UK, and by no means only by me. There are a lot of legal and political things going on: it's just non-stop. It's lawyers, politicians or people who are either celebs who have had trouble, or people who are not celebs who have trouble. I'm in touch with an awful lot of people.

MH I'm sure you're more interested in the "not celebs"?

MM Absolutely, because people like that get their lives completely destroyed and they've got no come-back at all. A former tabloid journalist said to me: "When you ring into the news desk and say you've got this blinding story about this couple, they immediately ask where do they live or what are they like? If they live in a council flat, that's all right: you're told you can do whatever you like. They can't sue." So, even if they're moderately well off, then the papers know they can't sue because however strong their case, they're never certain to win. If you lose, it'll cost you a fortune. The newspapers know this and they play on it. But there are now too many people who are too annoyed, in too many different areas. What exactly will happen is another matter.

MH Are you getting a lot of support for what you're doing, for actually taking them on?

MM Very much so. We had a very modest success against the *News of the World*, but that's encouraged a lot of people, particularly in the phone hacking business, to have a go. People are very frightened of newspapers, particularly somebody who depends on the media to some extent: an actor, politician or an author; any of those. If the newspapers have got it in for you, they can do enormous damage.

MH The phrase that seems to crop up is when the papers say: "In the public interest". What exactly, in your view, is the public interest?

MM You're talking about the distinction between what interests the public and what is in the public interest. The two are by no means the same. The tabloids want to make them the same, but the judges won't stand for it. Public interest is something that you actually need to know, or as they say in Strasbourg, 'furthers debate in a democratic society'. What they mean is if a member of the public has to take decisions, and if it's something they need to know to take that decision, then it's in the public interest. If it's about somebody's private life, nobody needs to know about it. Shall we order?

MH I'd like the sea bass, please.

MM Can I have risotto? No starter.

MH I saw you on the BBC's *Question Time*, the one where you were sitting between James O'Brien, a radio talk show host, and David Blunkett. That O'Brien bloke seemed very pleased with himself. I took an instant dislike to him.

MM Everybody says that for some reason. He's got a bad manner.

MH "I'm right. I'm speaking for the people. Listen to me." There was a bit of that, wasn't there?

MM Exactly. Unlike a previous *Question Time* I was on, this one was a bit boring because it never got into anything serious. The questions weren't particularly interesting.

MH The other programme I heard was with John Humphrys on BBC Radio's *Against the Ropes*. That was tough. You had to answer a lot of tricky questions about the *News of the World* story and its allegations about you, and also about the loss of your son.

MM I think he was fundamentally sympathetic. He was asking all the right questions. Certainly, it got a very good response from the public. Humphrys said it was one of the most memorable he'd done, which was rather interesting.

MH I would like to hazard a guess as to why. What impressed me was your directness and complete honesty. I suppose you'd say: "Well, I've got no alternative. I can only answer the questions as best I can." But these were very personal and tricky questions and I thought you came out of it extremely well. I couldn't have done that.

MM Thanks. With all those things, it's extremely important never to get caught out dissembling, never mind lying. The classic example of that was Lord Browne, the former head of BP. He said in a court document that he'd met his boyfriend while running in Battersea Park, or something. In fact, he found him on a gay escort website. Well, why not say so? There's nothing wrong with that. By trying to make it sound a little bit more respectable, he lost his case and therefore lost his job. It was an object lesson in going straight down the line, for better or for worse.

MH Let's get back to when you became president of what was first called FISA and then the FIA in October 1991. We happened to meet by chance in the big dining room at the Suzuka Circuit Hotel and we had breakfast together with a couple of my colleagues.

MM Yes, that's right. I remember; I'd just been elected.

MH Yes, and you said you were going to keep a low profile; that F1 was going to run itself. Which you appeared to do for 10 years or so. But then, in the latter part of your presidency, you were quite... I would use the word "confrontational".

MM Well, that's true. My view always was that if you're the manager, so to speak, like in an hotel, a good hotel, you never see the manager because you only see him if there's a problem. So if it runs properly, if you're the person in charge, you shouldn't be visible. If you're visible it means something's wrong. Obviously I became visible to some extent following Imola 1994. But then, for the next 10 years or so, there were road safety matters and things of that kind.

"BMW were making 600 F1 engines a year. Six hundred!"

But that really changed in 2002 when it was recognised that F1 costs were getting out of control. People forget that in those days you had a qualifying car, which was completely different from the race car. You had a qualifying engine that would do the necessary extreme lap, and that was it. Then a different car was presented for the race. A company like BMW would be making 600 engines a year for one team. That includes test engines. Six hundred! It was obvious that this was not sustainable.

There was a consensus among the teams that the costs had to be brought under control, but they could never agree. In January 2003, I called a meeting of the teams and said the FIA was going to adopt certain measures, such as parc fermé between practice and the race. I'd obviously prepared the ground a bit beforehand so that I wasn't going to have them all against me. The teams were split.

I know everybody thinks I don't like Ron Dennis - I do like Ron, he's fine - but Ron went completely silent. He went into overload I think, and he didn't really react. But then he and Frank Williams decided that they were going to bring arbitration proceedings. There was a huge row.

In the end, the measures were applied. If it had gone to arbitration, I was on fairly thin ice. I had an argument but it was by no means guaranteed that I was going to win it. But it was obviously the right thing to do.

In 2004, we had the meeting of the engine suppliers in Monaco. They were collectively spending €1.4 billion on engines. They came up with a proposal, but there was also a minority report from Renault and Ford, which was going much further. I looked at both and thought: "We'll go for the minority report."

MH But it turned a bit nasty after that, didn't it?

MM Yes, BMW and Honda threatened arbitration. That's when we had the thing of me saying to them: "Look, I'm being helpful to your main company in Brussels and if you cause me enough trouble, I'll stop being helpful. I don't want either of your companies coming into F1 and messing it up."

MH Is that when we heard stories that you were quietly threatening their road car divisions in some way?

MM I think they thought that I would cause problems with the Euro NCAP for them - which I couldn't do. I didn't have the power to do that. But what we did have was the power to stop supporting the industry in Brussels, which we were doing. We were saying to them: "Okay, we've got to do these things on safety but we'll also help you on all sorts of other things." We'd become quite influential in Brussels and I said we would simply stop helping them with other matters. That was quite effective. In the end there was no arbitration.

MH But surely the problem always was, if they have the money, they'll spend it?

MM True. The fascinating thing was that these very tight regulations completely failed to reduce the costs because all that we did was reduce the horsepower gained per million euro spent.

So then we said, "Right, we're going to freeze the engines." The experts told me you've got to freeze all the moving parts; that's the expense. That happened but then the engine people started doing research on air intakes and exhausts. This was in areas where, I'd been told by the experts, they would find maybe two horse power. So, if they spend millions, it doesn't matter. One company found 30bhp just in the airbox.

We started reducing the number of the engines and all of this was massively confrontational - which brings me back to your original point. But, if you were to ask Sir Frank Williams now, I think he would confirm that if we hadn't done those things five or six years ago, then they wouldn't be in business now. So, yes, it was confrontational. But there was no alternative.

MH Okay, so we're talking about necessary legislation. But what about Spygate? That was massively confrontational.

MM First of all, on the mobile, I had Ron saying they'd just raided Mike Coughlan's house and taken this information, which they knew nothing about. That it was a great shock.

Then Jean Todt, Ferrari's team principal, came on and told me his side of the story and this fascinating thing about the information being taken to the photocopy shop. I was on holiday at the time and I just sat there, thinking: "Oh, no..." Because that meant the end of the summer as far as I was concerned. I knew this was going to cause endless aggravation.

Hamilton, in the wars at Monaco 2011, here collecting Massa

MH It was massive! We knew there had always been a bit of furtive spying here and there – but never anything on this scale.

MM Exactly. So we summoned McLaren in front of the World Council. It was blindingly obvious they were guilty and most of the people on the council wanted to convict. I said we hadn't got the evidence and if we find them guilty, we'll be challenged in court and we'll lose. So, we acquitted them.

Then we had the McLaren emails which showed that it was quite simply untrue that nobody else knew. But they still went on, trying to pretend. We sent in a team of IT specialists and they went through 1.3 terabytes of emails; that's something like 85 million pages, but there are ways of doing this. Then we found the killer email, the one from the chief engineer on the '07 car to his equivalent on the '08 car, saying something like "Are we sure about this? Did we get this from our mole at Ferrari?"

It was getting to the stage when, really, they should have been thrown out of the championship. We'd had a big argument on the World Council because I wanted to exclude them from the championship, and probably for the following year. But that would have put them out of business, which nobody wanted. There were 1300 jobs there. So that's why they came up with the $100 million fine.

Then, you see, what you might call the stupid section of F1 – which is quite extensive and well-led by a fully qualified person – said the £100 million was disgraceful, and so on. Well, it was a lot better than putting McLaren out of business. That's why they didn't appeal. The fact that that company didn't miss a beat and won the championship the following year shows that the 100 million was by no means disproportionate.

MH The impression, rightly or wrongly, was that there seemed to be enmity between you and Ron - perhaps going back to certain things you'd said. I can remember one press conference...

MM I know what you're going to say..

MH It was at Magny Cours and you referred to Ron as perhaps not being the sharpest knife in the box.

MM Yes.

MH So you'll understand why we felt that.

MM I've actually tried quite hard with Ron. I once had dinner with him. I said look you've been really successful, just relax. I think he thought I was patronising him. It's quite sad for someone not to be able to enjoy life and be pleased with his success. He just seems unable to do that, which is a shame.

MH Going back to Indianapolis 2005. That is one area where I found it difficult to agree with what you were doing - as you're probably aware. I was re-reading the full page comment we gave to this in *The Observer* and, looking at it from my angle, you were in Monte Carlo and you appeared to be not very accommodating. We had this situation - and never mind the fact that Ian Phillips and I had to talk about six cars racing for an hour-and-a-half on BBC 5 Live! - I thought it was handled badly. How do you look back on it now?

MM At the time, I thought I was doing the right thing, but I wasn't certain. Subsequently, I'm absolutely certain. There were three points. The first is that if we changed the circuit without going through our procedures and there was an accident and somebody got hurt, there would be nowhere to hide.

MH Yes, I understood that.

MM Point two: to change the rules because some of the competitors had brought the wrong equipment was wrong in principle. Take the Hahnenkamm: if some of the teams turned up with the wrong skis, not the proper ones for downhill racing, you wouldn't then change the course into slalom to suit them. You'd say: "Well, do the best you can."

It's a sporting matter and you cannot change the rules to suit the majority when it's they who have brought the wrong equipment. There was no excuse because Michelin raced there the year before. They went to the edge - and got it wrong.

The third point is that Flavio Briatore and Bernie Ecclestone and some of the teams had decided that, if they refused to race, we would have to give in because we would have a nothing race. The drivers wanted to race but were told: "It's okay, go out, come into the pits and then they'll change the course and we can have a normal race." I knew they were going to do that. It was an attempt to strong-arm. But there were at least three solutions - I can't remember what they were now.

Indianapolis 2005: fan reaction to a six-car race

MH One was to drive through part of the pit lane; one was for the Michelin runners to stop and change tyres, neither of which were accepted by the teams.

MM That's right. They were determined to have a confrontation and win. I couldn't, even if I wanted to, give in on the first two points. The fault - and I suppose I would say this - the fault was entirely theirs because they didn't appreciate that even if I had wanted to, it would have been wrong for me to give in. I don't like giving in, anyway. But it would have been wrong. We also said you can slow down going through the troublesome banked curve.

MH Ah yes, I remember; but I just couldn't see how that would work.

MM The way it would work is that you'd have a speed trap and any of the Michelin runners that exceeded a certain speed would have a drive-through.

MH I couldn't see how those drivers would know by how much they had to back off.

MM After one or two drive-throughs, the Michelin runners would have found a way!

MH But surely it's dangerous to have such a speed differential on a fast part of the track?

MM They're used to it. You race at Le Mans and you have a much greater speed differential.

MH Michelin refunded the gate money and, to my surprise, the fans, or most of them anyway, came back the following year. So, I suppose you're going to say it worked out okay?

MM It was absolutely the right thing to do. But it was a very, very difficult decision.

MH Going back to our breakfast at Suzuka in 1991, you were replacing Jean-Marie Balestre. Have you seen *Senna*? The clips with Balestre talking to the drivers...

MM Yes, it all came back to me!

MH The thing is, we've never seen behind-the-scenes stuff like that before. We weren't fully aware of just how barking mad he appeared to be.

MM I went to see it as the guest of a firm of lawyers in a private cinema. When it got towards the end, I left. I couldn't really face talking to people about it. You see, I didn't go to Ayrton Senna's funeral; I went to Roland Ratzenberger's instead. All the beautiful people went to Senna's and I thought somebody needed to go to Ratzenberger's because, to his family, it mattered just as much. It was awful for them; for everybody. Terribly sad.

But, as you say, when I saw Balestre in the film, I was thinking: "I can't believe what it was like back then!" One forgets. Extraordinary behaviour.

When they have American soldiers in a camp, every three months they make them go out and camp in the woods for a week. You know, really cold and horrible. You give them a really hard time and as a result it seems so nice by comparison back at the camp that they won't complain. Well, I should have arranged for Balestre to come back for a month each year, just to remind people how bad it could be! It might have made things a bit smoother for me.

MH Were there any other memories invoked by the film?

MM Senna won the championship and then he let rip in a press conference. Ron, quite rightly, was very alarmed and concerned that Balestre, who was still president of the FIA and very powerful, would do him by not giving Senna a licence or whatever. Ron came to me and said: "Ayrton needs to apologise but he absolutely refuses to. Will you talk to him?"

So I invited Ayrton up to my little suite - I always got on quite well with him - and I said: "Ayrton, there's two kinds of people in the sport. There's amateurs and there's professionals. The amateur does what he feels like doing; the professional does whatever will further his career. What you did about Balestre was amateur."

He thought for a long time, and then he said: "Yes, you're right. But what you've got to understand is that I've been doing this since I was six years old and it's all I do." And his eyes started to well up. He was so emotional. We cobbled together a weasel statement that was put out. It wasn't really an apology, but it was close. And that was the end of it.

MH The problem was that Balestre was so inconsistent, particularly in his treatment of Prost and Senna in successive years in Japan.

MM When Senna and Prost had their coming together at the chicane in 1989, Balestre just fixed the whole thing [*which had Senna excluded and gave the championship to Prost*]. I was outraged. It went against all my instincts. I would never do that. People used to think I spoke to the stewards; I never did in the entire 18 years. There was one occasion when, wrongly, they rang me up to ask my view. I said: "Well, I'm going to give you my view but you don't need to follow it."

In 1990, Balestre was furious with poor old FIA Race Director John Corsmit saying that he should have penalised Senna for having Prost off instead of letting Senna win the championship. Arguably, that was right. But it wasn't Balestre's role. Balestre was the legislature, not the judiciary. He didn't understand about the separation of powers.

It's like these half-wits in Parliament and the House of Lords who "out" people under Parliamentary privilege. It's an abuse of the constitution; it's absolutely and fundamentally wrong in a democracy - but they're too stupid to understand that.

MH Do you think Ayrton's behaviour in 1990, when he drove Prost off the road at Suzuka, and the fact that he got away with it, set a bad example? Michael Schumacher seemed to adopt that tactic more than once.

MM I think, possibly, it did. It was wrong. It was understandable - but wrong. But it started with the great wrong of the previous year.

MH Talking about Senna, 1994 became a very difficult year for you in the aftermath of Imola - particularly following Karl Wendlinger's accident two weeks later at Monaco. I remember *L'Equipe* becoming hysterical and publishing a full front page picture of Wendlinger's car and shouting from the headline that this should be stopped. You had to be seen to be acting. And quickly. How difficult was that?

MM It was becoming pressing within some of the company board rooms. For instance, as you say, that picture of the crashed car with the big Mercedes symbol on it. The annoying thing is, you try to get something done about safety and nobody will listen. "No, we haven't had an accident for years." Then an accident occurs, which is going to happen sooner or later, and people start running around like headless chickens. You need a bit of balance.

You need to appreciate that it's a dangerous sport and you must do everything you can to make it safer. When an accident does occur, you've got to be quite calm, saying this is really unfortunate and there may be lessons to be learned, but we've done everything we possibly can.

People talk about living on the edge and things like that. Then when somebody actually gets killed, it's a total disaster in the minds of the same people. There's no balance. So you have drivers 20 to 30 years of age and our job, my job, was to see that they lived to 70-80 years, whatever.

MH Seeing Sergio Perez's accident at the same spot as Wendlinger's 17 years before and watching Perez being removed almost unharmed... did you take some comfort from that? In 1994, he might not have survived.

MM Yes, there is a lot of satisfaction in that. But the most far-reaching thing after Senna was that I set up this committee with Professor Sid Watkins. I said to Sid quite early on: "Let's have a look at what the governments are doing for the roads because they're killing 50,000 people a year in the EU. There must be some massive research going on and we can feed off that and learn."

But when we looked into it, we found that they hadn't changed the crash test regulations for road cars since 1974. There was a massive lobby from the industry to downgrade some of the tests. For instance, in side-impact tests, rather than focus on the door, which is more realistic, the industry were trying to get the test down to where the sill is because that is a natural strong point. So, we mounted a campaign to stop the industry doing that. We started Euro NCAP.

There were a lot of crash tests going on, but to different standards. It was obviously necessary to form one group and we managed to get the governments together. The opposition to NCAP from the industry was massive. Then Louis Schweitzer, who was the head of Renault, saw the opportunity to move Renault from being seen as not at all safe to being right up there among the safest. And very quickly. Renault suddenly became the first manufacturer to get five stars.

The NCAP has saved, I think I can say thousands, certainly hundreds of lives. The European Commission said it had advanced road safety in the EU by five years. That is the biggest improvement in safety since the seat belt. It's massive. That all came from Senna; that's what gave it the impetus.

MH That must give you more satisfaction than anything.

MM In the end, when one is finally sitting in a rocking chair, you want to feel that you've made a difference - and that's made a difference. There are lots of other things that have been satisfying - but that made a difference.

MH Okay, you were a racing driver, then you started March Engineering in 1969 before moving on to assist Bernie and FOCA in the fight with FISA and then you became president of the FIA. When you're sitting in that rocking chair and thinking back on such a varied life, which aspect will give you the biggest glow? I don't necessarily mean the most successful period of your life, but the one you enjoyed most.

MM That's a good question. I think probably the period after stopping March, when I was concentrating on FOCA, and we started organising the odd Grand Prix; stuff like that. It was fun. The FIA presidency was very satisfying, but my whole 18 years was spent in a constant haze of irritation. There would always be something happening that you really didn't want; something annoying or people being tiresome. A big person in F1 asked me recently if I would come back and I said nothing would induce me.

MH The days you're referring to - the battles with FISA, Jean-Marie Balestre and so on - must have been right up your street. It required a bit of politics, manoeuvring and out-thinking the opposition, a bit of fun, getting the teams together, going racing. You're still a racer at heart, aren't you?

MM Yes, very much so.

MH Bringing us up to date: what is your view on Lewis Hamilton as a racing driver? I love his free spirit behind the wheel and would hate to see that crushed. But perhaps he's been trying a bit too hard; overdriving, if you like.

MM Yes, I think he overdid it - in Monaco, certainly. And he probably knows better than anybody. He's been trying to make up for having a slightly inferior car, which is understandable. But the thing that upset me about what Lewis said afterward the 2011 Monaco race was that nobody got the point of the Ali G joke. You see, the whole thing about Ali G was that he wasn't black; but he wanted to pretend he was and he wanted to absorb this culture as a young white person. Any time anything happened that he had the slightest objection to, he'd say: "Is it because I'm black?"

The way I interpreted Lewis was that he wasn't saying it because he was black; he was using the catch-phrase as a joke. But the unfortunate thing is that most of the British press would fail to get it because it's a long time ago now. And, of course, the continental press would completely think it was racist.

MH Are you saying you were an Ali G fan, Max?

MM Yes, I used to love watching him and his successor, Borat. It just makes me laugh so much. But, getting back to Lewis, I thought, 'Lewis, you can't do that', because people just won't get it. And there was so much pompous stuff written as a result. I think he is a thoroughly good person. I like Lewis.

Sorry, I think I've got abandon you. I have an appointment at 2.30 and the traffic is terrible in this part of London.

MH Not at all. It's been most interesting, as ever.

MM Lovely to see you and catch-up. I must say it's nice to be able to do things like this and to sit at home, watch the races and not think when something goes wrong: 'Oh dear, everyone will say that's my fault.'

At lunch with **JEAN ALESI**

"Being in a Ferrari is like going into the grandstand, taking the biggest fan and saying, 'you go and drive'. When I drive the car, I'm so happy. I give my maximum!"

I'm often asked which of my lunch interviews I enjoyed the most. I can honestly say that each and every one has been a joy, quite often for different reasons. But if you were to ask which one makes me smile and chuckle over more than any other, it has to be the day spent in company with Jean Alesi at his home in Avignon.

Only Jean Alesi could have Pepe, a mad Italian who runs a pizzeria, come to his 15th century mansion and cook a three-course lunch, accompanied by wine from my host's vineyard. And then, after a wonderful few hours spent reminiscing, drive me round his home town and have us go for supper at Napoli Mia, Pepe's crazy restaurant - complete with Lambretta scooters hanging from the wall.

Then, the final bonus. Jean had booked on our return flight to London and he needed a lift to Marseilles airport. It goes without saying that he drove the 90km. I would not have believed that a BMW 1 Series hire car could go that quickly. I don't think he lifted once. And somehow - don't ask me how - the traffic seemed to melt from the outside lane of the Autoroute de Sol as Jean casually flashed the headlights and continued to chat nonchalantly - as if this was the sort of thing he does every day. Which, of course, is exactly what he has always done. It could hardly be any other way with such an effervescent character so in love with driving quickly.

Maurice Hamilton This is a beautiful home. You've come a long way since you left your parents' place here in Avignon and moved in with Eddie Jordan and his family in Oxford.

Jean Alesi I was not speaking English at all and my brother, Jose, came with me. I always mention my brother because he's looked after me since I was a little boy; he means a lot to me. He stayed with me for two days and then had to come back to France. The next night, Eddie says we going to have dinner with Rick Gorne, the guy who was working with Adrian Reynard. They had a lot to drink. A lot! I had to put them in the car and I drive these two through the centre of Oxford and I'm thinking I've made a huge mistake. But, after that, everything was fine! It was really a good time.

MH Eddie says he wanted you to stay there because he felt you needed to have a family around you.

JA Yes, it's the way I grew up. I was living in my family home, here in Avignon. I was pretty young although when I was doing F3 in France. I had my truck and my car. I was doing everything myself; mechanic as well as driver. But I'd never lived outside France. So Eddie was the key to the proper start of my racing life.

MH What I find difficult is that even though I'm from Ireland, I cannot understand what Eddie says sometimes. So I don't know how you managed!

JA For me it was okay because I thought that was the way to talk!

MH Dear God!

JA Eddie did so much for me, particularly the deal to get into F1 with Tyrrell - but he insisted I keep doing F3000 for him to win the championship in 1989; which we did.

MH The first time I met you was at the British GP that year. You probably won't remember but there was a driving promotion on the Thursday, with Camel I think...

JA At the Green Man pub?

MH Yes! You won a little trophy for driving a Land Rover or something in a competition.

JA I still have it. Do you want to see it? The only trophy I have here in my house is for my victory in Canada in 1995. Otherwise, my mother keeps my trophies, my overalls; everything.

MH You and I have spoken many times about Ken Tyrrell. What a wonderful place to go when you're starting F1.

JA I have many stories with Ken, but the one I like the most was Monza in 1989. It was only my fifth race in F1. It was raining in Friday practice and nobody was going out. Ken asked if I wanted to have a try. At Curva Grande, I spun; a 360 degree spin at 300km/h. But I didn't touch anything.

I came back to the box and Ken asked if everything was okay. I said: "Yeah, it's a bit wet, I prefer to wait." There was no telemetry then, of course, but Ken could tell something was wrong. He came back and asked if something had happened. I said: "Well, I had a small spin." He said: "Okay, we have a T-car, so don't worry. Go out and get some confidence with the car." It was unbelievable because, basically, he was saying okay, you can go and crash! But he gave me a lot of confidence because that spin had really scared me. And he understood something had happened.

MH That Tyrrell 019 was a nice car, wasn't it?

JA It was a dream car. It's like when you put on a glove and it fits your hand 100 per cent. A good front end; good traction. When you lost the rear it was okay to control. It was fantastic.

MH You were working with Harvey Postlethwaite who was a very clever guy: very British. He told me a story about you at Monza in 1990. You knew that car was going to go well there and, in qualifying...

JA I remember! Qualifying tyres were good for one lap and then they'd be finished. We had Pirellis and you could have them shaved and they would be good for another lap. So, they wanted me to wait...

MH The way Harvey described it to me was: "So we agreed with Jean what we would do. Jean said: 'Yes, yes, okay; we wait.' So I'm standing at the pit wall, with my back to the garage, and I hear an engine start behind me. I turn round – and Jean's gone!"

JA [*laughing*] That was my really weakest point. No patience. And specially for qualifying. I wanted to do it now, now, now! I don't care if the track is going to be faster later. The car was so good. I had to do it!

MH Your enthusiasm's incredible. You've always had this?

JA Always, always.

MH For everything in life? Everything you did, or is it driving you love most?

JA I would say only for driving because I have a passion there, you know. So you can imagine what it was like at Ferrari. I had the best time of my life because of the passion I had from the fans and the mechanics and everyone. Unbelievable.

MH That must have been fantastic for you. Particularly with your Sicilian background, and you speak Italian.

JA Yeah, but in Italy it's not always good if you are from Sicily! What I loved was the feedback I had from the public, because they want the guy in the Ferrari; it doesn't really matter where he is from.

MH How did you deal with the Italian media? Was that something you hadn't experienced before, particularly when the car was uncompetitive?

JA No experience, but I loved it. They gave me shit when I deserved it, what can you say?

Canada 1995: Alesi en route to his single Formula One win

MH What a difference to go from Tyrrell in that little wood yard, to Ferrari. A massive difference from the point of view of the way the team was run, the culture, everything. How did you find that?

JA It's all on the good side because you have more assistance, you have more support at Ferrari. It's not something more complicated actually; it's just better. Also, in my time, the F1 driver had more space, more privilege. Ferrari respected the driver a lot more. Now they control the driver. In my time it was more or less the opposite; the driver was controlling the team.

MH Do you not think Alonso's got control and a say in the team? Are you saying it's not as much as he would have had in 1994, had he been there?

JA Yes. In my time, it would have been a bigger place from his point of view. We had the T-car, we had the testing: we had more ways to show the power of the driver. Now, everything's less. Even when the driver talks, there's always someone next to you, to listen to what you are saying.

MH You had a bad start at Ferrari and 1994 was a difficult year. To my surprise, I discovered that your first-ever pole position was at Monza that year. You're the guy that's always fast and full on. But only two poles. Why do you think that is?

JA First, I drove a Tyrrell. So I was never going to be on pole. Also, Senna was there, so nobody was ever to make a pole position when he was around. Nobody! Then I moved to Ferrari when the car was not competitive. But, yes, that was a very dramatic year for me. First I broke my neck. After I finished third in Brazil, I came back to test in Mugello. At Arrabbiata I spun and flew into the wall. My car was destroyed. When I hit the concrete wall, I broke the C2, C3 and C4 vertebrae in two. I woke up in the hospital with a big pain in my arm. The doctors said to me: "Nothing is broken, you can go."

I took my car and drove back to Avignon. When my mother asked if I was okay, I said I had a small accident but it was okay. But my mother was not happy about this and she organized an X-ray. When they saw I was not 100 per cent, I called Jean Todt and he immediately arranged a scan in Paris. They put me in a collar immediately and I didn't race at Imola.

I was on the pit wall when Ayrton died. So it was a dramatic year for me in many ways. I was still hurting but I came back at Monaco.

MH I seem to remember 1994 Monza: you were leading, you needed that win so much and... you're holding your head, Jean! Sorry to remind you.

JA It was the pit stop. Then, you had to do it in neutral. When everything was ready, I opened the clutch - I used the foot clutch because it was faster - then the throttle and, when I took first gear, the revs were too high, the gear came in and exploded everything. The race after that, we had a limiter, so no problem. But, for Monza - bang!

MH You were very upset. You threw your helmet against the wall and you left immediately.

JA I was very upset because it was so difficult to put everything together. When everything looked like it was together, something always happened.

MH And you drove back to here, I think.

JA Very fast! A record! With Jose. Monza happened three times like that.

MH Okay, let's move on to something more positive; your win in Canada in 1995. How do you look upon it now?

JA It released the pressure I had in me, having felt so close a victory before. Finally I had won and I could tell myself everything would get better. So it was a very, very good feeling. But it was not an exciting feeling like when I finished second with the Tyrrell in Phoenix 1990 [*after fighting for the lead with Senna's McLaren*]. It was totally different. During the last laps in Canada, I was listening to everything; really taking care. I wanted to cross the line. It felt like an endurance race.

MH At least in Montreal, there was a good atmosphere. A lot of Ferrari fans come to this race in North America.

JA When I was leading, the grandstands exploded! The first win for Gilles Villeneuve was in Canada, with number 27. For me, it was my first win with Ferrari 27. So, the people linked Gilles Villeneuve and my win. They seemed to adopt me after that.

MH There are many similarities to your attacking driving styles.

JA Gilles was my hero because, this was when I was growing up. The things he did...

MH Zandvoort... dragging the wheel behind him in the 1979 Dutch Grand Prix after the Ferrari punctured the left-rear going into the first corner and Villeneuve drove a complete lap back to the pits?

JA Yes, and Monaco 1981, when he won with a car that was jumping and sliding around. Incredible. And his fight with Arnoux at Dijon for second place in 1979.

MH I'll bet you enjoyed the last lap of this year's British Grand Prix with the fight between Hamilton and Massa. Maybe this is a good point to ask what you think about racing in 2011?

JA The last 10 laps always seem to be the best time because of the tyres.

MH Do you think the tyres alone are enough? That we don't need DRS?

JA I do, because the DRS makes overtaking fake. You should be on the limit when overtaking. The problem they face now is the steering wheel, with all the buttons. People believe the driver presses a button and he overtakes. They believe he presses a button and he brakes. Press a button and the car turns. All those things on the steering wheel give an impression that kills everything the driver is actually doing. If the steering wheel had no buttons, I'm sure the drivers would have more respect from outside.

MH What about the race tracks these days?

JA Abu Dhabi, for example. There's no corners; it's just chicanes, left, right, left. There's not somewhere like Tosa or the corners at Suzuka. I think you know what I mean, because we've been together at Abu Dhabi.

MH Yes, we have! They've only got those quick corners at the back of the circuit, two right-handers and you tried to take the second one flat when I was with you in the two-seater F1 car.

JA [*laughs!*] Yes, yes! I remember!

MH We'd had dinner the night before with Johnny Herbert, and Johnny was winding you up, saying you couldn't take the second right-hander flat in the two-seater. I was with you when you went out for the first time...

JA Yes, and they say one out lap, one flying lap and in.

MH Exactly. So, on the flying lap, you try to take it flat and have to lift. But then you don't come into the pits. You start another lap! I'm thinking: "Jeeezzz... I know what's going to happen here!" Sure enough, you take it flat - and we end up on the Astroturf and then onto the run-off, all sideways. The guy gives you a bollocking when we get back. And we're killing ourselves laughing because I knew exactly what you were trying to do. Fantastic!

JA [*giggling*] Yes, I know! I knew you'd be okay, so I had to try!

MH That's the sort of thing Gerhard Berger would have done. You were with Gerhard for five years; three with Ferrari and two at Benetton. That must have been a great time.

JA Ah, Gerhard... He's the most political guy I've ever met; so clever to get the team on side with him. He's fantastic. I'm a bit sensitive, particularly when he was making political stuff that was not nice for me... like when he decided my engine was better and I'd find they'd be changing my engine and when I asked they'd say: "Gerhard says this will be okay."

There are lots of stories. Like qualifying at Monza in 1994. When I crossed the line, the flag came out. I'm on pole for Ferrari and it was a fantastic moment for me. I've loosened my belts and I'm responding to the crowd. When I arrive at Ascari, I see a small red image in my mirrors. It's Gerhard, coming flat out, even though I know the chequered flag has been shown. I didn't know whether to go left or right; he was coming like a rocket. I made a decision - but it was where he was going. Gerhard spun and crashed into the barriers. It was a massive shunt, but he was okay. I thought: "This guy is going to screw my best moment."

So, when I arrive in the pits, everybody was panicking because they think he's dead! I said: "No, he's not dead! I saw him." But Jean Todt says: "Let's go to the medical centre."Gerhard was laid on the trolley - and he was covered in dust! He says: "You're a fucking asshole." I said: "Gerhard! The session was finished! What were you doing?" He said, "Me? You were trying to get out of the car!" I said I could do what I liked because the session was finished. I had pole position! He said: "Ah, okay, okay". And that was it! But no one was celebrating my pole position!

MH Gerhard tells the story about testing at Silverstone with Benetton. He was on rain tyres, came into the pits, said the track was dry and you could go out on slicks. But it wasn't dry, was it?

JA I say: "Okay. Slicks. Let's go!" I arrive in Becketts flat out. It was wet. Big spin! That was a typical trick. I loved it! Okay, Pepe has lunch ready. Let's go through.

MH You've got to tell me the story about putting Jean Todt's car on its roof. Is that true?

JA Yes, yes! We were at Maranello. I was doing some things in the office and Gerhard was supposed to be testing across at Fiorano. He came into the room, wearing his overalls, and asked if I could take him to the track. He said he would find a car. Outside in the car park was a brand new Epsilon 10 with leather upholstery, everything. He said: "Okay, let's take this one."

He gets in and pushes the passenger seat as far back as it will go. We go through the factory gate onto the street and he pulls the hand brake. But we do not have much speed and so the car just goes a bit sideways. Then flat out to the track, through the gate and past Mr Ferrari's house. When I make another turn near the garage, he does it again. This time we have more speed - and the car goes onto its roof. The roof was touching the steering wheel!

Home fit for an F1 extrovert: Alesi plays host in Avignon

I was not wearing a seat belt, so I was on the floor. But Gerhard was hanging upside from his seat belt. He was laughing so much, he undid the belt and fell down. The car was so badly damaged that the mechanics had to open the back to get us out.

Jean Todt and John Barnard arrive. I think I'm in the shit because Gerhard says this is Todt's car and it's not his problem because I was driving. The mechanics have covered the car over and Todt didn't see anything.

He asked if everything was okay. I said yes, although I had a cut on my head and was trying not to show it. Typical Gerhard, he then asked Todt: "Have you spoken with Jean yet? He had an accident." When he asks me what Gerhard means, I say we were driving to the box - and we turned over. He says: "What do you mean?" He doesn't know! I said we came to a corner and Gerhard used the handbrake. Then Jean saw his car - and went completely mad! "What have you done? For six months I've been waiting for this car!" He called Montezemolo. It was so typical Gerhard.

MH You're very trusting, Jean. You're what we'd call an optimist.

JA Always! Because I believe if you live your life and do the best, you have the best. That is the way I feel. That way, I'm very affected when it's finished and I didn't reach what I wanted to reach. For a moment, I'm really down. But the next day I wake up and say: "Let's try again."

MH This food is superb. What have we got here?

JA Mozzarella with artichoke, prosciutto, egg plants and salad, with vegetables from here. Then two specialties of Pepe from Napoli: seafood pasta and limoncello tiramisu.

MH And a glass of your own Clos de L'Hermitage. Santé! You probably didn't feel like saying that after some of the drives later in your F1 career.

JA Yes and no. I went to Peter Sauber and said I want to drive with you. I wanted to find a place more or less close, like Tyrrell, a team with a real owner and not just a director like Flavio Briatore [*at Benetton*]. I believed this was a place to restart again, or finish very well. I faced some technical problems at this time; we had a gearbox with the clutch behind the gears and it was breaking all the time. Except for that, I felt good. But when Alain Prost asked me to go with him, I went there because we were very, very close friends and I believed it would be good to finish my career with him and a French team. But it didn't work.

MH I have to say I was a bit surprised when you joined Prost's team. Was Alain finding it one thing to be a winning driver and another to run a racing team? They're quite different, aren't they?

JA Definitely. Alain is very good in many things but in this particular position, he was not good. There was a lot of pressure, from Peugeot and so on; it was not an ideal moment for him.

MH Have you ever thought about running a team?

JA No. Because I'm sure I'm not able to do it. What I like is the atmosphere. I have the feeling for what is going on. When I go to a race, I understand completely what's right and what's being done wrong. I feel it. But to be the boss and say: "Do this, do that." No way.

MH And then you went back to EJ for a few races. What was that like?

JA I loved this time! It was not easy as a driver because Jarno Trulli was with me; he was very competitive in qualifying. Then Eddie took me to one side and said: "Look, Honda want to have Takuma Sato, so I don't know if I will keep you or not." So I said: "I don't care; I'll do my best and we'll see." When they decided to have Sato, that was when I immediately said: "Okay, I stop." But it was so good to be with Eddie again. I had good races - Spa, for example where I finished fifth. It was not easy because we had the two McLarens and two Ferraris at the front; it was very competitive at that time.

MH Had Eddie changed much in the time since you last raced with him in 1989?

JA Yes. He had changed because now he wanted to save the team. He was getting to understand how difficult it is to find sponsorship, so he was very busy all the time working on this.

MH He'd gone from the excitement of going forward with F3000 and thinking about F1, to the point where he was keeping an F1 team going and not having much fun.

Hockenheim 1996: Alesi gives Gerhard Berger a lift to the pits

JA Exactly. It was a huge responsibility.

MH Talking about old friends, I'm thinking of Martin Donnelly and wondering if you've seen the film *Senna*?

JA No, I've not seen it.

MH It shows clips of Martin's accident at Jerez and it really reminds you of how severe that crash was.

JA Martin is a fantastic guy. When he crashed, I could see it was not good. There were 10 minutes of qualifying left and Ken said I didn't need to go out again if I didn't want to. I decided not to. Ayrton went back out and put the McLaren on pole.

MH Yes, they make that point in the film. The film also reminds us what a mad man Jean-Marie Balestre was.

JA Ha! You probably only know the half of what he was like! But, you know, Balestre was influenced a lot by Alain. He was doing more or less everything Alain wanted. This is a funny story but it shows what I mean. We were at Monaco in 1991 and Balestre came to speak to him. Alain was carrying an open-face helmet for the scooter. He said to Jean-Marie: "I have a problem. Can you help?" Balestre says: "Yes, yes. What's happened? Tell me!" Alain says: "Look, I want to race with this helmet because in the streets, in the town, it's difficult to breathe, but the FIA say 'No'." And immediately

Balestre says: "No, no. You can do it! I say it's okay!" Alain starts laughing and he says: "What's wrong? You don't like?" Alain says: "The helmet is for the scooter!" Balestre laughed a little and then he left. But he was going to agree – just like that!

MH If you had the chance to race competitively again – not in F1 – would you like to?

JA Yes, I would. And I prepare myself now for the moment when it arrives.

MH So, you have something planned?

JA Yes, but I can't tell you what it is!

MH Okay, can you go as far as saying it might be something you haven't done before?

JA That could be true. Enough questions, Maurice!

MH That leaves plenty of scope for speculation! [*It turned out to be an unsuccessful attempt at the Indy 500*]. I see you have your gym here, so you are working hard. I hope whatever you do allows you to race in the wet; you always were fantastic. What's your best memory?

JA Suzuka 1995: I'm second on the grid. It was wet but I'm penalised for a jump start. I'm so pissed off because the grid is downhill and I'd said the car might roll a little because I was using my left foot for the clutch and I needed to get on the throttle with the right as soon as the lights come on. I came in for the penalty and it was not raining any more. I said I will be back straightaway for slicks. My engineer said it was too early but I was not listening to anyone! I came in for slicks; I was last. After 15 laps, I was second, one second behind Michael. Just like that. I did a 360 on the straight – I did everything! But, I caught Michael so fast that he went on the radio and asked: "Is he on the same lap as me?" And then my gearbox explodes. Pah!

MH I also remember Magny-Cours when you were on slicks. Very spectacular. Remind me of the story.

JA Ah yes... During the race, it rained and everybody stopped. Except me. And I was going faster than everyone because I had found grip in the wet during practice. At one stage, there was so much water, I made a 360 on the straight. And then the engine broke.

MH Do you know what strikes me? I had forgotten how many good results you were denied by mechanical problems of some sort. With the reliability we have today, you would have been winning loads of Grands Prix.

JA Please! Don't remind me. I finished second 16 times! But, eight times I had the lead in the pocket and then – boof! It's fantastic what they do now. Incredible.

MH Okay, best not to think about that... This tiramisu is to die for! Wonderful. I put a message on Twitter to say I was coming to see you, and had lots of responses.

JA Really?

MH Yes, loads. One guy said to tell you he was in Canada in 1995 and will never forget it. Another said: ask him about Martin Brundle!

JA Ah okay! We had a few moments! Martin was a super driver. I mean, he fought with Senna in Formula 3. So he was part of the Senna era which, I have to say, is not fair for Martin because he deserved more than what he got. But sometimes he had a way to drive which had me exploding! But nothing bad. We're okay. I respect him very much, as I think he respects me.

MH Have you ever thought of going into television, like Martin?

JA I do work for Italian TV in Milano, before and after the races. It's good to keep my name in front too, because in Italy we have the best audience in Europe. Ferrari is the reason.

MH And, of course, you were very much in the mould of what people expect a Ferrari driver to be. Doubtless you know about the banner at Monza in 1996 saying: "One Alesi today is worth 100 Schumachers tomorrow"?

JA I loved being there so much. I try to explain it by saying being in a Ferrari is like if you go into the grandstand, take the best fan and say okay you go and drive the car. It's the same. I'm such a big fan of Ferrari. When I drive the car, I'm so happy. I give my maximum.

MH That doesn't seem to have changed at all, Jean! Thank you for such a wonderful lunch in this magnificent home. It's been fantastic.

JA No problem, Maurice. Now, I show you round Avignon. We take your car... I'll drive.

MH I was hoping you'd say that!

At lunch with **Niki Lauda**

"Ferrari gave me this medical check which I hated and felt was unnecessary. They drove me crazy, the Italians, with their mafia-like organisation."

This was classic Lauda. I offered to fly to Vienna and have lunch with the minimum of disruption to his day job as boss of his airline, Niki. He replied, saying he would talk but he hadn't time for lunch or any of that social nonsense. He would be at the Nürburgring, working for German television (this predated his current role with Mercedes F1). We were to meet in Bernie Ecclestone's personal hospitality area run by Lauda's old friend and fellow Austrian, Karl-Heinz Zimmermann.

To be honest, it was less than ideal, particularly on a cold damp day and in a busy period at the motorhome just after qualifying had finished. At least, I knew if Lauda had promised to talk, he would.

Sure enough, he arrived on time, walked briskly to the table, sat down and barked: "Okay, start!" Lauda doesn't suffer fools gladly; you have to be prepared. There would be no small talk; I would somehow have to get the point across that this was a chat as opposed to just another interview.

I produced a photograph I knew he had never seen before. Having engaged his sharp mind, he eventually undid the toggles of his typically unpretentious duffle coat and leaned forward: a major concession; we were getting somewhere. In the end, the coat was undone and he was reluctant to finish.

I had been concerned that this might not work, but I should have known better. Ask the right questions and Andreas Nikolaus Lauda never sells you short.

Maurice Hamilton I want to show you this photograph.

Niki Lauda I'm like a little boy! Where's this?

MH It was Mallory Park, March 1971. I believe it was your first F2 race?

NL Could have been... don't remember. How did you get this?

MH I took it! I was just a fan at the time and in those days it was very easy to get into the paddock. But I don't know why I took a photo of you; you were a nobody at the time!

NL Correct! The thing that interests me is the ring I'm wearing. This was my family's signet ring; look, there's a family crest on it. I don't know how to say in English, but it was handed down from my grandfather and my father...

MH We would call it an heirloom.

NL Okay. It was given to me and, at this time, I was still thick enough to use it! My family was a kind of, what's the word: aristocrat? These funny people; in England there are a lot of them! In Austria, there are less. Anyway, I was very young - you can see here the way I looked - and I thought that wearing this ring was the right thing to do.

MH But it's on your left hand, which suggests you were married.

NL I wasn't married; nothing like that. I didn't even know how wear it properly; just shows how stupid I was. I remember soon after this, I threw away the ring, left behind the images of my family's upbringing and good manners and all that and decided to try to be a proper racing driver. So, this is a very interesting picture because I had completely forgotten I actually had this ring on when I started racing. Thank you for showing me this.

MH This is such a fascinating period because you were in F2, which was a really important series with all the top drivers doing it as well as F1, and here you were, aged 22, in a works-supported March. I know you paid for this by the extraordinary business of borrowing money from a bank against an insurance policy on your life, but what a way to start your top-line career. You had Ronnie Peterson as your F2 team-mate! How good was that?

NL Ronnie was my master at the time. I stayed one apartment above him in a house near Heathrow. It was a big place and I shared the flat of Mike Hailwood; he let me live there.

MH Ah, was this the famous flat at Heston?

NL Yes, correct; Heston! Ronnie and Barbro lived below me and he was the master because we were together at March. He had this big Mercedes, a V8 or something, and I remember very well driving to the March factory in Bicester, and he was always braking with the left foot. I said: "Why are you braking with the left foot?" and he said: "Because this is training." I was thinking, what's he training for? In those days you had a clutch and changed gear with the left foot: the right was for the brake and throttle. But he was so flexible that he could brake with either foot, without even showing that he was braking. That really impressed me at the time.

So when I was racing against him, I knew what he was doing because he was the fastest man. I only beat him once in a F2 car. That was at Rouen and it was only because I was using a different rear wing. Mine was better for the very fast bends on that track. But otherwise it was really hard to beat him because Ronnie was just so bloody quick.

MH There were other downsides to having Ronnie as a team-mate; such as the way he would think a bad car was okay because he would drive round any problems. I'm thinking specifically here of one car: the March 721X, the one with the transverse gearbox. This was your first F1 car – and it almost wrecked your career in 1972.

NL Correct! I remember Ronnie was testing this thing with the sideways gearbox for the first time. He was the number one driver, I was the schoolboy, and he ran and ran and said the car was good. Then I got in at the end of the day. I did two laps and said this is the worst car I've ever driven. Robin Herd was impressed by my words; he was not happy – but impressed. Ronnie didn't understand what I was talking about because he was balls out and couldn't even tell how good or how bad a car was. And then, as it turned out, the car really was a piece of shit. A total disaster.

MH You had to race that car and I remember seeing a picture of you spinning it in the wet at Monaco.

NL It was completely unpredictable; impossible to drive. It would oversteer, then understeer, had no downforce and was slow in a straight line! It did nothing right. But the worst thing for me came at the end of the year when Max Mosley told me that I can't drive for March anymore because they had no more money. So, I'd paid for this drive in F1 and was suddenly sitting there with a load of money owing to the bank and no drive after a disaster year with this 721X.

MH And yet you managed to convince BRM to give you a drive in 1973. You wouldn't have got that for nothing. How did you manage to persuade Big Lou Stanley, boss of the BRM team, if you had no money?

NL I told him that I had a sponsor – which I didn't have! I convinced him to run a fourth car [*alongside Jean-Pierre Beltoise, Clay Regazzoni and Vern Schuppan*]. Stanley was negotiating with me in Vienna airport with a bank manager I brought along. I had borrowed money to convince Stanley the bank could be my new sponsor. The bank manager didn't speak English very well and I was translating – to suit me, you might say. I made a deal that I had to pay the first amount of sponsorship to BRM in May.

So, we get to May and, in Monte Carlo, I was lying third in the BRM for a while and the Ferraris were behind me. Stanley called me afterwards and he said: "Where is the money?" Of course, I didn't have it. I thought that was the finish. Then he said: "I know that you have difficulties but you impressed me so much that I'm going to give you the drive until the end of the year without sponsorship." I signed the contract that evening.

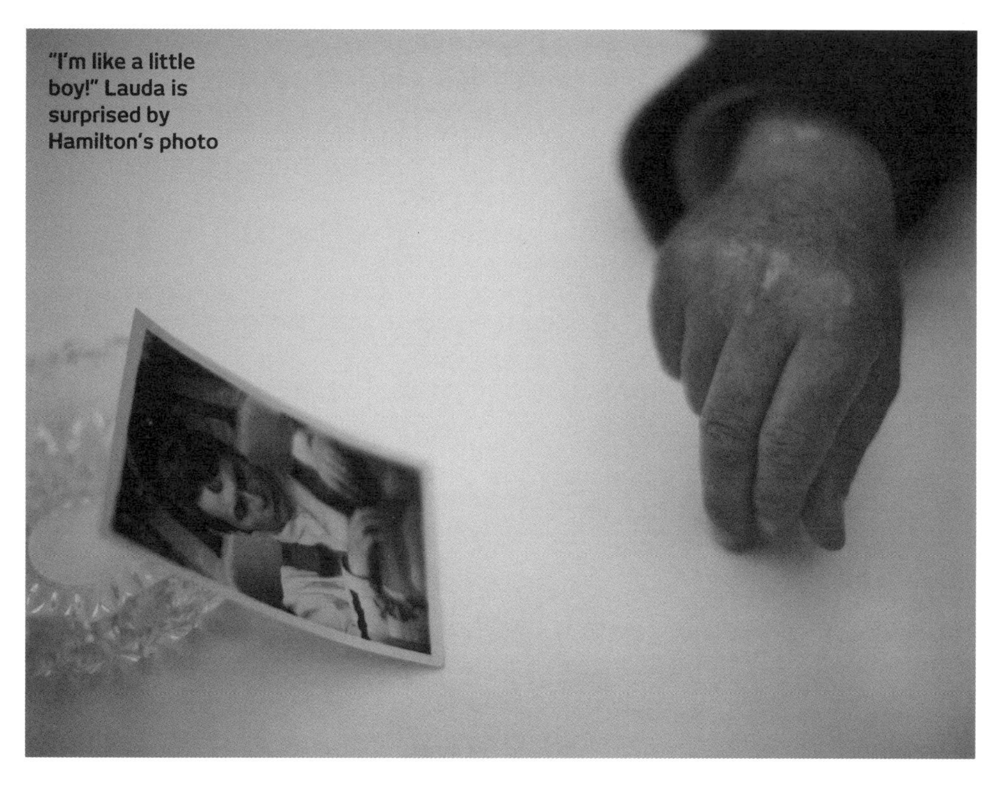
"I'm like a little boy!" Lauda is surprised by Hamilton's photo

MH I didn't realise you'd actually signed a contract.

NL I did, and that caused a problem I didn't expect. I had my cousin's secretary work for me in a little office. We had this joke running for about a year; every time I'd leave the office, I'd say: "Whenever Ferrari calls, then tell me!" On the Monday when I got back from Monte Carlo, she said: "Ferrari called." I said - something not very nice! She said: "I tell you, Ferrari called! Look! Here is the number. Here is the name, Mr Montezemolo". I thought: "Shit! She's not joking."

Next day I was down in Italy and Mr Ferrari said he wanted to sign me up. I said I had made a deal with Mr Stanley and Ferrari said he would take care of that. I signed with Ferrari on the Tuesday.

MH That started okay because the 1974 Ferrari was a good one. But I remember being here at the Nürburgring in 1974. You were leading the championship, and...

NL Crash! And I didn't win the championship.

MH Yes, on the first lap, you collided with Jody Scheckter's Tyrrell, just over there, at the Nordkurve. You won the championship the next year but, if you're going to talk about crashes, then obviously I have to mention your big one here in 1976.

NL Like Vettel today, I was leading the championship that year by far. And then, as you say, the big crash, the big mess. I got the last rites and all this which you know; I don't want to repeat all that again. But I was still in the lead of the championship before the last race, in Japan, and lost it by one point to James Hunt. I didn't lose the championship because I didn't drive in the rain in Fuji [*Lauda stopped after a few laps*]: I lost the championship because I missed three races.

MH Germany, Austria and Holland. And James won two of them and scored points in the third. Despite all the stories - certainly in the British press - about you, the nasty Austrian in a Ferrari, against the dashing British blond hero, you had a really good relationship with James, didn't you? Why was that?

NL Of all the drivers, James was the one I was able to communicate with best because I knew him from F3 when we raced against each other before F1. So, I had a good relationship with him and I liked the way he lived his life.

MH He was like you; a bit of a rebel. Is it true that, when you were fighting for the championship in Canada, you actually had hotel rooms that happened to have an adjoining door and, on race morning you marched, fully kitted in overalls and helmet, into his room, gave a Nazi salute and said: "Today, I vill vin ze championship!" and then marched back out?

NL [*laughing*] I cannot remember that exactly but it's possible because we were always doing things like this, and making jokes about each other and him being bloody British.

MH I think that story was in James's book. I also recall seeing a photo of James sitting in the cockpit of your Ferrari in the pit lane somewhere. Can you imagine that happening today?

NL No way! It's so sterile today.

MH For me, one of the greatest stories of 1976 was your comeback at Monza, six weeks after the crash. That really was a big deal, not just for you, but for the media. Take a look at these cuttings. This one is of a piece by Ian Wooldridge, sadly no longer with us, but one of the finest sports writers of his generation. Very British; very old school. Wooldridge rarely covered F1 but your comeback story was so big he was sent to Monza. You probably guessed what would happen. You were hidden away in some remote hotel.

NL That's right. I can't remember where, but it was away from everyone else.

MH Wooldridge, the crafty old fox, used his contacts in Milan to track you down. He says in the piece that he was the only journalist to do so. He was waiting for you at the hotel - and you weren't pleased.

NL I don't remember him - but that would have been the case!

MH Look, here's the story across two pages - and the only quote from you is this single paragraph, stuck in the middle. That's all he got! Apparently he said, in his very British way: "Mr Lauda, I have been sent from London to speak to you" and you replied: "You haff two minutes!"

NL [*laughing*] Probably. He was lucky to get that much! There was a lot of pressure because they did this medical check for me, which I didn't expect. Ferrari was trying not to make me race there. Mr Ferrari told me at the test at Fiorano: "Don't go to Monza because if you lose the championship, it's better like this." I said: "Commendatore, if I'm ready to race, I race." Then, on Thursday, they gave me this medical check which I hated and which I felt was unnecessary. They really drove me crazy, the Italians, with their mafia-like organisation.

On the Friday I could not drive. I got out of the car because I was frightened. I went to the hotel, thought about it, took it easy on Saturday and then got going again. But there was a huge pressure - so your poor journalist guy had no chance of getting anything!

MH What was the medical all about? They didn't have those as a matter of course in those days, did they?

NL Correct. They said it was to improve my racing! On the Thursday the organisers came to me and said I had to go to the hospital and do a medical check. But in those days there was no law requiring this. Willi Dungle [*Lauda's health guru*] went with me. They checked me and I said: "What the hell are you doing? I'm fit. It's my decision."

But the worst thing was at the start on Sunday. Nobody told me that they had changed the start system to lights. I came to the grid and looked for the fucking man with the flag. I'm out of gear - and the light comes on. I didn't know and therefore I was 13th on the first lap. Ferrari forgot to tell me that the system had changed while I was in hospital. So, I was way back. I was frightened in traffic again. I hated this.

MH And the whole thing must have been made even more difficult because you were making this comeback at Monza - of all places.

NL A crazy place. I remember walking out of the paddock and there was a woman at the fence with a little baby. I had the police around me to protect me and she was holding the baby towards me and I'm thinking: "What's going on here?" It was like she was treating me as if I was God. I'll never forget this sight... Crazy!

MH So here we are at the 'Ring, 35 years on from the accident. Do people still ask you about it?

NL All the time! But that's okay. I was doing something just now with German television and they showed the accident again. I said: "Why the hell are you showing this again? Do I have to cry or what?" They thought I was serious!

MH You've been to the scene of the crash at Bergwerk a couple of times, haven't you?

NL Yes, I went out with Karl-Heinz and Bernie a couple of years ago to do something for television. It was so funny because six Germans cycled by and they saw me. "Oh, Mr Lauda! What are you doing here?" Karl-Heinz came right in the middle and said: "We're looking for his ear!" These people, they were so upset, they nearly hit him! "You cannot do this to Mr Lauda..." But just before they came, Karl-Heinz had thrown a pig's ear into the grass. So then he produced the ear and they suddenly understood it was a joke!

MH After all that, it must have been a wonderful feeling to win a Grand Prix again - South Africa at the beginning of the following year - but it wasn't an easy win, was it?

NL For sure, it was the best result ever for me. It was a race I will never forget because Ferrari put this stupid Carlos Reutemann in the team. They said he was developing the car - blah, blah, blah! In Brazil they gave him a special wing which I didn't get and he won the race. So he was the number one guy. There was a pressure on me like you would not believe. I was leading the race and I had two problems: I hit a piece of wreckage from Jacques Laffite's Ligier and my car started to understeer. And then Jody Scheckter started pushing me. I said to myself: "After my last year's experience with the accident and so on, there's no fucking way this guy will pass me." I remember this clearly. I had to drive tactically, blocking him through the last corner and then accelerating like crazy because the only place you could pass was into the first corner. I drove away from him, thank God, because in the last six or eight laps I had the oil pressure warning light because my radiator was damaged. So I had to brake less hard and make the engine survive - which was a clever move because the engine blew up after I went over the finish line!

MH Tell me about the time when you were consultant with Ferrari in the late 1990s.

NL It was good! Luca di Montezemolo asked me to help him. One of the things I did was call Jean Todt. He was running Peugeot then and I asked him to come to Salzburg. We had a talk and then I went to Montezemolo and said: "This is the only man for you." They wanted this other guy as team manager- a stupid, idiot Italian; completely useless. I got Todt in and after two or three years he was pushing me out. I didn't know why. I was only a consultant because I was running LaudaAir at the time. I really had no time anyway to do the job - which they had offered me in the first place; I hadn't gone looking for it. Then I had other things happen which meant I couldn't have done this consulting even if I had wanted to.

MH I think I know where you're coming from. A couple of years ago, I had to write a story for a monthly sports magazine. They had a regular feature known as 'Triumph and Despair' in which a sportsperson would discuss the highest and the lowest points of their career. I did one with you and you said there were two high points: winning your third drivers' championship by half a point from Alain Prost in 1984 and winning the South African GP we've just talked about. I fully expected you to say the Nürburgring crash was the moment of despair but you said no way; it was the terrible tragedy when one of your LaudaAir aircraft crashed in Thailand and the subsequent battle you had with Boeing.

NL That's correct. I was operating Boeing 767s, brand new airplanes and one crashed coming out from Bangkok, killing everyone: 223 people. When I was in motor racing, I had taken the decision to risk my life. But when you run an airline and more than 200 people want to go from A to B and they don't arrive - that's a different responsibility.

The first decision I took was to go straight to the scene of the crash. It was in a remote

Testing at Fiorano in 1974, with Enzo Ferrari looking on

forest. I've never in my life seen a disaster like this. I'd never seen dead people without heads, without arms, with the local people stealing rings and watches from the remains of these people. It was the worst experience you can possibly imagine.

I was flying these planes myself as a pilot and I had to find out why this airplane had come down. The problem was the flight data recorder was destroyed and the voice recorder, which was still there, showed that the flight was normal. Then, suddenly, there was a huge noise in the cockpit. The pilots only spoke to themselves, not with each other.

I knew something must have happened so fast that these two guys didn't even have time to communicate with each other. This was my first reaction but, as the flight data recorder was not there, nobody knew what had happened. So, for eight months, it was my fault and LaudaAir's fault that these people got killed. This was the worst thing for me. I had to give a press conference to explain what I knew and I said if this is my fault then I stop LaudaAir and I stop running an airline because I am not capable of doing it.

This was a tough statement at the time, but it would allow me to concentrate completely on finding the cause. It took a long time to get all the computers from the engines and everything worked out. It was a failure on the design of the thrust reverse system. Basically, an O-ring in a direction control valve failed and the thrust reverse deployed.

MH On just one engine?

NL Just on the left engine. Therefore the left wing stalled at 28,000 feet and the airplane turned over. The airplane crashed because of a design mistake on the thrust reversal system. I was pushing and pushing to get the truth. It was really annoying because all our airplanes were flying worldwide. What happens if the next one crashes? So there was a huge fight between me and Boeing to get this thing resolved because my only interest was to find the cause and fix the airplanes, so that travelling is safe. This was a huge mess. It was clear that the reverse thrust had deployed in the air but Boeing did not want to say anything.

MH I remember you saying that the moment your patience ran out came at a mass burial for the last unidentified passengers.

NL Correct. It was in Bangkok. I went there to pay my respects. There were 23 unidentified bodies. All their friends and loved ones were there and no one could tell them why this had happened. This was a very difficult time for me. I decided to fly straight to Seattle and have this dealt with properly.

MH Were Boeing suggesting the plane could still be flown, even if reverse thrust had been deployed?

NL Everyone thought that an airplane could continue to fly under those circumstances - but it was clear to me it couldn't. I flew via Hong Kong and there was a pilot from Boeing coming in the other direction. I met him at the airport and asked him what was going on. He said I should try to get in the simulator because they had tried to save it with reverse thrust deployed and no one could handle it. He knew they had done this.

When I got to Seattle, they would not let me fly the simulator. I said: "Listen, this was my fucking airplane, my name, my damage... so let me do it." They eventually agreed. I tried several times to recover the aircraft, but it was impossible. It was absolutely clear why the plane had crashed. As soon as the reverse thrust comes out, the airplane turns over. You can do whatever you want, but you cannot control it.

I asked Boeing to issue a statement. They said they couldn't because it would have to be checked by lawyers and it would take another three months. I said: "Okay, tomorrow I will hold a press conference here and say we are going to take a 767, load it up like it was with my two pilots, deploy the reverse thrust in the air and everything will be okay. I'll be on board and you can show me that it works. Simple. I will ask you to do that for the sake of all the passengers." I went back to my hotel - and they were waiting for me when I got there. They issued the statement.

Finally it was all over. This was the first time in eight months that it had been made clear that the manufacturer was at fault and not the operator of the airplane. But the thing I did not understand was why it took so long to do these things because this was a safety issue. My company had the plane crash, I felt responsible but out of it came the discovery of the fault and the knowledge that such a problem will never happen again.

MH On a lighter note, tell me the story about how people - Austrian Airlines, I believe you suspected - had tried to spike your inaugural flight from Vienna to Sydney.

"The best result ever": Kyalami in 1977 with runner-up Scheckter

NL On the day before the flight, I had a phone call from an official in Canberra saying my airplane books did not turn up in time. They were technical books for the 767, so they said they couldn't give permission to fly over Australian air space. I said: "What do you want me to do? I have 223 people all ready to go." He said: "I don't care." So I said: "Neither do I. I'm coming so, if you want to stop the flight, you'll have to shoot me down!"

MH [*laughing*] Did you actually say that?

NL I did! So I flew the plane to Bangkok and got start up clearance from there because, thank God, they didn't know about what had happened with the Australians. I flew down to Australia and there was the mayor of Sydney, the music band and everyone there to inaugurate the new flight. I told them it was easier to win three world championships than to fly to bloody Australia! We had given the passengers a voucher because it could not be a commercial flight. It was the best PR I ever had because, on television I said: "Whoever wants to go back to Bangkok free of charge, then come to the airport." Suddenly, lots of people turned up - and we got our permission.

MH What happened to LaudaAir in the end?

NL Very simple. Lufthansa was the first part-owner of LaudaAir. Then Lufthansa asked me if Austrian Airlines could be my partner. I agreed to it because on the economy side this was the most sensible thing to do. But my biggest mistake was that I tried to make two different cultures work; you had the state culture of Austrian Airlines trying to work with LaudaAir private culture. This never worked out because the Austrian Airlines shit destroyed LaudaAir. In the end they had an option to buy my shares. This was part of the original deal, so I sold them and left.

I was blocked from being in the business for three years, but then I started a new airline. It's called Niki, because I can't use the name Lauda anymore. We've been going for seven years – and I'm blowing Austrian Airlines off again. We've four million passengers in six years. It's funny because Austrian Airlines always blame me and everybody else, but now I have the second airline and, again, I'm profitable and they still lose money.

MH But you're not doing long haul, are you?

NL All Europe. It's like an easyJet concept, but better. Low cost with quality. We're working together with Air Berlin because I need the critical mass. We are 138 airplanes together. I've 21 in Vienna; Airbus and Embraer. I fly still myself, two or three times a week, but only the Airbuses.

MH And your television work with RTL means you can still go to the races.

NL I like it, it keeps me involved. I still do my work with the airline, but I enjoy this.

MH Knowing how pragmatic you can be, I presume you accept that change in F1 is something that happens. No point in being misty-eyed about the past?

NL Correct. It is a normal development. You have to live with it, but I think the paddock is a little sterile today. I tell you a funny thing. Ron Howard, the guy who made the film *Apollo 13*, and writer Peter Morgan were at Silverstone filming the movie *Rush* about the 1976 F1 season. I invited them in and Bernie was kind enough to give them tickets.

They both said: "What's wrong here? Because you come in, you've got these huge monsters of motor homes, but there's no life, there's no atmosphere, there's no emotions. Has it always been like this?" I said: "No, look at my time. This is why you're going to do this movie. It has not always been like this, but unfortunately this is the way F1 developed." It was interesting to see the reaction of these two guys. They were not speaking in a negative way. They liked being there but they felt there could be so much more. They were just asking if this was normal. You know what I'm saying?

MH Yes, I do. And it was doubly unfortunate because the new paddock at Silverstone is completely soulless. But that's the way Bernie likes it. Will you tell him about this?

NL No, I won't, I don't want to get involved. I've told Bernie a hundred times: "Let the people in. Get the whole thing alive!"

MH Sums you up, really. After your experience here at the 'Ring in 1976 and Thailand in 1991, you tend to see life a bit differently from the rest of us?

NL Correct. Okay, I gotta go to a stupid meeting somewhere. I've enjoyed this.

MH Me too. Thank you.

Argentina 1973: a relieved Lauda joins BRM after a miserable 1972

At lunch with **Sir Frank Williams**

"Adrian Newey should get far more than an OBE. What he's done for three British teams is an amazing achievement, when you think about it. No one else has come close."

Sir Frank Williams and his love of motor racing never change. The boyish enthusiasm remains undimmed, despite threads of tragedy and personal difficulty laced through 114 wins, seven drivers' championships and nine constructors' titles.

The 2013 season may have been one of the worst for Williams since the flaky days of the mid-1970s when he lived hand-to-mouth before the formation of Williams Grand Prix Engineering in March 1977, but such setbacks do not diminish the familiar grin as he contemplates the next race.

It has always been like that with Frank, from the day and hour I first met him at the launch of FW06 in the team's original factory in Didcot. If anything, the terrible road accident that almost killed him in March 1986 sharpened rather than dulled his desire. Life in a wheelchair is better than no life at all and allows him his continuing passionate involvement in an automotive world that has intrigued and driven Frank since he was a young boy.

This style of interview was made for Sir Frank. He likes nothing more than a good chat about all things Formula 1. Not one to dwell on past success or reach for the rose-tinted glasses, he nevertheless enjoys a lively discussion on the past, present and future of a business involving anyone driving racing cars - and driving them well.

Just prior to the start of the 2011 season, we met in his spacious office at the team headquarters in Grove, the place where he happily spends the majority of his waking hours. He's effectively 'At Home' there. With his team.

Sir Frank Williams Come in, Maurice. You've timed it right; would you like a cup of tea?

Maurice Hamilton That would be nice, Frank. Thank you. Good to see you. Look what I found. It's the original press kit - if you could call it that - for your first car, or the first car for Williams Grand Prix Engineering.

FW FW06 in 1978? Whoa! Look at that!

MH Not much to it, is there? A folder and slide-binder bought from WH Smith, your sticker slapped on the front and typed pages inside. Very straightforward. But that sums up you and the car at the time, doesn't it?

FW It does. This was our first proper car as such; Patrick's first car. A lovely looking car but it was a year out of date because ground effect had arrived. It was very good for what it was. We didn't have the size of company to operate a more sophisticated car. Patrick Head was relatively new at all this as well.

MH The launch was in your factory in Station Road, Didcot, and I remember you wore a suit and tie and you had these guys from Saudia Airlines coming in by helicopter. It was a big moment for you, wasn't it? We knew from your antics that this was important.

FW Antics! What a charming word for me being so well organised!

MH You know what I mean! I remember you turning round, winked and said to us: "Don't let me down, lads." There was quite a bit we could have told them! They landed, if I remember, on a football pitch out the back of your place.

FW That's right. We already had a connection with the Saudis and this was hopefully a way of tempting more to come on board. It was the start of a very successful relationship.

MH If we look at the way F1 has advanced since 1978, what has changed most?

FW The size of the calendar; the influence of television; the revenues paid to the teams by Bernie - they're very substantial even though they could and should be a bit more, but that's not something I'm going to get into now! Aside from inflation, there's a very big difference between then and now. There's the professionalism of it all and the development of technology.

MH This press kit says you had 21 people in total then. Now look at the various departments you need here in Grove to run a F1 team. It's colossal. How do you personally keep pace with what's needed?

FW We have a very good and professional business manager. He has several people reporting to him who are good managers in their own right. All the key departments are managed by the appropriate people with the right qualifications. We make sure we have very good communication between them.

MH But they must keep coming to you saying: "Frank, we need this now." Or "We must have that." And you go: "Gawd... what next?"

FW In September or October, wish lists are created by the various departments and they go to the business manager; he vets them and brings it up at the next board meeting, saying we've got a request for 'X'. We'll debate it but the fact is this company is keen to improve all the time. If the budget allows, we'll spend the money.

MH You've hit on a key point here in that perhaps you haven't had the budget you really need.

FW There are teams like McLaren, Red Bull and Ferrari who, while not awash with money, have what I would describe as very substantial budgets. All teams have to work hard to have a half-decent budget and pay the bills. Given the world's economies at various times over the years, it's never easy.

MH But getting that money depends largely on success. And, not to put too fine a point on it, you haven't had much of that in recent years. How difficult does that make it?

FW People don't say: "Oh, you haven't won for eight years" or whatever. Many of the people we talk to - particularly outside Europe - are quite unaware of that sort of statistic. People want to know what we can do for them; what F1 can do for them. If having very few wins is a penalty, then it's our fault and we have to weather the storm and get onto the comeback trail.

MH But that's not easy, Frank.

FW Well it's not easy to have a heart operation and survive - but you do it if necessary!

MH It must have been made even more difficult for you in recent years because F1 has become so competitive now. I mean, look at the margin between the teams; it's nothing compared to what it was. You can be there or thereabouts and yet be...

FW ...tenth, twelfth. Yes, that's right.

MH And then there's the reliability now.

FW That's astonishing. I'd say that's the single biggest change - and an admirable one in a way. There's no mercy out there now. It's superbly competitive. Extraordinary competence from one end of the grid to the other.

MH Do you love that side of it?

FW I admire it. I wouldn't say I love it because it makes life difficult! But, despite all we're saying, there's still a problem. It's called Adrian Newey. There's only one of him.

MH Since you've mentioned Adrian's name, I have to ask if, looking back - and hindsight is a wonderful thing - you regret not agreeing to his request to take shares in Williams when he was with you in 1996? Do you feel you should have done more to keep him?

FW He wanted some shares which I didn't want to give him at the time, which is arguably a mistake with hindsight. Adrian is quite a remarkable individual. And now the competition is such that if your car fails, you're going to lose. People make the effort to

Adrian Newey (second left) put Williams on top again in 1992

go the extra mile to gain reliability. It's remarkable where we are today. Boring in one way, highly admirable in another.

MH I agree. I used to enjoy watching a race thinking, "Well, one of them is going to drop out in a minute with mechanical trouble." Just doesn't happen now. So, really, you're talking in terms of, on the one hand, the show; and, on the other, the technical achievement. Which do you think should be the priority?

FW I think it's the show. Let's say for every TV programme, I would guess that 70 per cent of viewers are there for the race or, God forbid, the accidents. And 20 or 30 per cent are technocrats who want to see superb engineering whizzing around a circuit. I suspect that's the case. But, taking up your point, you'd want one or two cars to break down and change the order and get things cranked up a little. The correct thing to say is you want more circuits that are designed for overtaking - but with difficulty.

MH What about DRS? Does that work for you?

FW I think it's helped - from what I hear; the way the drivers talk. Certainly, I've not heard anyone say: "What a joke! Waste of money!" So it must make a difference.

MH But is there an argument for needing it in the first place? Do you think it's become too easy in a way because of vast run-offs and so on?

FW I think, actually, there's a lot to be said for massive run-off areas that allow you to make a prat of yourself, go way off the road and not damage your car, then come back on again. But some circuits are so restrictive, when you go off the road you're out of the race. So it means the driver won't make an attempt unless the guy in front leaves the door wide open.

MH Hmmm. I don't know what to think about that, Frank. My thought is if a driver makes a mistake, this is F1, the top of the pyramid, then he should be penalised in some way.

FW Yes, but if he goes wide, he's lost at least two seconds and probably a couple of places and has to recover his car. But he can rejoin the chase and try and catch up because he won't have suffered any damage. I've often thought there should be a little more encouragement for the drivers to take risks. And the way to do that is to remove the risk. The braking distances are so short now. So that reduces the overtaking opportunities as well.

MH I agree with you there; the braking distances are ludicrously short. How the drivers can spot a braking point when sitting with their backside on the ground at 180mph, I just don't know. I take it you haven't changed your opinion that racing drivers are special people?

FW They're remarkable, definitely. I think the idea of having two-seater racing cars should be revived, to let people see what it's like. I'd love to be able to experience that.

FW I've been lucky enough to be in a two-seater twice; with Martin Brundle and Jean Alesi, both times at Yas Marina Circuit in Abu Dhabi.

FW [*grinning*] Did you? Go on! Tell me! What was it like?

MH Absolutely unbelievable! I was half-ready for the acceleration and I thought I was ready for the braking - but I wasn't. It literally takes the breath from your body.

FW [*still grinning*] Go on!

MH What really caught me unawares was the violence of the cornering, particularly sudden changes of direction through chicanes. I was just wrecked at the end of it. And I had done nothing but hang on!

FW Fantastic! But it's all in a day's work for these guys, which is why they're so special. We need a bit more of what you've just explained for people who have no idea what it's like.

MH Do you think F1 could do more to help in that regard? The problem is that, unfortunately, television dumbs it down.

FW Maybe you get several well-known commentators - not from motor sport - to have a ride; people who would not be biased to F1 and who would say: "If I'm looking bruised, it's because of the experience I've just had. Let me tell you what's happened. And here's the film of me puking in the cockpit!"

Sir Frank during Silverstone testing in 2012, with Bruno Senna

MH Do you also think that F1 should give more information to commentators about tactics during the races and so on?

FW [*long pause*] I'm looking at you in a strange way because I'm thinking: 'Tactics? What's that in F1? I thought it was balls out from the moment the lights went out'. I'm not being rude to you! Okay, tactics; that's looking after your tyres, but really there's so little time. It should be about the driver looking to overtake a couple of cars in the first few laps.

MH I'm surprised to hear you say that because I know you used to be really into tyre choice during the days when there were maybe three different compounds and you could mix and run them how and when you liked; you loved that.

FW It would've been Patrick making the tyre choice, not me.

MH You say that, but Neil Oatley [*former Williams engineer, now Design and Development Director at McLaren*] tells me you were really into tyres - and you made some great decisions. The Swiss Grand Prix at Dijon in 1982 was a classic. It was your call and you decided to put, I forget what it was, but a harder tyre on the left rear or something and that's why won Keke Rosberg the race. You did like sussing that out, didn't you?

FW I know what you're talking about, yes, but I have to say I can't remember it that clearly. It was always about, and still is, trying to be a winner. Don't get me wrong; tyre choice was always a worry.

MH I take it you're looking forward to the new season? This time of year is always nice, isn't it? The unknown.

FW Of primary importance to me is how good is our next car? Is it going to be competitive or disappointing? The Renault engine gives us hope. We have three new technical people - one as technical director, one as chief aero and one running the cars. They have different backgrounds, coming from three different teams. Racing these days is all about first designing a car, then putting some aero performance on it and the third thing is operating it correctly. That job is split among three different people rather than one person doing everything. It's a very strong group.

MH So where did it go wrong last year?

FW I'm not an engineer but I've seen lots of good and bad cars and ours wasn't quick enough. Why not? It was deficient in most of the areas that matter. But we were lacking in the most important, which is aero. And probably a bit of horsepower. It just wasn't a quick car. And I don't think it carried much ballast. Some of our clever brethren created an enormous amount of ballast - which is a great performance benefit.

MH I suppose I'm really asking how do you deal with 2011 and just five points, when you consider all you've done in the past?

FW My wife, Ginny [*who sadly passed away in March 2013*], says I'm not a particularly responsible person. In the bad old days, the bailiff might have been in removing furniture, but I'd go to bed and immediately be sound asleep. And you couldn't wake me up for seven or eight hours. I'm very lucky like that. No matter what happens, I can sleep.

MH I take you didn't lose much sleep over Sam Michael's departure to McLaren?

FW I wouldn't put it like that, Maurice. I'm very fond of Sam. He loves racing. He would talk about racing any time you wanted - morning, noon and night. He was in the wind tunnel all the time - I'm sure he had a sleeping bag in there sometimes. A good man.

MH So, you're sorry to see him go?

FW Change was necessary.

MH Okay. But now you have also lost Patrick. That's going to be difficult, surely? You are the greatest of mates; working together for 40 years. You're going to miss his chats in this office over a cup of tea. Will he still be around?

FW Yes, but not as much as he used to be. Yes, at lunchtime he'd come in. He hasn't been in today - you can tell if he's been in; there are crumbs on the floor!

MH So you'll still have a sounding board - because that's what you two are good at.

FW Yes, absolutely. He'll still want to be in touch.

MH I take it you're happy with the role of Adam Parr as chairman [*Parr would leave Williams on amicable terms in March 2012*]?

"Very clever" Adam Parr with Williams in Hungary 2011

FW A very good man: utterly honest, hard working. very efficient and with good marketing acumen.

MH Are we saying that F1 has reached such a peak that you need to have a good businessman in charge rather than a racer?

FW All I would say is that Adam is a very clever individual with a strong sense of business. A lawyer by training, he's got a lot going for him.

MH And what can we say about drivers at this stage?

FW A driver is always coloured by his equipment. Ayrton Senna would have been in trouble from time to time last year if he'd been in our car. Rubens Barrichello is very experienced. I don't think he ever lost his temper or got angry about anything. A very calm, mature individual. He never had a fair crack of the whip. I'm sure we disappointed him. When he talks about the car and racing you can tell Rubens is very experienced. He talks about the right things, in the right order. He knows what he needs to get on the table quickly during discussion. In the car, he didn't disappoint. Very good at overtaking, very professional, one of the better drivers.

Pastor Maldonado is learning. He's a very charming, easy-going character. Yes, we needed the money, but he is not a waste of space. Being blunt, it has been us wasting his time.

MH So you're not saying who you're going to have! [*Frank would replace Barrichello with Bruno Senna*]. I often wonder if your feeling about drivers was coloured by what happened with Alan Jones when he announced at Monza in 1981 that he was going to retire at the end of the year. Did that affect your view of drivers and how to treat them?

FW I think I knew it might be coming because he was talking more than usual about [his native] Australia. I thought he might be preparing his retreat. Everyone gets homesick. But I think he stepped down at least a year too early because the car was a championship-winning car in 1981. Alan led a lot of races and threw it off the road in a few them - which he'd never have done the year before. He had a winning car - we almost won the title with Carlos Reutemann but I don't think Alan took the 1981 championship seriously, having won it the year before. That's not to be critical, but I think, between us, we allowed ourselves to lose the championship.

MH But did it make you think drivers are simply another thing to deal with from a business point of view - a box to be ticked?

FW Yes, that's true. It needs to be an unemotional decision.

MH Bringing emotion into the discussion, of all the cars you've had, which stands out as a favourite for you personally?

FW I think FW07, the 1979 car. It was superb; a very clever car. It won five races - and remember, it came out late; missed the first four races.

Barricello in his last race (Brazil 2011) chases Maldonado

MH Yes, you tend to forget cars were introduced during the season in those days. But that moment during the Silverstone test when Patrick and Frank Dernie - I'm not getting into the debate over which of them thought of this! - closed off the rear underside of the car, around the exhausts, and suddenly you found over a second!

FW [*grinning*] Just astonishing! The lap times kept coming down. You looked at your stopwatch in disbelief.

MH Today, you find a couple of tenths after spending a million quid and everyone is going crazy. But if you told them about what happened - finding more than a second - they wouldn't believe you, would they?

FW It was an incredible amount. The trouble is, the regulations are so tightly restricted these days, where do you make a breakthrough? Then again, Adrian does it.

MH I think you're right about the regulations being very, very tight. And the point with Adrian is that it's the whole package, is it not?

FW Yes, it is. He finds a bit everywhere on the car. "I'll get another tenth on the front wing, another fraction over here" and so on. The thing I like about Adrian is that he hasn't changed; he's quiet, introverted, nice smile, works very hard, motivated - but not big headed. He's totally unspoiled.

MH Nice that he got the OBE.

FW He should have got far more than that. If he keeps plugging away, I think they'll give him the promotion soon. It's what he's done for three fine British teams. An amazing achievement, when you stop to think about it. No one else has come close.

MH Well, he was the man behind about FW14B. How do you rate that car?

FW Technically brilliant but, speaking personally, not as pretty or exciting as 07. It's in the reception area downstairs. Did you notice anything when comparing FW14B with last year's car that's also on display? I was looking at them both the other day – I go pushing [*Frank's expression for taking his wheelchair on a tour of the factory*] down there a lot and, when you look at the new car it seems about 50 per cent bigger. Okay, I'm exaggerating, but FW14B is a midget beside FW33. It's gargantuan. What are we making these days?

MH I suppose a lot of that is the crash structures.

FW Yes, that and the length of the chassis for the aero and so on. Not pretty, though.

MH On a purely personal note, I don't like the front wings these days. And they cost you a small fortune.

FW They do. A lot of composite skills go into those.

MH On the subject of specialised technology, tell me about your latest connection with the Middle East.

FW We're focusing on Qatar. It reminds me a lot of the 1970s, when we had our first contact with Saudi – which has grown massively since. There's only 300,000 people in Qatar, which makes it easier from a communication point of view. They have spent their money on education for any and everybody there. They look after their people.

They started the Science & Technology Park. This is an area where people from abroad – people like us – can participate, lease a place, share facilities, do our R&D and share it. It's a clever venture. It attracts people who are looking for somewhere off line to conduct long term R&D at an affordable cost. A lot of world-class companies are in there from America and Europe. We have about 25 people working there now.

MH What are you working on; is it F1 related?

FW We have two projects there, one of which is relevant to F1 as well as the commercial market, and the other is for the commercial market but I'd rather not give any detail on that. It's a long-term venture; we won't get payback tomorrow or at the end of the year, but it's good to be part of an expanding economy.

MH Without wishing to sound morbid, Frank; is there a succession plan in place for when you're no longer around?

FW If, for whatever reason, I couldn't come in to do my job, Adam would fill the gap. He a young man, physically fit like I was at his age. He's not a racer but, in a way, that's probably an advantage in these distinctly commercial days. He's very good at making financial decisions and working out cost-to-benefit. And he can hold his own in the F1 meetings [*Since our interview, Frank's daughter, Claire, was appointed deputy team principal in March 2013*].

MH But that's for the future; you've clearly no intention of stopping tomorrow.

FW I'll be 70 in April. But, no, you're right, even though 70 would've seemed a hell of an age way back with FW06 in 1978!

MH That's the trouble, Frank, it's bloody hard to give it up.

FW You're right. It's a wonderful business we're lucky enough to be in. More tea?

At lunch with **John Surtees**

"I did the Mille Miglia about 10 years ago and we stopped en route. Who should turn up, but every one of the remaining lads from my Ferrari team. That summed up the true spirit of the relationship we had."

John Surtees may have turned 82 a few months before our interview in January 2012, but he still hustled his road car in the manner of the only man to have won world championships on both two wheels and four. You don't win 255 of your 348 bike races, many on closed public roads, without adopting a sense of space and speed that never leaves you - natural resources that stood Surtees in good stead when he switched easily to cars. He was driving his BMW 330d Touring estate, arms slightly bent and left-foot braking as we swept safely and swiftly through the Kent lanes towards the Castle Inn at Chiddingstone and its home-made shepherd's pie. It was a classic driving pose and environment for a true gentleman and champion the Italians reverentially refer to as "Il Grande John".

Looking back on it now, I was struck by John's power of recall and his continuing sense of what's right and what's wrong with racing then and now. Never one to mince his words, JS did not disappoint.

But more than anything, I still think of the way in which he drove that BMW. Mere words cannot portray the smoothness of touch coupled with precision and speed. And he was chatting all the time. It really brought it home how top racing drivers, and world champions in particular, really do possess a natural gift that is very special. It's not an exaggeration to say I felt very privileged to have been taken along for the ride to and from an engaging interview and lunch.

Maurice Hamilton Looking back at your career and your first four-wheel race at Goodwood in 1960, one of the things that strikes me is you were immediately on the pace; front row of the grid, fighting with Jimmy Clark in the race. Then you were second in a Formula 2 race at Oulton Park; again, you were right up there. Were you surprised at how quick you were?

John Surtees No, because that was obviously the objective. When I first sat in a racing car, it came from a suggestion by Mike Hawthorn. I initially said, "No, no. I'm a motorcyclist" and Mike came out with his famous words: "Cars stand up easier." We agreed to meet at another function which was coming up, but Mike was killed in a road accident while on his way to that function.

MH So, we're talking January 1959, when he was World Champion?

JS That's right. I didn't think anything more of it until my circumstances changed. I was racing for MV Agusta. I brought them their first World Championship in 1956, but, when it came to end-of-season races, I raced and won on bikes - mainly Nortons - that I'd prepared and owned. Agusta got unhappy that the Italian press were saying Surtees doesn't need an MV to win.

So, in typical fashion, Count Agusta said, "You don't ride bikes other than MV Agusta." That meant I would be doing a limited number of races. But there was nothing in my contract to stop me racing a car. Aston Martin and Vanwall had asked me to drive but I wanted to learn a bit about it first. I decided to buy a car and then I could be flexible about when I raced because I had my motorcycling to consider, championships to win.

I went to see Cooper with the intention of buying a little F2 car. John Cooper introduced me to Ken Tyrrell, who was running a team of Cooper-Austin Formula Junior cars. Ken didn't really ask me a lot. He basically said, "I've entered you for Goodwood. The RAC stewards will look at you and give you a full licence if they're happy. We haven't got time to test because it's going to be touch and go." As it was, the car arrived there unpainted. But I thought, "Why not?"

I put it on pole and then, as you say, I had a good dice with Jimmy. I finished a close second and then I finished behind Innes Ireland at Oulton Park.

MH Did you think, "Bikes are difficult, but this is easy"? You have to say that was an incredible performance.

JS It was a stress. As you get more experience, you acquire more inner calmness; everything becomes very much slower for you. But at any early stage, the degree of concentration and input needed is that much more intense. I was learning all the time. But I had no problem doing the lap speed from the moment I stepped in a car.

MH You were very quickly into the international scene on four wheels. Did your experience with bikes help in any way?

JS The first time I came across international competition was in my second race with the F2 Cooper. This was at Aintree where I'd ridden bikes, so I knew the circuit and got in the groove. I finished fourth behind the works Porsches. Basically, I was in front of the British entry. At which point Colin Chapman came up and said "Come up to Silverstone and try our F1 car."

I turned up at Silverstone. Innes went out and did his testing. Then it was my turn. I went round and round, and then made a bit of a braking error at Stowe, where I stuffed it in the bank. Not very hard. But Innes went berserk, saying Chapman shouldn't be putting amateurs in the car because he didn't have enough spare parts. Colin wasn't really perturbed.

MH Did Innes see you as a threat?

JS I was quicker, so I think that might have been the case. Colin said he wanted me to drive for Lotus in F1. I told him I'd only do it when I wasn't motorcycling. We shook on it, and that was it. I did the *Daily Express* International Trophy at Silverstone, where I didn't spend any real time on the track in the race because of problems with the oil pump. Then he said, "You can fit Monaco in." I'd never seen Monaco in my life and, if I had any difficulties at all, it was coming to grips with the car technique for slow corners compared with bikes. It was vastly different. There were tremendous problems with the gearbox and I didn't finish. Then it was Britain, where I had a reasonable drive and came second.

MH A podium for your second Grand Prix? I think that's more than reasonable!

JS It wasn't bad. Portugal was better in that I put it on pole and led the race. Then I made a stupid mistake. I caught up with Stirling Moss, who'd had a pit stop. I followed him down the main straight, which was full of tram lines. The tyres then were very narrow and coming up was a sharpish left. I pulled out of the slipstream but, unfortunately, a slight leak from the front fuel tank meant fuel had got onto the sole of my right shoe and my foot came off the brake pedal momentarily. I made the mistake of trying to turn into the corner instead of following the tramlines into the escape road. I just clipped the kerb enough for it to damage the radiator. I ended up with fastest lap but I could have won. The degree of relaxation I was referring to had not yet come in.

MH Of course, you were also winning motorcycling world championships.

JS Yes, 350 and 500. I won both of those. Then Colin said, "I want you to be team leader next year. You've got choice of team-mate, it's up to you. Who do you want?" So I said, "Jimmy, I get on well with him."

That lit a fuse. The next thing I had a call from Paris. It was Innes: "What the hell are you doing? Taking my drive, pushing me out. I've got my contract."

My start had not been totally without opposition from within motor racing circles. A number of people hadn't liked me coming onto the scene. One or two of the drivers, not the ones who really counted, were rather anti, and also the press people associated with them. Innes and I sat down with Colin, who told Innes he had arranged for him to be team leader for Ken Gregory's team, BRP.

But Innes insisted he had a contract. It was so unpleasant. I liked Colin but I didn't

Now 82, but still driving with the skill and ease of a champion

want my racing that way. I walked away from it and suddenly found, of course, that I didn't have a drive. Reg Parnell said he was going to have a second Cooper works team and that seemed a pretty good suggestion.

MH When was your first involvement with Enzo Ferrari, because he approached you more than once?

JS I was asked to go to Italy. I saw the Old Man and was told about the 1962 programme for F1 and prototypes – sportscars. But they had all these drivers on the books. Having had a bit of experience with the Italians, I wanted to be more complete; I wanted to go there with a degree of strength. So I said no. As I left, I was told Ferrari doesn't ask twice.

MH That must have left you in a quandary. Where could you go in F1?

JS There was no point going as a private customer. Eric Broadley of Lola was very highly rated and I thought he could perhaps compete with Chapman. Lola were in Bromley, one street across from where I lived, and so I asked about building a Grand Prix car and reached a deal with Eric. In that first year we didn't have the support of engine manufacturers like Lotus and Cooper had with Climax; we had sort of standard stuff to start with, but we did finish fourth in the World Championship in front of Ferrari and Porsche, which was something.

MH It certainly was. And you came close to winning at the Nürburgring.

JS Yes, lying second to Graham Hill in the BRM, which I knew was quicker than the Lola on the straight leading to the finish. It was very important to be tucked up behind and have the momentum and the slipstream. I was in the right place, pulled out, and what do I find? A backmarker! My chance of winning was gone.

I'd put it on pole at Zandvoort and then had the steering fail, which had put me into the bicycle park! The handling was very inconsistent. At Spa we made a breakthrough. Our mechanic was jacking up the car but it wasn't lifting all four wheels. Ah, there's the problem – the chassis is flexing. So, we stiffened it up and from then on it was very good. And then the phone call came through again: "Will you come to Maranello?"

MH So this time you thought, 'Okay'?

JS There had been a bit of a revolution. They still had one or two of their old engineers, particularly Franco Rocchi, a wonderful man, and also Mauro Forghieri. Mr Ferrari said, "Your responsibility is to work with the team, to test. Our first priority is Sebring and the prototype car, which we are evaluating now. You'll be number one driver." I said the stopwatch would show who's number one driver. I was a bit anti that side of things and I had enough confidence to say it.

MH You spent most of your time there but I guess that wasn't a problem because you knew Italy and the Italians well from your time with MV?

JS Maranello was its own little world. Ferrari said they hadn't got a lot of money but there were other advantages. I could stay at the Real Fini hotel, full board, for 1800 lire a day. That represented about £1! But you're right; it was very like MV which had been a team in the doldrums but looking for a way forward – and prepared to do anything to get there. And it was the same in that you went into shops and restaurants in Maranello and Modena and they'd say, "Ah, John from Agusta. *Disconte* 20 per cent, 30 per cent". I got a discount everywhere. It was part of returning to the Italian way of life.

MH Clearly, you enjoyed the way of life there.

JS I did. But it isolates you because, whereas I'd been a part of what you might call the English contingent, with people like Jimmy, Innes and Roy Salvadori, we were all together, piggy-backing all the time. Suddenly, in Maranello, I felt very isolated. In a way, I was Ferrari's link to the outside world, which was largely developing back here in England. I was doing things such as persuading them to take one of the V6 sports cars and extend the rear chassis members to take the V12 engine. I went to Modena autodome and I remembered reading an article about Vanwall developing the bodyshape with oil and wool tufts. We had no wind tunnel then, so I did the same thing on Ferrari – poured oil over it, put tufts of wool on the bodywork and they'd come along and take photographs to see where it had been going. That's how the first protoype car for Sebring was built; that was to be my first race for Ferrari.

MH How did you feel about the emphasis being on sports car racing as well as F1? Did it bother you?

Mexico 1964 and Surtees is the first world champ on bikes and cars

JS Yes it bothered me, because we fought F1 with one hand tied behind our back. But I came to realise that prototypes were part of the life blood of Ferrari and the way he dealt with various team patrons around the world - selling them cars and so on. It was a little bit old fashioned. In England they were building up dedicated F1 teams. It put Ferrari at a disadvantage, because we did no testing on the F1 car and nothing would really happen until after Le Mans. 1963 was very much a compromise year, in that they'd had a dreadful 1962.

MH But 1964 was your championship year. Am I right in saying it wasn't easy?

JS It should have been easier. It was all a little bit topsy-turvy; various things breaking or incidents in the races and so forth. Too much was being attempted with the limited resources available. There wasn't the manpower nor, I suspect, the money to do F1 and sports prototype.

MH I read somewhere that when you won the championship at the last race in Mexico, you weren't particularly satisfied because the car hadn't been running cleanly and Jimmy Clark was about to win the title when he retired on the last lap.

JS I was unhappy because the engine never really chimed in on eight cylinders properly; I was using a V8 because it was more likely to get to the finish whereas Ferrari's flat-12 was more competitive. And then there was an incident where Graham Hill had a coming together with Lorenzo Bandini [*Surtees's team mate*] which looked as if Lorenzo might have done it deliberately - which, of course, he hadn't. But I wasn't particularly happy because I was quite capable of winning on pure speed.

MH What about the 1965 Ferrari?

JS The flat-12, which I eventually drove at Monza - just before my big accident in the sports car in Canada - was probably the most competitive Ferrari I ever drove. I put it on pole there but I always seemed to have the V8 that season. I always say we should have concentrated on the 12 for 1965, and not fiddled around because it was so disappointing to have such a disjointed year after winning the championship in 1964.

MH Before telling me about the accident, how come you were racing sports cars in North America?

JS I had talked about it with the Old Man because I liked the idea of the American races. He said, "You should try one of the prototypes, but you'll have to do this yourself as we don't have enough people." When we took everything off the Ferrari to make it as light as possible, I said to Mr Ferrari, "We don't have enough engine capacity to compete against the 7.0 litres. It isn't possible."

Meanwhile, Eric Broadley had asked if I'd help develop his CanAm car, the Lola T70. So I went back to the Old Man and said: "Look, can I drive another make of car? Can I drive the Lola?" I pointed out it would allow me to look carefully at the American scene, which would be helpful to us both. He said: "Yes, as long as you don't enter it under Lola. You only enter it as Team Surtees."

So that's how Team Surtees came about. The plan was to do some races in America - it wasn't known as CanAm then. Since it was more economical to run two cars, Jackie Stewart drove a second Lola. I had won a race, things were going quite nicely, and we go off to Mosport. I'm driving my old car and Jackie is in a newer one which he wasn't terribly happy with. So - and this is the story I'm told because I don't remember a thing about this incident - I say I'll do a couple of laps to check it out.

Coming past the start-finish line, the right-hand front upright shatters. The car goes off, hits the rail, flips and drops on me. That smashed my femur, split my pelvis and pushed up my left-hand side by about four inches. The most worrying thing was that it also damaged my kidneys and I was losing lots of blood. I was taken to Scarborough General Hospital; it was a bit touch and go. But, luckily, it righted itself, because they couldn't do anything about it. The Old Man wanted to know how I was. Ferrari were very good because I didn't have any personal insurance, but Ferrari covered me.

I was given the option for treatment; it's either the USA or England. In America, it no doubt would be a knife; England the old fashioned way. Tony Vandervell [*head of the former Vanwall team*] had been over on business and came to see me. He said when Stirling had his problem, it was Mr Urquhart of St Thomas' Hospital who'd sorted him out. He rang Mr Urquhart, who more or less said, "Don't let the Americans get their hands on you. Get back here somehow." The hospital said travel would be a bit dodgy, but they could mummify me - wrap me tightly onto a stretcher. Tony got on to BOAC and blocked off a line of seats in first class. I was whistled off to London.

Monza 1962 drivers' briefing: Lola's Surtees (in open overalls)

MH Considering what you've just said, you made a pretty good recovery.

JS Mr Urquhart said, "You're consistent enough, but we need to get you somewhere straight. You see my registrar? Big lad, isn't he? Plays rugby. Okay, we're going to take you downstairs, put you on the table, he's going to get one end, I'm going to get the other and we're going to pull like hell and we'll get you somewhere near."

And that's what happened. He got me from four inches difference to three-eighths of an inch. Then I had to build up my strength. I was allowed to go into the water tank in the basement of St Thomas', which had been a war time water system tank but the doctors were now using as an orthopaedic tank. At the start, it was to get the legs moving lower down because they were held pretty tight at the top, and get the circulation going. Bit by bit, the recovery continued and they soon had me on crutches.

Mr Ferrari arranged what he called a 'convalescence car', which was in effect what should have been a Tasman car. I'd arranged to put a 2.4 V6 engine into a F1 chassis and the car had been built. It wasn't that easy getting in and out, so they had one of those engine A-frames which helped me to lift me up and drop me in. I went round and round Modena in that little car.

MH When you were out on the track, did you feel okay? How was your confidence?

JS My confidence was okay. Lola had told me what had happened. It wasn't my mistake. The failure had been a part supplied by an agent. It had been sent there for evaluation and somehow it had got mixed up in the assembly of my car.

MH Moving into 1966 and the arrival of the 3.0-litre formula, you were given the new V12, which you didn't want.

JS The problem was that Ferrari were going through a difficult period financially and so on. There were deals in the offing with Ford and then Fiat to take over Ferrari. And then, of course, there was also the threat from Ford relative to Le Mans. So it was a very difficult time for Mr Ferrari. Part of the plans for development of the brand new pukka 3.0-litre car for F1 in 1966 had been put back and they did a short-stroke sports car engine. It was announced as having 320 horsepower but, in fact, when I went in the test house, it had 290.

I was rather forthright when telling them that Stewart in the 2.2 V8 BRM had passed me up the straight at Silverstone in the non-championship International Trophy race [in April 1966]. Plus the fact that I was two-and-a-half seconds a lap faster around Modena in the Tasman 2.4 than I was in the new 3.0-litre F1. So this all created the foundation for what later transpired.

MH Which was for the first round of the 1966 championship at Monaco. Bandini had the lovely little V6 - perfect for Monaco - and you were given the V12.

JS I wasn't happy but I said, "Okay, I'll push this V12 along and I'll do something, but it won't last. We ought to be here to win the race; we have a faster car." Which was proved because Bandini was only just pipped by Stewart's V8 BRM.

MH But at least when you got to Spa, you were in a better position with the V12.

JS I put it on pole. It was dry when we started the race but, as I approached Burnenville, the rain really came down. The only one who stayed with me was Jochen Rindt in the Cooper-Maserati. Jochen came by and I took a conscious decision that it was a damn sight safer in his wheel tracks rather than leading the way because the conditions were changing so much. Then it gradually subsided, I went by again and cleared off to win. The only one who didn't congratulate me was Dragoni.

MH Ah, Eugenio Dragoni, the Ferrari team manager with whom you were having what could be described as a difficult relationship. How could he not congratulate you after a drive like that?

JS Because I allowed a 'Maserati' to be in front of me!

MH It was only the engine! You're joking?

JS I'm not. But the lads in the team were terribly enthusiastic and, to this day, I've still got a good relationship with them. When I did the Mille Miglia for Mercedes about 10 years ago and we stopped en route, who should turn up but every one of the remaining lads from the Ferrari team of my time. I felt that summed up the true spirit of the relationship we had.

MH And it all came to a head at Le Mans in 1966.

Monaco 1966: Surtees' V12 Ferrari leads winner Stewart

JS In order to try and break the Fords, we decided to have this tortoise-and-hare thing; the plan was for me to go like hell from the beginning. Then Dragoni said Ludovico Scarfiotti was doing the first stint. The pretext was that Gianni Agnelli would be at the start of the race and it would be nice for him to see his nephew drive the car. This was when we were supposed to be giving the Fords a hard time. It was the final straw and I left. The Old Man said to me shortly before he died: "John, we must remember the good times and not the mistakes."

MH You got on very well with Mr Ferrari, didn't you? I don't understand how Dragoni had so much influence.

JS He was a very useful link with Fiat. But in all that business, unfortunately Forghieri was relatively weak, which is a shame. Some of the others were terribly upset about it. Also, I do believe Mr Ferrari was under great pressure. The future of the company was very much in the balance. If you look at what he had to sustain compared with the teams he was competing against - they were totally dedicated little units. It was only when Luca di Montezemolo pulled Ferrari into what was then the 20th century did it turn around. Montezemolo did many of the things that I was trying to get done. In some ways, I think I paid the penalty for my enthusiasm. Perhaps I should have been a bit more calculating.

MH If I may move on to when you became a constructor. How did that come about?

JS We came into being a car constructor by mistake. The TS5 Formula 5000 car was a project I did for James Garner, the film star, who wanted to compete with Steve McQueen. Having become involved, we were left holding the baby. There were certain things being said against the car and so I thought, "Right, we'll bloody prove them wrong." We did a rush development programme and I got David Hobbs to prove the car could win - which rather shot some people down. I then made another mistake. John Surtees, racing driver, should have rung up Colin Chapman and said, "Colin, let's let bygones be bygones; let's see if we can get together because there are openings there." Instead, I took another challenge on, which was to try and lift up BRM.

MH Oh dear, I was trying not to mention BRM...

JS Well, there was that and other things, such as driving for Chaparral in CanAm. In the end, I said, "Enough is enough. I'll make my own car, here in Edenbridge." The team was established on £23,000. That was my total budget.

We built F2 cars and won the European Championship; F5000 cars, and won the American and the British championships. We thought we'd really arrived when we got sponsorship from Bang and Olufsen, but that was the beginning of the end. I made a lot of commitments on the back of that sponsorship, but the first payment turned out to be the last. Finally, having dragged on through the courts, I had to settle for costs.

By that time, I had a bit of a problem with my health and, at the end of 1978, I had to make a decision sitting in St Thomas' Hospital. I did a deal with Frank Williams and he took over my position in the Formula One Constructors.

MH How do you describe your business now?

JS Industrial property. The team episode very nearly wiped me out. Because we were insured, it took us a few years, but we paid everybody. I was left with one thing, which was the factory. I've always been interested in design and construction, so I did two things: I got involved restoring an old period house as occupational therapy; and two, I turned the factory into a letting site and then acquired another one, and another one, and built a business out of that. I didn't want to know about motor cars; I turned my back totally and utterly on that.

I didn't look at motor racing again until Mercedes rang me. They said their champions were getting too old and they wanted another World Champion to drive their cars. I think this was 1988. So began a long relationship going round the world driving their cars. That put me in touch with cars again and then, of course, my son Henry started his karting, which brought me back to racing - and then on to the charity...

MH Where you're doing a lot of good work. You've put a lot into that, haven't you?

JS A lot of time. We do put a lot in. The important thing is that we don't take anything out except satisfaction, and acknowledgment that we need people's help. Things like holding the event at Buckmore Park at the end of last year and being able to get such a super range of prizes together to give lads who are all trying to make their way in racing. That was very satisfying because it's a two-way thing. I think life is a balance.

I got messages saying how much the lads had appreciated the prizes.

MH Your brochure mentions 'Headway', which I assume is derived from Henry's freak accident at Brands Hatch? [*Son Henry Surtees, aged 18, was fatally struck on the head by an errant wheel from another car during a Formula 2 race on 19 July 2009*].

JS Headway is our main thing. It's a charity for assisting people who've had head injuries. It allows them to exercise and develop new skills. We got involved with Tunbridge Wells to start with because they were having to relocate and they were finding it difficult from the financial point of view. They wanted an additional unit and they were getting some silly estimates. I heard about it and said we'd try and help.

We've done lots of different things; the involvement with the Beaujolais Run has been fantastic. Not only have people been able to contribute, they've also enjoyed doing it. We've got two very exciting projects which we hope to announce a little later in the year and which will be an aid to the whole community. Henry would have loved it; he really would.

MH That's nice, John. It gives a very positive aspect to what must have been a truly awful time for you.

JS Dark, yes. One which provides a lot of anguish and a lot of other emotions.

MH I can't begin to imagine. But I'm sure everyone reading this will wish you all the luck in the world. Thank you so much for your time.

JS Not at all. Thank you.

At lunch with **Sir Stirling Moss**

"I was recognised wherever I went and racing seemed to take me around the world every weekend. I was lucky to have the name Stirling Moss. I was nearly called Hamish – which is a ghastly thought!"

Sir Stirling Moss has a thing about punctuality. Precisely three minutes before our appointment, photographer Lorenzo Bellanca and I rang the bell at his home in Shepherd Street in London. The town house on five floors has been the Moss abode in Mayfair for more than 50 years. I'd read all about it but never been inside; one of many reasons to look forward to this lunch with a motorsport legend.

The door was opened by Mandy Shepherd, Sir Stirling's PA. We were ushered past his ground floor office and onto a narrow spiral staircase, pausing at the first floor to be greeted warmly by the lovely Lady Susie Moss before continuing the climb to the kitchen. Seated at a desk by the window, that familiar stocky figure removed his spectacles and rose - slowly, it has to be said, after the horrendous accident in his lift shaft injured his ankles, legs and knees two years before our October 2012 meeting.

Once on his feet, that sense of urgency and energy became all too evident, just as it had been when SC Moss was one of the greatest drivers in the world. Moss is more famous for not claiming the world title than some champions are for having won it at least once. It is a mark of the man and the reason why, approaching 85, he is as busy as ever. On the day we met, he had just returned from a visit to the United States before preparing to fly to the Isle of Man the following day, then back to London and on to a function in York 24 hours later.

"As busy as ever, boy," he said, making room at the table. Then he paused before adding, "Thank God I am." He meant it. Sitting still and doing nothing is not an option in the world of Sir Stirling Craufurd Moss. Never was and never will be.

Maurice Hamilton I want to start by linking the past with the present. Mercedes is in the news because Lewis Hamilton has decided to go there for 2013 and I guess you'll have people asking about when you raced for Mercedes.

Sir Stirling Moss I have, and there's no comparison at all. In 1955, I was racing for a major motor manufacturer who was going motor racing. It was a racing department; part of a big company. There were lots of reasons why going to Mercedes made sense. Alfred Neubauer the team manager was there. And so was the chief engineer, Rudolf Ulenhaut, both of whom were exceptional in their own right. Particularly Ulenhaut from a driver's point of view, because he was talented enough to race if he wanted. Can you imagine that now? He spoke perfect English, which was enormously useful to me. But they wouldn't let him race because he was too valuable!

MH The standard of engineering must have been extraordinary at the time. You hardly had a single retirement, did you?

SM Just one! And the thing was, at Mercedes, whatever you wanted, you got. If you wanted square wheels they'd look up the book and say: "We tried it in 1928 and they vibrated too much." Or they would be fitted the next day. They used four-spoke steering wheels but I liked three-spoke, so that's what they made.

In one race, a stone came up and broke the windscreen, which was only a bug deflector, really. But I had to go in for a new one. Of course, we didn't have radios in those days and the first the mechanics knew of this was when I came down the pit lane, pointing in front of me - which could have meant anything. And yet, 36 seconds later, I was away with a brand new one fitted. But, better than that, at the next race, if that happened again, you pushed a button and another windscreen flicked up! Absolutely incredible. Go into the Maserati pit and they'd have a job finding the tyres.

We had one problem because of a design failure of the valves. During the whole time I raced with Mercedes, I didn't know what a desmodromic valve meant. I had no idea. To me it was a technical term. What it meant was that you couldn't get valve bounce. You could keep your foot in there until it blew up.

MH But you must have had a red line on the rev-counter?

SM Oh yes, a red line and a tell-tale needle.

MH So, could you go right up to that red line with complete confidence?

SM Oh, absolutely! If you wanted to, you could go up to it all the time. But I was following Fangio all the time and very rarely would you go up to 7000rpm and the red line. Depending on the layout of the circuit, I'd probably go to 6000rpm and over that if there were certain places where you needed to hold fourth for a long way.

MH From your point of view, the most valuable asset had to be having Fangio in the other car. You were, in effect, number two to the great man - and you were happy to accept that?

SM You bet I was! But I wouldn't have accepted it with any other driver in the world. I was not told or instructed to follow Fangio; it was a completely free situation. But I was very happy to sit right behind him. Neubauer said: "I don't like you going that close. What happens if Fangio goes off?" I said, "He doesn't!"

MH It must have been nice to know you could match his pace?

SM It was, yes. But he gave me what you might call a lot of hints about driving; about where to place the car. But he never, ever said "You're getting too close" or whatever.

MH I guess the learning had to come from what you were seeing because you had a language problem, didn't you?

SM Yes, he was Spanish-speaking and I could only manage a little Italian. But I tell you, boy, if you're only talking cars, crumpet and food, you don't need much! A few hand signals and you're in business! Our dialogue was kept to a minimum.

MH And team orders? Was there such a thing at Mercedes?

SM There was only one occasion which was during a sports car race in Sweden. Neubauer said, "We'd like Fangio to win this one." That was the only time I was given an order. Otherwise the rule was, once a Mercedes had got 30 seconds lead on the rest of the field, they would put out a sign 'REG' which meant 'Regulare' or 'Hold your position'. Then you were under team orders.

MH This leads us to the British Grand Prix at Aintree in 1955, which you won. You came out of the final corner, moved right to let Fangio through – but you kept your foot in it! He couldn't have overtaken you at that point if he'd wanted to. What about earlier in the race? Did he let you through?

SM He said afterwards I'd won fair and square. He said, "It was your day." But what does that mean? He could just as easily have meant it was my day because it was the British Grand Prix. He was the sort of guy that would have felt it was correct and right for me to win my home Grand Prix. After all, he had won all the other races!

MH Yes, but you had pole, fastest lap and you led the final laps. So it was your day in many ways, wasn't it?

SM I'd caught him while he was behind somebody else and I managed to get past both of them. Then I went as hard as I could.

MH Fangio always seemed such a gentleman. And he never gave the impression that he felt threatened by you. I say that, not in the sense that you weren't as quick, because you were, but because he was confident and mature enough to cope. That's always the sign of a top performer, isn't it?

SM Exactly. I was faster than him in sportscars. When I asked him why, as far as I could make out it was because he liked to see the front wheels. I can't really understand that because, apart from when in a hairpin, you never looked down at your front wheels.

Nothing topped the Mille Miglia: Hamilton and Moss reminisce

MH That's interesting because you'll remember when he had the streamlined W196 at Silverstone, he was hopeless - by his standards, anyway.

SM Yes, he kept hitting the barrels marking the inside of corners.

MH The W196 was quite a big car. Did it feel big when you were in it?

SM It wasn't an easy car to drive. Not like the Maserati 250F. That was the most user-friendly F1 car - you ask anybody who has driven one. But the Merc was a large car; not what you'd call an easy thing to throw around.

MH I seem to remember you saying there was something trick about the gearshift?

SM It was back-to-front! Very difficult until you got used to it. My problem was that I was racing every week. So, if I wasn't racing a Mercedes, I was driving something else. I had to remind myself about the gearchange each time I got into the Merc. It had an off-set first [*indicating top left*] then second back here [*down, across left to right and down*], then third up here [*straight up*], down, across and down to fourth, and then up to fifth. So, in any other car, you would flick it across and back one when changing down. Which I did in Argentina in the Merc!

MH So, you went from fifth to third?

SM: Exactly! But it was actually no problem mechanically because that was where the desmodromic valves came in [*they were opened and closed mechanically, so used no*

valve springs]. Had it not been for that, the valves would have bounced. Do that once at speed and you soon learned! I don't know why they had the gearbox like that - I never asked!

MH What exactly was Neubauer's role?

SM He had nothing to do with the technical side at all, it was the running of the team. You'd see him timing, but he was never timing a lap; he had people doing that. He would be timing how long it took to get from second to third gear or whatever it was. He would purely use his watch to tell how the car was performing, how many seconds it took to get from there to there. If it took longer then he knew something was wrong. Maybe the engine was dropping off or something because, of course, there was no other way of telling as there was no telemetry then - or anything like it.

His first concern was his drivers. Before booking accommodation for a race, he'd go there and check everything out beforehand, making sure the drivers had the quietest rooms and all that sort of thing. He really did look after the drivers immensely. He had a great sense of humour. I remember we were on a DC6B, which was the latest aircraft at the time, and he went off to the toilet. The next thing we heard a call as he pretended he was stuck in the toilet - which was possible because, as you know, he was a big man! He had a 44-year old secretary which he joked he would swap for two 22-year-olds. And at Le Mans they said only people with armbands would be allowed in the pits, so Neubauer took out his handkerchief and tied it round his arm. Nobody dared stop him.

MH Talking of characters brings us to Ferrari. Sadly, however, you never got to race for the Prancing Horse. You were about to in 1962. Indeed, if the car had turned up as promised at Goodwood, you wouldn't have had the accident that ended your career. I often think, and I'm sure you do too...

SM ...that if the Ferrari had arrived, I wouldn't have been in the Lotus and I probably would have continued racing until I was 50? It was a dream deal. Ferrari would have made whichever car I wanted. And it would have been painted, not red, but in the blue used by Rob Walker [*Moss's private entrant*]. Absolutely amazing, really.

MH That is such a public admission of how much Mr Ferrari wanted you as a driver.

SM It is, particularly when you know what the man was like and how he really couldn't care a sod about his drivers. In fact, he preferred to have different drivers winning because, for the Old Man, it was all about his cars rather than the driver. He would say it was the best car - which wasn't necessarily true at all.

MH But this deal you had with Ferrari is all the more interesting because you got off to such a bad start with the Old Man, back in 1951. He promised you a drive at Bari, you went all the way to Italy, only to find he'd given the drive to someone else! I don't blame you for being pissed off.

SM I flew down there with my father and we went to the Fiat garage where the racing cars were being prepared. I saw the four-cylinder car, knew that was mine and I was

Dutch GP 1955: Moss follows Fangio to a Mercedes 1-2

about to get in when the mechanic asked me what I was doing. I told him I was Stirling Moss and I was driving this car. He said something like: "No you're not. Taruffi is driving this car." I was, as you say, really pissed off. Ferrari didn't even have the manners to call me and say, "Look, sorry. I've changed my mind." I thought: 'That's it, boy. I'm never going to drive for you. Never'.

MH You were only 20. That's a terrible thing to happen. And 'abroad' as well. Bloody foreigners and all that stuff!

SM Exactly! It was awful. Terrible.

MH So when this incredible offer came along in 1962, you really had to put all that behind you, swallow your pride, and accept.

SM Absolutely. It was the car to have. Apart from anything else, I couldn't think of anyone who had been killed in a Ferrari because of a mechanical failure. Not one. And that was saying something in those days. That sort of thing was fairly high in my mind because I'd been driving Lotuses and there was a 10-to-one chance that something was going to fall off!

MH On top of that, you would be driving Ferrari GT and sports cars, which was a very important consideration. What a dream deal, as you say. The F1 car should have been ready for the non-championship race at Goodwood on Easter Monday. It wasn't, so you drove the Lotus 18/21...

SM ...and then I crashed and that did it. [*Brief pause while Sir Stirling serves smoked salmon and a glass of chilled white*].

MH Before coming today, I started to re-read Ken Purdy's book *All But My Life*, which he wrote about you. I was reminded what an incredible effect that book had on me when I read it for the first time in the late 1960s.

SM A fantastic book! Absolutely fantastic. It was the only one of its kind in that era. He wrote in a vicarious way. Although he knew nothing about racing when he started out, he wanted to be part of it. He contributed articles to all the very big magazines and *Playboy* sent him over from the States to do a piece on me. But after a while he said there is so much material, this is a book and not just an article.

MH Purdy had started all of this before the accident and he was with you right through the recovery, which meant he could provide a tremendous insight to the Stirling Moss before and after. He more or less lived it with you. Which is the perfect situation, not for you, of course, but for a writer. He described you at one point - and I want to quote this - as being "beyond doubt the best-known sports figure in the world". He went on to make the point that, for example, the World Heavyweight Champion in 1962, Sonny Liston, was well known mainly in the USA, but your name, because of racing here, there and everywhere, was global. That's a big claim to make. You probably wouldn't have said that yourself. But do you feel, looking back, that was correct?

SM I suppose I was recognised wherever I went and, as you say, racing every weekend seemed to take me somewhere around the world. But I was lucky to have the name Stirling Moss. I was very nearly called Hamish - which is a ghastly thought! It also helped to be viewed as the underdog because I drove so many crappy cars early in my career. The English people get behind that sort of thing and, of course, they knew I was always looking for the British win.

MH Yet you ultimately had to go for a Maserati 250F as a privateer in 1954 if you were to make any sort of mark in F1. Did you feel uncomfortable with that?

SM I called in the British press and told them, "Look, I want to drive a British car, I've tried it and there's nothing suitable. I have to go with the Maser." They agreed it would be better if I'd had a British car, but if I had to have a foreign car to win, so be it. I needed to get that endorsement. It was political as much as anything else.

MH Saying that, you wouldn't leave the pits until your car - be it a Maserati or a Mercedes - had the Union Flag showing somewhere on its flanks.

SM Oh, absolutely!

MH So there's that and the BRDC badge on your overalls; the nice young Englishman, winning races, with an eye for the ladies afterwards...

SM Chasing crumpet. Exactly!

Two all-time greats: Moss beats Fangio at Aintree 1955

MH And yet Ken Purdy also wrote that you were, or are, shy.

SM Very much so. I wouldn't go into a room if I was on my own. If you were there and I could see you, I would come in and say hello. Or take somebody with me. But otherwise, I find that quite difficult.

MH And yet you chat away nineteen to the dozen; you are very easy to get on with. But you're saying it's the initial approach. Do you put this down to British reserve, or what?

SM Lack of confidence, if I'm honest. I don't know why. I knew I was pretty good at what I did because of the success, but when I got out of the racing car, my disguise had gone. In the car, I was perfectly at home. But when the race stopped, the reality came in. I had confidence in the car, but I didn't have confidence to walk into a room of people.

MH It always struck me that you looked so relaxed at the wheel, your facial expression, everything. You appeared completely at ease and in control.

SM There were bad cars when I probably wasn't quite at home, but I'm lucky in that of the 108 cars I drove, probably 100 of them were pretty good.

MH On that subject, this is a good point to bring in the fact that one of them was a Sunbeam Talbot saloon car with which you won the Alpine Rally, not just once, but three times to claim the coveted Gold Cup. That's an immense achievement in its own right because that was a very tough rally.

SM We were on public roads and you could really get your foot in. The cars we were driving were relatively slow, I think the Talbot had a top speed of about 105mph, but it meant I could work harder and make the difference. If I had done it in, say, a Jaguar XK120 then to me that would have been far less of an achievement. It was all about time controls and on one occasion I got in by a gnat's cock. The whole thing hung on this. I had tears in my eyes, boy; it was so emotional.

MH For a speed test somewhere, you changed all the oil, engine, gearbox - for thin spindle oil; you blanked off the radiator and raised the tyre pressures. You went for it.

SM Oh yes! Do whatever you need to do. But, you know, there was trouble with my gearbox and I had to cheat. It was a four-speed box and I only had second and third. It was the end of the rally - you couldn't change the gearbox of course - and someone pointed out to officials that my gearbox wasn't legal because it didn't have all four gears. An official was told to sit with me and check. I started in second, took it out (it was a column shift), waggled it around, flipped the overdrive switch and shoved it back into second and said "Deuxieme". The official said "Oui". Then I went into the real third. "Troisieme". "Oui". Then I took it out, hit the overdrive switch and slipped it back into third and said "Quatrieme", to which he nodded and said "Oui". And everything was okay. It would've have been fair to be disqualified because the car wasn't working. In fact, I think I should have had extra points for managing to bring it home in that state!

MH You drove touring cars when you made a racing comeback in 1980 with Audi in the British championship.

SM Biggest mistake I ever made, boy. I never researched it. I'd never driven on slicks. I had no idea at all that the tyres had no grip whatsoever if the track was wet. But I wasn't ready for the driving standards. It was like stock cars.

MH Not your style, is it? So, what do you think when you see the start of an F1 race today and the guy on pole swoops straight across the track in a blatant movement to block the man on the outside of the grid?

SM There's certain things they're allowed to do. I presume it's done within the regulations, so that's it. I can see why they do it under those circumstances. My attitude is that you learn the rules and, if it's within the rules, you push the envelope as far as you can. But I'm not saying the rules are necessarily right to allow it.

MH What would you say about incidents such as Senna and Prost at Suzuka in 1989? And Michael taking Damon off the road in Adelaide in 1994?

SM Those things happen because the cars now are so safe. If you want to live, you get in a racing car. It's remarkable what they've achieved. The shunt Mark Webber had in Valencia - unbelievable! That's the way it is. If the cars were as dangerous as they were in my era, I don't care how big balls you've got, you simply wouldn't do what people do today. It was a dangerous sport. That was one of the reasons I entered it; I like playing with fire. I wouldn't swap my era for now.

Moss, in his privateer 250F, took pole in the 1956 British GP

MH Why is that? It is because, despite the tragedies, it was a happy time in your mind and everyone got on so well?

SM I think the danger added an enormous amount to it. If you and I are playing cards, you want to try and win. If I give you chips, you want to try and win a bit more. If I give you cash, it becomes even more important and you really concentrate if you're losing your money. The fact that there is danger on your shoulder certainly sharpens up your attitude towards what you are doing.

MH And I presume racing in cars like that generated more respect between drivers?

SM It did. There were certain drivers you knew damn well were likely to cause problems - Willy Mairesse was one; people who were competent to a degree, but not great. When you caught someone like that you had to make allowances. You'd say, "Okay I'm going to take two seconds to get by rather than go straight past."

MH In Purdy's book, there's a reference to a sportscar race in Sweden where you deliberately gave one slow driver a little tap.

SM I did. I hit him in the arse. It was on a little circuit, in some former gravel pit somewhere. He kept blocking me all the time. When we went into a hairpin, I just nudged the back and he spun off. It wasn't dangerous. But that was dirty driving and I meant to do it. It was the only time I ever did something like that.

MH This really was a different age. People today would have difficulty getting their head around the fact that when officials tried to throw Mike Hawthorn out of the 1958 Portuguese Grand Prix for going against the traffic after he had spun, you sprang to his defence. You had no hesitation.

SM No, certainly not. Mike did go up the escape road and that was penalty enough in itself.

MH Yes, but it was you, not Mike, who pointed that out, although he was going in the wrong direction, he was on the pavement and not actually on the track. The officials agreed and allowed his second place to stand.

SM But I can't see how this is open for debate. He was not on the circuit.

MH Yes Stirling, but if you hadn't said anything and he lost the six points, you'd have been World Champion! He was your only rival. That didn't come into your thinking?

SM No! [*Words cannot convey the genuine incredulity in Sir Stirling's expression at this point. It really did not figure then - and doesn't now. Hawthorn was being hard done by. End of story!*]

MH I suppose you could say you have gained more notoriety for never winning the championship.

SM Absolutely!

MH And you have 16 wins in classic places such as Monaco, Pescara and the Nürburgring Nordschleife.

SM Yes, but 16 wins in my mind has no bearing on it. If you're talking about the skill of driving - and I don't care if you have 25 GP wins - not one of them equals winning the Mille Miglia in 1955. That was way beyond anything I would have expected to do. Averaging 97.7mph over 1,000 miles of public roads, and that included three mountain passes and stops for fuel. It's pretty surprising.

MH Surprising? Phenomenal more like! One of the truly great feats in sport, never mind motor racing.

SM The pleasure was remarkable.

MH I'll bet! You have often referred to the difference between taking a corner on the limit and there being a wall on the outside and taking the same corner with grass outside.

SM Yes, that or a drop on the outside. Big difference! That's the thing, you see. Now there's no difference because they can have a go knowing that the worst eventuality is spinning off. There are drivers today who would enjoy the challenge we had and there are drivers who would think you're bloody mad doing it. I'd wonder, for instance, how Michael Schumacher would be if it was dangerous? I really don't know. Do you?

In the early '60s "the best-known sports figure in the world"

MH Hmm... I don't think he'd be one who, as you say, would enjoy the challenge. What was your view of Michael's comeback?

SM He should have stayed out. Having said that, if I'd been in the position to come back, I probably would have done so. In my time, Fangio was winning at 47.

MH After your accident in 1962, you tried a Lotus sportscar at Goodwood, but it was too soon and you had not fully recovered.

SM The reason it was too early was purely because of the press. I was only 32 and all the time they were asking, "Are you coming back? Are you going to race again?"

MH Interesting, because the sport didn't get the press coverage it gets now. So, for the media to pursue you in this way says a lot about the importance of your comeback.

SM Yes, I suppose that's true because in my day motor racing was either on the first page or the third page. The first because someone had been killed, or the third because it was of editorial interest. I've got more than 180 scrap books and you'll hardly find a single mention on the sports pages. But the continual questioning contributed to me going sooner than would have been wise. If I'd been able to stand back and say I'm not going to make a decision for another year, I'm sure people would have shut up.

MH You didn't allow for the length of time it would take your functions to fully recover from the brain injury caused by the shunt. You were unconscious for how long?

SM One month. And paralysed on one side for six months. But so much had happened in between. Jimmy Clark had arrived and he was looking over my shoulder.

MH You eventually got over that injury. But, nearly 50 years on, how did you recover from that fall down the lift shaft?

SM I opened the doors and got in at this height [*two floors up*] but didn't realise there was a malfunction and the lift was actually on the floor above. I must say my knees and my ankles aren't as good as they were before I did it! When I get up, I have to take my time before I take some pressure. And when I wake in the morning, I'm a bit stiff.

MH But you must have such a strong constitution. The shock alone...

SM It wasn't that much of a shock. It wasn't a case of, "God, it's not there" because the next thing I knew, I'm hurting in my legs and ankles. I was lucky I didn't bang my head; just rubbed my shoulders - and not very much. Broke both my feet, ankles and the rest of it. A few rather depressing people said recovery was going to take a long time because of my age. Well, age is what you make it. There are times when I feel older than I am, but most of the time I feel really good, I must admit. When you've been through what I've been through in racing, you become professional about injuries and take them in your stride, so to speak. You name it, and I've broken it.

MH Well, you look fantastic on it, I have to say. It's been a lovely chat. Thank you.

SM A pleasure, boy.

"The drivers' professional status has been shot to pieces"

Barcelona 1994: Hill beats Schumacher and Mark Blundell

TAG HEUER
SIEMENS
Communications
SCANIA
HIL

Hill, brakes discs
aglow, en route
to the win at Spa
1998, for Jordan

Max Mosley: was direct and honest during his tabloid fights

Mosley was outraged when Balestre 'fixed' Suzuka in 1989

Hamilton's single most enjoyable interview lunch? With Jean Alesi

Alesi spun his Tyrrell out when running third at Monza in 1990

His enthusiasm for the sport conquers all for Frank Williams

In a Williams 1-2 at Hockenheim 1979, Alan Jones took the win

Lauda doesn't suffer fools: the p51 photo was the ice-breaker

When F1 thrived on camaraderie: Stewart, Lauda, Fittipaldi, Pace

Monaco 1973:
Lauda qualified
his BRM P160
sixth but retired

TEXACO
TEXACO

When Hamilton meets Moss at home: "As busy as ever, boy"

Dutch GP 1955: Moss follows Fangio for a Mercedes 1-2

Surtees: "Only the Ferrari team manager didn't congratulate me"

John Surtees leads Bandini to a NART Ferrari 2-3, Mexico 1964

ERGOL
BP
26

Monaco 1960: Surtees makes his F1 debut in a Lotus-Climax

Having shared a mic with Murray, Hamilton is lost in admiration

In a typical media scrum, it's Walker who has Mansell's ear

No one prompts more affection in the pit-lane than Barrichello

Suzuka 2003: Rubens's win secures Ferrari's championship

Sir Jackie: "In F1 you must be able to remove all emotion"

Mexico 1966: Stewart qualified 10th in his P83 BRM, but retired

At lunch with **Murray Walker**

"The public at large are gigantically intolerant. I often read quite vicious criticism of somebody and I think: 'I wonder what you do for a living and how good you are at it?'"

Whatever you may say about Murray Walker OBE and his 53 years at the motor sport microphone, the man is a legend - ranking alongside great sporting commentators such as Sir Peter O'Sullevan, Eddie Waring and Bill McLaren. Each had a distinctive voice and unique style that automatically linked them with their respective sports. And each had detractors who felt they could do it better.

The critics didn't know what they were talking about - I speak from experience, having bumbled along as the lead commentator for BBC Radio 5 Live's F1 coverage for a few years. I was only too happy to hand over to David Croft when he replaced me at 5 Live. Crofty's elevation to fatherhood meant he had to miss the 2007 European Grand Prix at the Nürburgring and in a moment of genius our producer, Jason Swales, persuaded Murray to pick up the radio microphone as a substitute five years after he had retired. For a couple of hours each day I was to have the privilege of sitting in on a master class. My admiration for Murray Walker, already at a respectable level, rose to new heights during those times.

As I was to discover over lunch at The Montagu Arms at Beaulieu, Murray, 90 in October 2013, has lost none of his ability to tell a story in that oh-so-familiar voice. A few days after our lunch, Murray had a bad fall, fracturing his pelvis and injuring a shoulder. Happily, he made an amazing recovery, but when I initially posted the news on Twitter, I was overwhelmed by the reaction and concern for someone the nation clearly holds dear to their collective hearts. Somehow, all seems right with the motor racing world when he talks about it.

Maurice Hamilton We had to do a bit of juggling to find a convenient date, Murray. You seem to be as busy as ever.

Murray Walker I'm as busy as I want to be. I do stuff for the BBC F1 website, for Radio 5 Live, the column in *F1 Racing*, after-dinner speeches and talks on cruise ships.

MH The talking we know you can do, probably quite literally with your eyes closed. But the writing... do you enjoy it?

MW I enjoy it, Maurice. But I can't just sit down and do it like you professionals can. When I think about the *F1 Racing* column, my first problem is: what am I going to write about?

MH You're not alone there, Murray!

MW I'm sure you're right. But I only do it once a month and you do it all the time. Once I've decided, I'm okay. But I go over and over it. What do you do when you're writing?

MH I write the piece and then go away, do something completely different, and then come back and read it afresh. Sleep on it if there's enough time. You need to stand back at some point because you can get too close to it.

MW Yes, that's what I find. Of course, there's a difference when I have to write to length for television. In your case, it's X number of words, whereas I have to write for X number of minutes or sometimes seconds. Saying what you want to say in the time you've got isn't always easy.

I enjoy doing it and it keeps your brain active. I really think that's important for someone like me. If you've led a busy, interesting and stimulating life and all of a sudden you stop because you're 60 – not for any other reason – and you're still healthy and mentally alert, it's an absolute killer. Literally.

MH When you did your book, did you write it yourself?

MW Every word. When I stopped commentating – I don't want this to sound bigheaded – I had eight publishers who wanted to do a book. I talked to all of them. Basically all I had to do was to say 'No' until there was just one publisher left. And that was Harper Collins. The next decision was do I write it, or do I have a ghost writer? I decided to have a go myself. I worked out the format. It took about a year to write – and it went very well. We've sold 560,000 copies.

MH Blimey. That's huge! Particularly for a hard-back on a specialist subject.

MW I know. I was amazed. I didn't think for one moment that people were going to be that interested in it.

MH Did you have to write it to a certain length or did you write it until you stopped – and that was it?

MW They told me how many words they'd like. I can't remember the figure, but I do remember nearly falling over at the thought of having to write that many words.

Murray Walker, painting F1 pictures with his microphone

MH That was going to be my next question. Did you get to a point, say halfway through, when you counted the words you'd written, think about the effort that took and then realised you were only half way through? It can be a daunting thought that tests your motivation.

MW Yes, it can. Saying that, I had the opposite problem at times. I would send one chapter at a time to the editor, Tom Whiting. One chapter was on my time in the army. I wrote 20,000 words and I sent it off. When I called and asked if it was okay, Tom said it was fine - but a bit long.
"Do you want me to cut it down a little?" I asked.
"Yes," said Tom, "that would be good. Sharpen it up."
"Okay. How much would you like me to cut?"
"About half," he said [*laughs*].

MH That's really hard to do, isn't it?

MW It certainly is. But it's a great way to learn to be economical with words.

MH When it comes to speaking rather than writing, do you have specific topics in your after-dinner repertoire?

MW It depends on the audience. If you're doing something for Cunard, for instance, and it's a long voyage, they'll want three talks. I'll do one which I call 'A funny thing happened to me on my way to the race track', which is largely anecdotal. If you're doing a talk to people in these conditions, it doesn't matter whether you are a nuclear scientist or a Belgian carpenter or a F1 commentator; they don't really want to hear a talk about whether or not we should have the atom bomb or whether one carpentry joint is better than another; they want you to make them laugh. And because you're a nuclear physicist, it doesn't mean you're also a stand-up comedian.

Over time, you find out what's needed. I have a speech that I know from experience is relevant to what I'm talking about, but which makes people laugh. So if you're talking to the United Glassblowers of Sheffield, you'll start it one way, and if you're talking to the Bideford Ford dealers, you'll start it another way and probably finish it differently. But the central part of the speech is the same.

MH With after dinner speaking, do you get a lot of approaches?

MW I do, but not as many as I used to. Just as there are people now – can you believe it? – who have never heard of Ayrton Senna. I stopped at the end of 2001, which means its 12 years since I did television commentary, so for anyone to have heard me, remember what I've said and have any opinion on what I was like, they have got to have been at least 10 years old in 2001. That means to say that anyone below 24 now will be asking: "Murray who?" Fortunately, there are people around older than that, of course. But my point is that time is continually marching on.

MH I think you retired at just the right time; the period when Schumi was dominating was the dullest I've known. So difficult to commentate on. I really struggled.

MW I was lucky. James Allen had to commentate on that. I had 2000 and 2001 but James had the next three years at an even greater intensity than I did; that must have been very tough going.

MH Of course, things have changed a great deal. There is so much information available to commentators now.

MW If I get the tapes out, which isn't very often, my commentary seems to be very stilted and repetitive because – and I'm not saying this vaingloriously – I did the interviewing, I did the commentating, I did the time keeping, and Mike Doodson did the lap scoring by writing down the numbers on a piece of paper as the cars went past. There were no graphics at all. You were continually saying who was fourth, fifth and sixth. Now, with so much showing on screen, the viewer knows who is in the top six.

MH The trouble is, the viewer knows as much – if not more – than the commentator. Whereas in your day, and less so in mine, we could bluff our way.

MW Oh yes – and did so!

MH Do you remember coming back and doing Radio 5 Live with me in Germany in 2007?

MW I do. I enjoyed it enormously. Not just because it was coming back and doing something I enjoyed doing. But because it was radio, which was where I cut my teeth. I was

"We could talk for hours": Walker and Hamilton at ease

a radio commentator at the 1949 British GP. It was wonderful to go back to something that involved just talking and not relating to pictures.

MH Yes, in the days before the Red Button, you could control it completely because, unlike now, the listener didn't have information coming in from other sources. You could paint the picture but, even then, you'd get some stick.

MW The public at large are gigantically intolerant. I often read quite vicious criticism of somebody and I think: "I wonder what you do for a living and how good you are at it? I'd like to come and see you at work and then tweet about how incompetent you are."

MH I tell a story about when we did that commentary together. John Inverdale was doing the link into the programme from Carnoustie, where the British Open golf was...

MW I was furious about that. We were told we would be doing continuous commentary. When I say "we", I don't mean just me, I mean BBC Radio. The afternoon's programme was actually being controlled from Carnoustie, so they kept giving themselves priority. And that irritated me. You were talking earlier about getting into the flow of writing; as you well know, you've certainly got to get into the flow with commentating. But when you're having to listen to some chap braying on about golf - I've got nothing against golf, except when it interrupts F1. Sorry, I interrupted you!

MH No problem. So, Inverdale eventually comes out with this flowery introduction about how he never thought he would have the privilege of welcoming an icon of sports reporting back to radio, the place where he started all those years ago and went on to be loved by the nation. All that stuff. A really great welcome back.

So, I'm waiting for you to say: "Well, thanks for that John. It's nice to be back on radio. An emotional return..." and words like that. But, oh no. As soon as Inverdale's finished, there's not so much as a "Good Afternoon" or "Thank you John". You immediately shout: "Round 10! The 2007 F1 World Championship! And qualifying for the European Grand Prix here at the Nürburgring *has begun*!" No messing about, Murray. Straight in there! I glanced at Jason Swales, the producer, and the pair of us just cracked up.

MW [*laughing*] People used to ask me: "Did you get nervous?" I'd say: "No, I didn't get nervous but I certainly got excited." It's a fast-moving, dramatic, colourful, dangerous sport and your job is to communicate to people sitting at home watching their televisions, or listening to their radios, the minutiae of what is actually going on at the circuit. And if you can't get excited about what's going on, then you certainly can't expect them to. It was a passion for me and it genuinely came from the heart.

MH I don't think anyone is in any doubt about that, Murray. Why did you stop commentating? Was it the travel schedule?

MW That was one reason. At least half the races are long haul. I was 78 when I stopped. I'd like to think now that I could do the job or I could do the travel - but I know I couldn't do both. I just don't have the stamina. Any job in F1 is enormously taxing, both physically and mentally. You work long hours under pressure. Yes, it's enormously enjoyable and gigantically satisfying, but it's also tremendously demanding.

MH So, what was the other reason?

MW During a race in 2000, I made an absolutely hideous and unforgivable mistake. Michael Schumacher was in pole position and Rubens Barrichello was 12th on the grid, or something like that. The race started and a Ferrari went off. My brain wouldn't let me accept that it was Schumacher who had gone off. I said it was Barrichello and made a great song and dance about it. Then I realised it was Schumacher and, somehow, blagged my way out of it.

The next day, there was a really vicious piece in the *Daily Mail*. "Time for the old fool to go"; that sort of thing. I thought: "I don't think that's fair, but there's an element of truth there. I got it wrong and I shouldn't have got it wrong." I was with ITV at the time and I went to Brian Barwick, the head of sport, and said I thought it was time to stop. Brian said: "Well Murray, it's your life, your decision. I'm not going to ask you to stop but, if you feel you ought to stop, then okay. But, if you're going to retire then give yourself time so that every Grand Prix you go to, you'll know it's the last time you'll be at that particular race. And we'll give you a jolly good send off." That's what I did. As a result, 2001 was an absolutely magical year for me.

MH I remember there was a great send-off for you in the F1 paddock at Indianapolis. It wasn't quite the end of the season, but it was a chance for everyone to pay justifiable tribute. What did you make of that?

Germany 2007, and Walker still had a few tricks to teach MH

MW I knew something was going on - but I didn't know what. I was taken to the Williams place in the paddock and, when we got there, I found Tony George, owner of the Indianapolis Motor Speedway, Flavio Briatore, Bernie Ecclestone, drivers, mechanics; an enormous number of people all standing round drinking champagne. Michael Schumacher was there so I thought if whatever's happening is good enough for him, it's good enough for me. I went and sat beside Michael.

Tony Jardine was compere and he was getting the drivers to come up and read from pieces of paper on which were written things I was alleged to have said. Then it's Michael's turn. Tony gives him a piece of paper which has on it: "Here comes Michael Schumacher, son of Ralf Schumacher." Poor bemused Michael looks at this piece of paper and says: "I don't understand. What am I supposed to do?" Tony tells him he has to say it like I say it. Michael then says: "Yes, but when Murray says it, I'm in the car and I can't hear him." I said: "Come on, Michael, we'll do it together" and I put my arm round him - I've a lovely photograph of us doing this together.

He came up to me afterwards and said: "Can you help me, Murray, because there's something I don't understand. This party is in your honour - but they were all making fun of you!" I said: "Well I suppose that's our way, Michael." He asked if this was the English sense of humour. I said I supposed it was. He said: "Oh! I see." But I don't think he did.

MH So much happened in your career. Do you miss it?

MW I was at a lunch for my wife's golf club, sitting next to a very grumpy bloke, trying to make conversation. I said: "What do you do?" He said: "I've retired, haven't I." He said he was the chairman of a major committee in farming, quite an important bloke by the sound of it. So, I said: "Do you miss it?" "Miss it!" he exploded. "Of course I bloody miss it!" I feel like him - but not so grumpy, I hope. How else are you going to feel when you're suddenly cut adrift from something that has been the central focus of your life?

MH Do you watch the races?

MW Yes, I do. I watch as much as possible. Do you think F1 is as enjoyable as it used to be, or are we looking through rose-coloured glasses?

MH You obviously get asked that question a lot. My answer is that, along with everything else in the sporting world, F1 has changed and some parts are better and some parts are worse. For me, having been through that dreadful Schumacher period we referred to, I'm loving it now; the unpredictability.

MW Yes, I think we're living through a golden era now. But the thing I would miss is the camaraderie we used to have. You don't get the chance to chat with the drivers and everyone else because they're so busy with all the information they have to sift through.

MH There's two ways of looking at it from a media point of view: things are much more regulated now, and each time you talk to a driver a minder puts a micro-recorder on the table. So you've no chance of getting anything off the record. On the other hand,

'Of course I bloody miss it.' Murray reflects on retirement

if you want to talk to Button or Webber or whomever, you're told by the PR people: "You can have 10 minutes at 4.15 on Thursday." You turn up at 4.15 on Thursday and the driver is there, as promised.

I say that because when I started as a professional journalist in the days of James Hunt, there was no organisation and I can remember sitting for hours - and I mean hours - outside the Texaco trailer and coming away with nothing because James either forgot or couldn't be arsed because he was chatting up a good-looking woman.

MW I once spent four hours sitting outside the Marlboro motorhome at Monaco, waiting for Senna. This was in the days when, like you say, you would go to the driver and ask if you could do an interview. Senna had said: "Yes, okay, after the debrief." I knew, having said that, he would do it.

This was at the height of the Senna-Prost animosity and, after four hours, the motor home door opened and Prost came out. I said: "Alain, what in God's name have you been talking about for four hours?" Alain said: "Oh, zis and zat. But, you know Murray, I do not like to be the first to leave..." And you knew why. Because the moment Alain left the room, Ayrton would say: "Okay, put more pressure in my rear tyres and adjust the front wing."

MH You must have talked to Senna quite a lot.

MW I interviewed him at most grands prix. I remember doing so on the Friday at Imola in 1994. Over the winter, I'd got out some tapes of Formula 3 from 1983 when Ayrton was fighting hammer and tongs for the championship with Martin Brundle. I realised I had been using the correct pronunciation back then by calling him 'I-ear-ton' but had since become very sloppy, calling him 'Air-ton'. I vowed to put that right in 1994 and used 'I-ear-ton' in my commentary at the first race in Brazil. I got such a volley of abuse from the British public that I thought: "Well, it's them or it's him - so it's going to be him" and I continued with 'I-ear-ton' in the second race in Japan. So, we're sitting down with him at the third race at Imola and I said: "Well, Air-ton, Schumacher beat you in Brazil, Schumacher beat you in Japan, you're 20 points down. What do you think about that?"

"What happened to I-ear-ton?" he said.

I said: "How on earth did you know that?" And he said: "Oh I keep in touch with these things, Murray." Another manifestation of what an incredible bloke he was.

MH I guess you must get asked if you have a favourite interview - or interviewee?

MW In Brazil, in 1980-something, early in the morning when the temperature was about 38 degrees, I did a 20-minute interview with Nigel Mansell. It was only afterwards that the BBC engineer realised he'd forgotten to turn on the microphone. So I had to ferret out Nigel and ask if he wouldn't mind coming back out in the heat and doing it again. He made a few comments, but we did it again. And every time thereafter, when I appeared before him, I'd get [*imitates a Midlands accent*] "Have you turned the microphone on, Murray?"

I got on really well with Nigel. He used to wear this Canon cap which he was paid a lot of money to wear. When I was doing interviews, the BBC would tell the cameraman to have just Nigel's face in the frame; not the cap. Nigel isn't stupid, of course. As the interview progressed, Nigel was sliding lower and lower in his seat. By the time we'd finished, he was almost under the table.

MH You had a good rapport with the drivers. Do you feel relaxed interviewing them?

MW Some more than others. People believe that you and I have unfettered access to the drivers and, not only that, we're personal mates with them, go on holiday together, have Christmas lunch in each other's homes and are deep in each other's pockets. But it's not like that. It's a professional relationship and I got on better with the British drivers - especially Nigel.

MH The questions have to be right, don't they? And a lot can depend on where we are in the championship.

MW You're right - and here's a good example of both. I remember doing an interview with Damon Hill towards the end of his championship year and he was as tense as a violin string. He also had to cope with Jacques Villeneuve, who was not at all bad at the mind games. I think Damon was doing six hours a day in the gym; his cheeks were sunken. When we sat down, I said: "Are you all right? You look a bit peaky."

"What did you say that for?" he exploded, and got up and stormed off. I gave him a little time to simmer down before going up to him and saying I'd obviously said something that offended him but it was unintentional and I was sorry. He said not to

Murray picked the wrong time to tell Damon Hill he looked 'peaky'

worry because, before we sat down, he had just been interviewed by a foreign journalist, who had asked Damon: "What would you give to have your father back for just one hour?" I mean, how insensitive can you get?

MH I want to go right back to the beginning, when you were working in an advertising agency and commentating at the weekends. How did that schedule work?

MW I look back in amazement at what I did. I don't how I did it but the answer is, if in life you want to do something badly enough, you find a way, don't you? This was in the 1960s when ITV were doing what is now called motocross but what was then known as scrambling. Every Friday, I'd leave the office in St James' Square at 5pm and get on the tube to Cockfosters, at the northern extremity of the London Underground system. My wife Elizabeth would be waiting in the car, with the dog and provisions, and we'd then drive to Yorkshire - and this was before the motorways and the M1 - to somewhere like Wakefield, Rippon or Leeds, work all day Saturday for the national network and then, with the same riders on the same bikes at the same circuit, do the whole thing again on Sunday for the northern network, ABC.

When it got dark at 4pm, I would drive back in our Triumph Herald estate with the Boxer dog in the back. It makes my blood run cold to think about this, because we had one of those gas stoves which Elizabeth had in the footwell; she would heat up some stew which I would eat on the move. On Monday morning, I was back in the office. One year, we did this for 32 weekends in succession. And I loved it! Adrenalin conquers all.

When I got into F1 on television in 1978, I was lucky in that I was by then a director of the company. If I wanted leave early on Friday, that's what I did. We didn't have a conventional holiday for 20 years. I'm not saying that looking for sympathy. It never crossed my mind. As far as I was concerned, I was on holiday all the time.

MH The job got you into some interesting places. I know you were in the Tank Regiment during the war and you got to drive one again for a TV programme.

MW The BBC did an hour-long programme on my life and times, during which we went to the Bovington Tank Museum - the best in the world, in my view - and I put on the khaki and drove a Sherman. They're not difficult to drive. The difficult thing is getting the best out of them. You can make it go forwards or backwards or sideways, but it's all about being able to position the thing and stop in the right places.

MH So, much the same as driving an F1 car - which I also remember you did.

MW Yes, that was when Niki Lauda and John Watson were paired at McLaren. I was at a function and Ron Dennis asked if I'd ever driven a F1 car. When I said I hadn't, he said he would be in touch. I thought I wouldn't hear any more about it. But Ron isn't like that.

I got a call to be at Silverstone. I got on my BMW bike and, when I got there, Ron gave me a duffle bag. It had a set of Niki Lauda's overalls and two pairs of racing boots; one size 8 and one size 10, which was typical of Ron's attention to detail in that one of those sizes had to fit me. I had my own helmet because I'd ridden up on the bike. Ron said I would be going out in the lunch hour. People started saying they were looking forward to the lunch break. I realised then that I was at a Goodyear test day and all these people I'd been slagging off for years were now going to be watching me drive an F1 car for the first time.

James Hunt was my mentor and he said there were two things I had to know: you must not stall when you leave the pit lane and when you come in, you must stop at the right pit. I didn't stall the car going out the first time. But I did stall the second time and, needless to say, that's the clip the BBC always shows. I was supposed to be out for two laps but I got so engrossed in getting my line right for Copse, I didn't see the pit board with the arrow. I stayed out for eight laps I think it was.

When I came in, I was sitting in the car feeling rather pleased with myself. I looked up and there was Ken Tyrrell standing over me. And you know what he could be like - all stern-faced with his arms crossed, glaring down at me. I thought: "No! I've stopped in the Tyrrell pit." But I hadn't. Ken had watched me going round and he had seen the arrow go out. So he came down to McLaren and, when I stopped, he leaned into the cockpit and said: "When you're told to come in, you bloody come in! Understand?" Then that classic Tyrrell cackle.

James said to me: "Well done Murray. You've done something any F1 driver would give his eye teeth to do."

"Oh, really James? What was that?"

"You've improved your lap time by half a minute!"

James was such a multi-faceted character. And that was a good example. Sometimes he could be the nicest bloke in the world and an absolute hoot and, at other times, he could be an unmitigated so and so.

MH I saw both sides. I hated having to work with him on the *James Hunt Magazine* in 1977 but, later on, when he was commentating and broke - by his standards - he was one of us; such a top bloke. I know exactly what you mean.

Murray, this has been wonderful. We could talk for hours.

MW I've absolutely no doubt about that. It's been very enjoyable. Thank you.

At lunch with **Rubens Barrichello**

"There is no question that Michael was better than me on average. But if you put us in a cage with a lion, I'll be the only one to come out. Because I'll find a way. In six years at Ferrari, I was finding my way."

Typical Rubens. Having experienced a disappointing end to his distinguished and lengthy F1 career at Williams, you'd think Sir Frank's team would be the last place Barrichello would want to be seen having lunch. He doesn't give it a second thought. No problem at all; we'll meet in their paddock hospitality restaurant on the Friday of the 2013 Spanish Grand Prix weekend.

Not only is Rubens made welcome, he immediately feels at home and happy to see his old friends. The ever-efficient Jo Turley has reserved us a table at the window to assist Glenn Dunbar's pictures but also, as it turns out, to provide occasional diversions. Passers-by, seeing Rubens, pop in to say hello. We have Brazilian journos, there's Dickie Stanford, the Williams team manager - not to mention Alan Jones and Alain Prost - stopping by the table, and Ferrari personnel saluting cheerfully as they walk past. The hour or so we spend in conversation fills in detail of the impromptu display of widespread affection for this most popular of drivers.

He's been part of the scene for a long time - as I know only too well, having kept company with Rubens while writing a fly-on-the-wall account of Jordan during his debut season with Eddie's team in 1993. Then, by another stroke of good fortune, Barrichello happened to be driving for Stewart when I recorded that extraordinary first year for the team in 1997. Subsequently our relationship became more distant owing to the red media defences erected in the very different surroundings of Ferrari, a situation that was reversed completely during an eventful and unique season with Brawn in 2009. A lot of ground to cover, then, as he arrives, smiling and bang on time. Typical Rubens.

Maurice Hamilton It's a nice surprise, seeing you again at F1 races. What are you up to?

Rubens Barrichello I'm doing 10 races for Globo TV, including all the European grands prix, Abu Dhabi, Singapore and Brazil.

MH Have you done TV commentary before?

RB They invited me to try it for first time in Brazil last year. To be honest, I've always liked working on camera. People think F1 is very technical, which it is, but if I can make my son understand, I can tell others as well.

MH Apart from expressing it in layman's language, drivers can get across what it actually feels like in the car, whereas the rest of us obviously would have no idea. But the thing that always impresses me is that drivers can look at a car on the move and detect all sorts of things about the fuel load or the effect of tyre degradation, set-up or whatever.

RB Yes, you can point out something and people suddenly say, "Oh, right! I see that now." In the Bahrain Grand Prix, for example, I noticed there was a problem with Alonso's rear wing before the TV cameras picked it up. When I saw the drop in his performance, I began to look really closely at the Ferrari and, when he went by the commentary box, I could see the DRS flap was way beyond its limit.

MH You've always enjoyed the technical side, haven't you? I was reminded of that when recalling your first F1 season in 1993 with Jordan. They didn't have any other driver initially and there you were, doing all the testing with the new car and the new Hart engine; a novice but carrying the responsibility of giving feedback.

RB Before that, I remember my first test at Silverstone at the end of 1992. They only allowed me six laps because Stefano Modena, a team driver that year, was going around. So it was like, "Okay, let this Brazilian kid who has brought money do some laps." And I went faster than Modena ever did.

After that, I took care of the test. I had a great relationship with Gary Anderson who was Jordan's technical director, and he could see that, although I had very little experience, I had such a feeling for the car.

MH But weren't you overawed by that? I mean, here you were, what age were you?

RB I was 19 at the time.

MH And you are in an F1 car after F3000 and, before that, F3 and Opel/Lotus. In the space of three years you are into a F1 car. But the team was growing as well; it was only the start of Jordan's third year in F1. How do you look back on all of that?

RB It was a great experience, a great way to begin my F1 career. It was a small team with not a lot of cash to get things done. The 1993 car wasn't great to qualify but it was okay on full tanks. The best thing I remember was running seventh when I had a hydraulics problem in Brazil, which was only my second race.

MH But it was the next race that really mattered, wasn't it?

RB Yeah, Donington, the European Grand Prix. I started 12th, and at the end of the first lap I was fourth. Unfortunately, there was a problem because the race was wet, dry and then wet again: the traction control was working too hard and using too much fuel. They calculated it wrongly although, at the time, they said it was a fuel pump failure, or something like that.

MH We all remember that race for Ayrton Senna's fantastic drive. It was such a shame you couldn't get on the podium with your hero because you were running third when the car stopped.

RB If I had finished third, I would not have been able to stand up on the podium. I had a modified seat because I was trying to compensate for a lower back pain problem. The seat was pushing my lower back forward. When I got out of the car, I couldn't stand up; they took me straight to the medical centre.

Saying that, I probably would have found a way of standing beside Ayrton if I'd finished. Then we almost got a point in Magny Cours. I had a very long brake pedal and I lost a position to Michael Andretti's McLaren two laps from the end.

MH You have fantastic recall. Can you remember all of your 326 F1 races?

RB Yes, I have memories of all of them. My wife thinks there's something wrong with me! But when I do my book, it won't just be the straightforward facts - even though I remember them all. I will want readers to know there has been much more to my life, coming from a poor - financially, I mean - background, when you think of what we have achieved, it's been a phenomenal life. The way my father went to great lengths and through great hardship to make sure I had the best equipment.

MH I was always impressed by the way your dad was quietly in the background, never got in the way, but made sure he was there for you.

RB I had a lot of support. He was a fanatic, he loved racing, but he didn't understand very much so, at one point, we were learning together.

MH Have you learned from that when dealing with your boys?

RB Absolutely. Eduardo is 11 and he is already racing. I was there for his first race. He did very well and when it was over, I asked him, "Did I talk too much? Is it something that I need to watch?" He said it was okay although sometimes I was talking about two or three things at the same time and it was a bit much. So I need to step back, and the fact that I'm not there for two or three races is actually good. He will have a lot more pressure than I did.

MH Are his helmet colours like yours?

RB Yes, mainly white but, if you remember, there was one which he painted for me when I was racing for Williams. That's become his helmet colours, with the orange at the sides having splits instead of being round, like mine.

Rubens enjoys his return to the F1 pits, meeting old friends

MH That reminds me of Interlagos in 1995, the first GP in Brazil after Senna's death, when you had Ayrton's colours incorporated into your helmet design. I don't think I've ever seen you so stressed as that weekend. That was a lot of pressure, wasn't it?

RB If I could re-live that weekend, I would never do that again. I felt it was like I was doing something for somebody else. I wasn't being myself. You may have seen the moment when I embraced my father and I cried, big time.

There were a lot of other pressures that weekend. This was when I was trying left-foot braking for the first time. The telemetry then was not as good as it is now. I didn't know it, but I was touching the brake pedal a little when on the straight and it was putting temperature into the carbon discs. I was something like 6-7km/h slower than Eddie Irvine on the straight. But we didn't know why. I felt it was like putting my hand in front of the air box and the engine power dropped.

I told my father I was going to have a big accident because I was overdriving. I couldn't understand why I was quicker than Eddie in most of the corners but still losing out. After five or six races, when I went back to right-foot braking, I finished second in Canada and the pressure eased off. But it was a tough time in Brazil.

MH The pressure seemed to ease all round when you went to Stewart in 1997 - even though there was more responsibility in a sense because you were leading a new team into F1. As you may remember, I was lucky enough to be able to watch the whole thing come together.

RB Yeah, you seemed to be following me! But for me, and I guess for you, it was very special to be with a team that was starting off. A fascinating experience. So much to learn, an incredible ambiance. But the thing that made it for me was working with Jackie Stewart. He was the best teacher you could have. People sometimes make fun of him - you know, the things he says and the way he says it - but I disagree with them. He is a guy who really put his heart and his passion into being a racing driver. And to make the show better.

MH And how about as a driver? How did you feel about his words of advice?

RB He loved my smoothness with the steering wheel. He never told me anything about my driving because, when you choose someone to drive for you and you are really sure, then it works. Maybe we wouldn't agree over this or that, but we would talk it through. We never fell out over anything.

MH I remember Jackie had a thing about appearance, not you personally, but the appearance of drivers generally.

RB I still have the suit he had made for me.

MH And the hand-made shoes?

RB Yeah, everything was perfect. I haven't changed much physically, which means I can still wear the suit. It's so nice.

MH And then there was the story with the Rolex watch.

RB Ah, yes. My watch was a Timex and, as you know, Jackie had a thing with Rolex. So I said to him as a kind of joke: "Jackie, you need to give me a Rolex Daytona." He said: "Okay, if you qualify in the Top 10 for the first two races, I'll get one for you." The first race, I qualified 11th, so, no watch. The second race, I was 11th again. I asked for one more chance. I qualified fifth for the next race in Argentina. I have this picture which one of the mechanics took and you can see the Timex in the air as I throw it from the cockpit! I got my Rolex - with an inscription from Jackie on the back.

[*Alain Prost comes to the table to say hello*]

AP Your turn for one of these interviews, huh? [*Nodding in my direction - and then, to my relief, smiling*]. Good to see you, Rubens. Are you working?

RB Working for Globo TV and doing some racing in Brazil; it's good to be closer to the family. But it's good to be here too. Maybe some driver has a stomach ache and I jump in the car! Well, you never know!

[*Prost laughs, excuses himself and leaves*]

RB What age is he now?

MH Err... I should know because I had lunch with him for one of these interviews a couple of months ago. I think he's about 57 [*he was actually 58 at the time*].

Prost drops by mid-interview; he's been 'done' by MH already

RB He looks amazing. Great to see him. I know Jackie always rated Alain very highly and it was nice to have our driving styles compared.

MH Monaco 1997 with Stewart must be a great memory. How does that rate?

RB The wins with Ferrari and Brawn mean more for obvious reasons, but second place with that car at Monaco was as good as a win. It was our fifth race! I watched it again the other day with my kids. They love to watch races they were not able to see at the time and I can talk them through it.

MH That must be a wonderful thing to do.

RB Yeah, it is. I love it. We watched the 1996 Spanish GP, the one in the wet, which Michael won. I was doing so well with the Jordan and then we had a problem with the hydraulics. They said it couldn't be fixed. I was getting changed when they shouted: "It's fixed! Get back in the car!" I put my helmet back on without the balaclava and without earplugs. I didn't get too far before the car stopped again - which was lucky for me because it would have exploded my ears if I'd been able to finish. I can tell you, never, ever, drive an F1 car without earplugs. I had that buzzing in my head for weeks.

MH I interviewed you when you left Stewart for Ferrari and I questioned the wisdom of it all, given the fact it was more or less Michael's team. You said you felt your talent would be enough; just get in and drive the car. Which is, in effect, what you did. But it didn't quite work out as you'd hoped, did it?

RB When I had my first meeting, I told Jean Todt: "If it's written in my contract that I will not be able to race for myself and win, I'm not interested. I want to be free to race." He said that's what Ferrari wanted from me. I knew that Michael was really good and I felt sure this was good for me as I was going to be able to prove myself.

In the first few races, nothing much happened because Michael was quicker. Michael didn't have bad days... but I was getting faster and faster, closer and closer. Then they started to talk about things that were not written in the contract. Like the T-car, for example. They said it was always Michael's. But why? It wasn't written in my contract - but it was written in his. They talked about strategy but, when my engineer left the room, they turned their chairs away and they started to talk. Instead of fighting, I took my chair and sat with them. So, I've always taken it positively without much blah, blah, blah.

There is no question that Michael was better than me - on average. I've always said this in Portuguese, so, hopefully in English it will come out okay. If you put myself and Michael into a cage with a lion, I will probably be the only one that will come out. Because I'll find my way. I'll make it happen. So, in the six years that I was there, I was finding my way. Driving for Ferrari was such an enormous, great feeling. There was a lot of pressure, but I've always liked the pressure. But things started to collapse because they never allowed me to be... good enough. At the end of the day, they didn't want it to change. That's why I said to myself, "I have the best car available, but am I happy?" I wasn't happy any more and I left one year before the end of the contract.

MH Was there a particular turning point when you thought, enough is enough?

RB The US Grand Prix in 2005. There were only six cars.

MH And you had the pit stops and almost collided when Michael rejoined.

RB Yes, but that wasn't the thing. Something happened in the middle of the race that I will reserve for my book, if you don't mind. That incident you referred to, leaving the pits, was a pure racing incident. I tried on the outside and he hung onto his line. That was okay. During the race, there was talking and... well, there were only six cars and that's what made me frustrated. The way the conversation developed made me furious and that's when I decided to leave.

MH I can't wait to learn exactly what went on there. It must have been significant for you to feel that way. Moving on to more positive experiences at Ferrari, which of the wins stands out? I'm sure the first, in Germany 2000, means the most?

RB The first is always the most emotional. The reason I cried on the podium when I looked at the sky was because, for some reason, I remembered my father selling his car - the only car we had - to enable me to race in the Brazilian go-kart championship in 1987. If he hadn't sold that car, maybe I wouldn't have been driving in F1.

But I have three top wins. Silverstone 2003 was magic in a place that I've always loved. Even if I had bad days, I had something over Michael that day. I knew Silverstone a lot better than I knew Interlagos.

Monaco 1997: Rubens takes a brilliant second for Stewart

MH Really? Even though Interlagos is over the fence from where you were brought up?

RB Yes, really. Don't forget, I was 16 when I came to Europe. I had only done a couple of tests at Interlagos, whereas I raced so much at Silverstone. So, that race, and Suzuka in 2003, was also special because I rate Suzuka and Spa as driver's circuits. And then Valencia 2009. That was super.

MH But your time with Honda, from 2006, wasn't so super, was it? Initially, it must have seemed a good deal because you had Gil de Ferran there, people like the designer, Geoff Willis.

RB It was a good car; aerodynamically, it worked okay. But, sometimes, you would have a problem with grip level and the car was stalling too much in the downforce phase. Sometimes it would work perfectly; sometimes not. It took me a while to learn how to work with the Michelins because this was a tyre that had a lot of grip - but only if you kept a lot of temperature in it. It was the only year that I didn't drive Bridgestone, apart from the early period with Goodyear. The longest time was with Bridgestone.

Driving with Jenson was nice. I liked it. He was a good team-mate but we both suffered in 2007 and 2008 with cars that were really bad. The team was going through a lot of different strategies, people going away, and we lost Geoff. It was tough, but I've always found that the tough years in my career were always before years that became better. I kept on smiling and I had those three or four months without knowing what I would be doing in 2009.

MH That must have been a really long winter because it did seem you would not be driving anything at all.

RB It was really horrible. But, for some reason, I knew it I would be okay. My wife was thinking I was crazy. My friends thought I had lost it. But I had two little guys who knew their daddy would go racing again some time. When Ross Brawn called me, I was actually by myself in the pool area of our country house, thinking about life. When he asked if I could be there by Friday, I said, "I can be there any time you tell me." He said, "We have a contract". When I went to tell my wife - I still become emotional when I think about it - it was the best day of my life. It was such a great feeling. I'm going to be driving!

To make it even better, it was here in Barcelona that Jenson had the first run in the new car. There was a lot of fuel on board and he came back and said: "We're going to have a lot of fun this year!"

MH And if you hadn't had such a difficult start to the year with the brakes, the story might have been even better.

RB That might sound like an excuse, but it wasn't. Jenson used Brembo and I used AP. In 2006, I couldn't get Jenson's brakes to work. So I changed to AP. In 2007 we tested again; no way for me with Brembo. In 2008, the same thing. In 2009, I started with AP as usual but for some reason I was running hotter rear calipers than Jenson, which affected the tyres. It was minimal but I was always a little bit behind even though I sometimes qualified ahead.

After six races, they suggested we try the brakes again. We changed the brake materials and they worked perfectly for me on the 2009 car. After that, Jenson never qualified ahead of me again [*apart from at the Hungarian GP, when Rubens suffered a mechanical failure in Q2*] but, by then, Red Bull were coming strong, so I couldn't get as many points as I'd have liked. It was a phenomenal year. If you ask me when was my best chance of becoming champion, I'd have to say it was 2009. I won in Valencia and Monza with a car that was not the best any more. But Jenson had won six races at the beginning of the year. That package with the Mercedes engine was just phenomenal. It was a lovely car.

MH Do you have one of the Brawn cars?

RB I have one of the Honda cars. But I wish I had a Brawn.

MH I'll bet you do! There was talk of you going to McLaren after that. What's the story there?

RB I had a contract with Williams for 2010. I really thought about McLaren but I've always had a good relationship with Sam Michael. I went to Williams to make it work with Sam. I was happy with that, but I have to say the offer from McLaren was very tempting. I'd like to think that if the F1 paddock remembers me for one thing, it will be for my honesty. I couldn't do that to Sam, or to Williams. I say that without any regret whatsoever. Unfortunately, I came in when Sam was about to leave.

Rubens' Rolex, courtesy of JS, makes its star debut in Japan

MH So things never really went as planned at Williams?

RB Adam Parr was a financially driven man. The rules had changed inside the team. Adam needed money so, it was not going well and the car was not fantastic. The first year with Nico Hulkenberg was okay; I rate Nico very highly. There were a lot of politics in the second year and even though I tried very hard to be in for my 20th year, I was happy enough not to be involved in any politics. If F1 didn't want me any more, I didn't want to stay.

MH Before we leave Williams and F1, I have to ask you about Hungary and Michael Schumacher in 2010. I remember you said that it actually looked worse from outside the car than it did from the cockpit. Even so, it looked pretty bloody awful from where I was sitting.

RB I have always fought really hard, any time, anywhere, for one point. But seeing Michael in front of me that day was special. It was a present from God.

MH What do you mean exactly?

RB It was special because I was fighting Michael without anyone in my ear telling me shit about what I could and couldn't do.

MH Ah, right! Sorry, carry on...

RB I thought to myself, "If I have one chance I'm going to take it." Although I had a softer tyre and it was coming good, it was very difficult to follow Michael. I think I had about six laps running behind him and I was trying to find a way. I could only manage if he made a mistake. He made one going onto the pit straight and I thought, "This is it! He's going to go on the inside and I am going to go outside, and that's the way it will be."

I thought it was strange when he went to the middle of the track because he was not protecting his line. So I went on the inside and he started coming across. I then realised he knew he had zero chance of staying ahead because, if I came left or right, I was going to be faster. So, when I decided which way to go, he would close the door and I would back off. Well, that's what he thought! When people ask me how close to the wall I was, I say I don't know - I closed my eyes.

MH Did you go into a year of Indycar with your eyes wide open?

RB I did. And I'm happy to say that even though F1 people think it's crazy stuff. But it was a difficult decision to start with. I had been watching the race when Dan Wheldon died. When my wife looked at me, I said, "No way. Don't worry, I'm never going to do that." When I went testing, she thought, "There's trouble there." But, in the end, she said, "If you're happy doing it, then I'm happy for you to do it." That was important.

So, yes, I enjoyed it. The paddock, the way they do things and the way they go racing is really nice. But, although the cars are very safe, the tracks are not. You race in places where it's so bumpy, your feet cannot stay on the pedals. I think if I had stayed there, I would have tried to become a president of the drivers' association and do something, because there was a bit of a lack of respect.

I struggled with the lack of power steering. Not because I was weak but because I lost my smoothness. To drive an Indycar fast you've got to be brutal. But when I went to the ovals, I got my smoothness back because they had no downforce and all of a sudden I was up at the front when everyone was expecting me to be at the back.

It's a great feeling to say that I have done it and raced on the ovals. But I had to ask myself if I needed that for my whole life? Because, like Michael Schumacher, you won't see me backing off if I have a chance to overtake. But you finished the races with such a stress. In Texas, for example, in 24°C and you have a guy who is suffering in front of you and he uses the whole track. He crosses in front of you and you lose downforce; you're just like a spectator. I lost a little more hair in the first year.

I worked very hard to get a second year because I thought I could do better, knowing the car and trying different things. But like F1 now, they need money. I told them they didn't need to pay me anything, but they still needed $2 million on top. I said I wasn't going to take it from my pocket, because I don't deserve that. But don't get me wrong; I never disliked my Indycar year. I'm proud I achieved so much in my first year.

MH So, what are you racing now?

RB Stock cars were always something I'd wanted to do. I thought, "I'm gonna go back home and do that." When I did three races at the end of last year for charity, I found the stock car was much easier to drive than an Indycar, so I decided to have a go.

MH One final thought while we have our coffee. I'm not sure you know this but, at the time you were joining F1, Eddie Jordan was talking to Ayrton Senna about 1993. It was a very slim chance obviously but, if you remember, Ayrton was looking to leave McLaren and the deal EJ proposed was to have Honda come to the team on the condition that Ayrton would be there and he would make it his team, run the team the way he wanted with his mates at Honda. It appealed to him. And you would have been the perfect number two; a young Brazilian he liked. Unfortunately, as we know, it came to nothing.

RB I didn't know that. That would have been perfect. I tell you, just to have Ayrton some times sit at my table for dinner was great. Imagine having him as a team-mate. I had such a passion for him as a person and a driver. Thank you for telling me that.

MH Not at all. You can put it in your book!

At lunch with **Sir Jackie Stewart**

"Emotion is less today, partly because of the danger. Martin Brundle's grid walk wouldn't get anything like the same responses in my day, because somebody was likely to be killed."

There was a surreal feeling about hosting this 2012 lunch. In 1967, I remember waiting patiently by the BRM truck for Jackie Stewart's autograph, then watching in awe as he provoked the hefty BRM H-16 into a power-slide through Becketts during practice for the British Grand Prix.

Seven years later, as a fan posing as a journalist, I blagged my way into a 7-Series BMW as he took a bunch of writers around the Nordschleife during a lull in practice for the German Grand Prix. I never uttered a word. But I wrote a story about that journey - how could you fail to find the right words after such an experience - and the piece was published, thus providing the leg-up I needed into the world of motorsport journalism.

Since then, our paths have crossed in a number of ways, from keeping lap charts during his days as a commentator for ESPN to joining his birthday dinners which usually fall at the time of the Canadian Grand Prix.

And here I was in the Old Plow in the tiny Buckinghamshire village of Speen, watching Sir Jackie Stewart walk across the pub car park in that familiar bouncy manner of his. It was a reminder that, despite his fame, fortune and status, the triple World Champion remains exactly as he was at Silverstone in 1967. I knew instinctively this lunch would be insightful and wide-ranging. And so it turned out. But it was slightly surreal nonetheless.

Maurice Hamilton Before we get going, I wanted to ask about the podium interviews you did at Silverstone for the 2012 British Grand Prix [*the first of their kind*]. Where did that come from?

Sir Jackie Stewart I have no idea. On Sunday morning they asked me. They said we'd like you to ask each of the guys a question or two, but keep it short. They said, by the way, the drivers will not know it's happening and it'll come after the champagne spray. I thought, well thank goodness for that! It was straightforward but all three drivers delivered very well and they took the chance to thank the crowd after all they had been through with the weather and so on.

MH What sort of reaction did you get?

JS Everybody seemed happy. As I was walking back, Bernie came out of his place and said thanks very much. He said the podium is a new design, much smaller. I said it was a little awkward because I was on the lower level, which meant I had to reach up with the mic, which wasn't good. But, typical Bernie, I see they learned from that.

MH It was making a connection between Formula One and the crowd, because they don't normally get that. Do you think F1 is still guilty of not connecting properly with the fans; the people paying the money?

JS Yes, there's much more to be done. Frankly, a lot of drivers will go a long way to avoid the autograph bit. The only opportunity the fans get is when the drivers come in the morning and go out at night. I think it's very important for fans to have the opportunity to meet everybody.

Okay, I know a lot of autographs are going to ebay. You can see the guys who are the pros at this. They've got a lot of different pictures of you but, the moment I see the second picture coming up and it's the same as the first picture, then it's likely to be ebay and you want to avoid that. But it's difficult when there's so many people around you; sometimes it can be 10 deep. But, no matter what, I've always taken the view that you've got to be courteous. People will be courteous to you if you're courteous to them. A huge number of them have autograph books. I've still got the autograph book I had as a wee boy.

MH Me too.

JS I still do my signature in a way that you can read it. It takes longer but I remember when I went home at night from Silverstone when my big brother was racing, I was awfully disappointed if the signature wasn't clear and I couldn't read it. The drivers now are just doing that [*imitates a squiggle*] and I think it's a mistake.

MH Are we talking long term here? Because you are still in demand nearly 40 years after you last raced.

JS That's the point. The drivers are too short-sighted. If I go to Goodwood or a Grand Prix in Italy or Spain or wherever, there's still a huge number of people who want autographs. It's easy when you're at the top to think autographs are unnecessary. But it's part and parcel of your duty as a World Champion or a top-line F1 driver. You never know where tomorrow is going to take you.

MH Is this also part of your insistence about a smart appearance? I remember when you started Stewart Grand Prix, you had Rubens Barrichello walking about in hand-made shoes!

JS Drivers don't think it's important to present themselves well. When you're earning good money, you think you're never going to need any more. But it's wrong. There's got to be life after driving cars and I think there's a missing factor in nearly all F1 drivers at the present time. You've got to look clean, look tidy; present yourself so that you're appealing to everybody.

I don't care whether you're talking about the top people at Microsoft or Apple or wherever. Mr Microsoft is now wearing a collar and tie because he's now bigger than just being the genius that he was. He's stepped up a level. He's dealing with governments and monarchs and world leaders. This is not being pedantic; this is a realistic observation. David Beckham is bigger than he has ever been and he's better presented than he's ever been. Jean-Claude Killy was on the board of Coca-Cola - USA, not just France. And he's on the board of Rolex. He was a skier in a very casual world and yet he's at the top level 40 years later. F1 drivers need to think of that.

MH You have to be living proof of how this works at the age of 73.

JS I've been lucky enough to establish long-term relationships. I've been with Rolex now for 44 years; with Moet since I first sprayed it at the French Grand Prix in 1969 - I'm now on the board of Moet Hennessy. I was with Ford for 40 years. I'm earning considerably more today than I ever made as a racing driver, but still from being, if you like, the racing driver. My business interests are because of that. It's no good to me saying it's because I'm a really good business man. It's because I saw the need to deliver back then.

MH You mention the autograph book because, as I say, I've got one - which has your autograph in it, by the way - and if you go back over time it's interesting to see how these days drivers just do a quick squiggle and it fills a page whereas back then, drivers would carefully write their name and there'd be two or three to a page.

JS Quite right. I would think it presumptuous of me to take a whole page; it just wouldn't be the right thing to be doing. I think all of that stuff is more important than the guys think. Yes, it's intoxicating when you first start to win. But there are other times you get annoyed because you're being intruded upon. It's wrong to think that; totally wrong.

MH Can we blame poor driver management here?

JS I think one of the really important missing links in F1, and motor racing generally, is that we're the only major sport where we're so clever, we don't need coaches. How can that be? It's absolutely nonsensical. The best skiers, cricketers, rugby players, boxers, golfers, tennis players; they've all got coaches. Grand Prix drivers don't need them?

"Every other top sportsperson is coached – why not F1 drivers?"

Rubbish! Sir Frank Williams has taken on Alex Wurz to try and help Maldonado and Bruno Senna. That's absolutely right and I think Alex is the right guy; he's intelligent and he's got the experience and the vision.

MH You've always talked about mind management – it comes up when, say, we've talked about Lewis Hamilton in the past.

JS It's the single most important thing that a top sportsperson of any kind has to have, and it's missing with some of our racing drivers. Lewis allows himself to get put into circumstances that he doesn't need and, the point is, there's nobody there to tell him. I'm not being unkind to Lewis, but he doesn't think he needs anybody. His father would have been trying to tell him but that doesn't always work. In fact, I said to his father quite a few years ago: "Anthony, it's a mistake, you being his manager. It'll break up your family if you're not careful." If you went to Anthony now, I hope he would remember me saying that.

Lewis needed an outside manager who knew the business – but that's not to be confused with a coach. As I said, I think that applies to every grand prix driver, even those who have won a championship. Alonso's won it twice and I think he's got the best toolkit mentally of all the drivers in F1 at the present time. Once you start allowing your emotions out of the box, you're in trouble. Particularly at the wheel of a racing car.

MH Again, you're touching on an interesting point. How much can you tell just by looking at the pictures from the on-board cameras?

JS Look at the hands on the steering wheel. Some drivers are all over the place; everything's an adventure. What you don't need is a challenge; what you really want is an invitation. The Matra MS80 I drove to win the championship in 1969 was an invitation. I gave it time to do everything and it allowed me to do things that I would not have been able to do if I'd been trying to keep up with a difficult animal. You want to try and lead a placid animal into a corner. If I overdid it under braking and it became too busy, suddenly I'm trying to consume this busy-ness just to get the apex. But if everything is calm, on the way in I'm thinking of the exit, not the apex.

It's sometimes difficult to have a young driver understand that because he thinks he's just got to drive it. When you get into F1, it's a whole new package. Suddenly there's not as much space between the exit of one corner and the entry of the next. You're up through the box and you're working the steering wheel and the buttons. You get to the next corner and you're not prepared. It's about being able to find time and create very subtle improvements which suddenly make the lap times more consistent.

Most of the present F1 drivers turn in much too fast; you can see it on television. Vettel turns in microseconds slower, and so does Alonso. Microseconds slower, but that little bit is taking all of the tensions within the car. It's really very simple. But there are no coaches out there to tell them.

MH You say that, but I can't imagine a current F1 driver wanted to listen to anyone, particularly a coach who hasn't won a grand prix.

JS Again, that's missing the point. David Leadbetter didn't win any majors, yet he was the best golf coach ever. Same for Butch Harmon, who didn't win a lot, yet he was dealing with Tiger Woods at his peak. Why are drivers so clever that they don't need help?

MH You're working closely with Lotus and Genii now. What's your take on Romain Grosjean?

JS I'm concerned that one of the anomalies of F1 is what I call the second year factor. Regrettably, in a lot of cases, the second year is not as good as the first. Right now, Grosjean is one of the fastest drivers; I've been very impressed. But I have been desperately hoping he wins a Grand Prix this year because history shows there's every chance the second year will be disappointing – I'm obviously not including that period with Renault in 2009. It's not that he will become big-headed or he won't be trying; it's because whatever the 'second year' anomaly is, it has a consistent reality in almost every case, including mine.

I finished third in the world championship in 1965, my first year. I won the Italian GP and had three podiums standing beside Jim Clark. For me, it was unbelievable to be there. I was thinking I've learned so much in this first year; boy, next year is gonna be good. And it wasn't. I can't take much personal blame for that; it just happened.

MH How do you cope, as a young driver, with setbacks which are bound to come?

JS I was lucky that when I got into the car, I was able to remove all emotion. That was something I learned to do and I think it's to do with my shooting, which I did before

I got into motor racing. In shooting, once you've missed a target, you'll never get it back. Once you've missed an apex, you can't get it back.

I thought at one point I was God's gift to shooting. The other competitors were of mature years and here was a kid, who'd never had success in his life, doing well and getting slightly carried away with himself. Then I suddenly went for ages not winning. I had to realise that I wasn't going about it the right way. I was trying too hard. I didn't know what I was doing at the time and that's when the mind management came in. I later realised that if I removed emotion, I drove better races.

MH But is it not true that drivers, in the 1960s particularly, had to deal with totally different emotions?

JS Very true. I think emotion is less today than it was before and, frankly, that's partly because of the danger. The grid walk that Martin Brundle does, you wouldn't get anything like the same responses in my day because somebody was likely to be killed. I don't care who you are, when you've been to that many funerals and memorial services and you've seen the father and the mother at home after the burial and the whole family just in shock through suffering such a huge loss, it's very difficult to switch that off.

MH How do you rate the current drivers - for example, that podium at Silverstone: Mark Webber, Fernando Alonso and Sebastian Vettel. You'd have to say Alonso and Vettel would be in the top echelon.

JS Absolutely. And I think Mark, if he keeps his emotions under control, is as good a driver right now as any of the others if the car is good. Last year, he overdrove the car; emotionally, he tried too hard. This year, so far, has been much calmer. He is a more focused, capable driver in my opinion; considerably better than he was last year.

MH Is the ability to win at Monaco a good guide? Certainly, it's a race in which you excelled.

JS I think so, yes. Webber's race in Monaco this year was put under great stress coming to the end because he wasn't as quick as the other guys and they knew they couldn't pass him unless he made a mistake. That's the problem at that point; calculating enough to keep going and yet not to overdo it - which, as many drivers have proved, can happen so easily at Monaco.

MH You mentioned earlier the work the driver has to do making adjustments on his steering wheel. But could you not argue that the drivers from your era actually were much busier because you had a manual gearbox and a clutch and needed to synchronise your downshifts with the braking? Could you argue that you had to have more co-ordination?

JS No, I think they've got considerably more to do today. Then again, it could be said what I had to do was probably more than Stirling Moss or Fangio, because it took them longer to get from corner A to corner B. Saying that, it took me longer to do the same distance than the time the current F1 driver has to work with. We had one hand off the wheel changing gear but the driver now is constantly having to make adjustments while travelling much faster.

MH Mention of Vettel leads to the question of winning three world titles [*now four*] in a row. Fangio and Schumacher have done it. But no one else. How difficult is that?

JS Michael was with Ferrari each time but Fangio had swapped teams during that 1954-1957 period and I think that's an important consideration. Winning the championship once puts a big strain on any team. Do it twice in a row and everyone is wiped out. Therefore, going for a third in succession puts a huge expectation on everybody, not just the driver.

Saying that, Vettel is lucky in a way because he's with Red Bull and this is not what I'd call a normal team in that respect. Vettel doesn't have as much to do away from the race track as, say, Lewis Hamilton and Jenson Button, because they are running around servicing McLaren's sponsors [*Lewis switched to Mercedes for 2013*].

MH I seem to remember you were incredibly busy, probably for 12 months of the year when you were reigning champion?

JS When I won the championship the first time I had Ford, I had Goodyear and I had Elf Aquitaine; three of the biggest companies in the world at that time in their own industries. So I did a world tour; three countries a day; that sort of thing. I would have breakfast in Argentina, lunch in Brazil and dinner in Venezuela. The next day I'd do Central America, go up to Panama or somewhere because there was a big Goodyear dealer. I would go to India for Goodyear and Ford. And then Lagos for Elf because Nigeria was the seventh largest oil producer at that time. Everywhere you'd go, you'd be presented with another trophy and another gift, another round of applause.

MH And, correct me if I'm wrong, but you seemed to be doing a lot of testing in those days because, of course, there were no restrictions like there are now.

JS You could test whenever you wanted. It was down to money in a way but the real driving force was tyres. If Goodyear had something ready to try, off you went. We did a hell of a lot of testing. For example, it would not be uncommon to go to Kyalami in South Africa for a minimum of two weeks. And we didn't have test drivers on the team then. That was unheard of. It would be François Cevert and me.

MH Okay, so you had a hectic schedule through, let's call it, official F1 work and the unavoidable commitment that brought. But weren't you running yourself ragged, criss-crossing the Atlantic, doing television stuff in America, racing in the CanAm series and so on?

JS That's true. A guy called Roone Arledge took me on at ABC Wide World of Sports. Roone was the most creative man that's ever been in sports television. He directed the Olympics and was the president of ABC Sports and ABC News. He was a genius. So when he put me under contract for 1971, I was doing the Olympics, summer and winter. I was doing all the stock car races, IndyCar races, sprint car races. I was doing the

Stewart lapped the field to win the 1969 British Grand Prix

Highland Gathering! And the bobsleigh, the luge, the cresta. I was in 25 American television shows a year, prime time. So the Jackie Stewart factor became big in the US.

Drivers today don't understand the dimensions of that. You talk about the Vettel factor. Just think of the intoxication for Sebastian, winning the world championship. Probably £20 million. Can you imagine 20 million pounds coming your way? When I was doing it, I was earning a lot of money but, in those days, you had to do more to get that money. You were having to deliver.

MH So, are you saying that Vettel doesn't have to work so hard?

JS As I say, he's a lucky boy because he's with Red Bull and I understand he may have as few as 12 days a year of obligations. I had 40 days with Ford alone. Sebastian travelled to the US after Canada to drive on the New Jersey circuit. That was part of an Infiniti deal and, if I were him right now, I'd be doing everything for Infiniti that I could touch because it could be a life-long relationship. I did that with Ford. Forty years. That's a lot of money; a couple of million a year.

MH Your association with Ford led you to Stewart Grand Prix. You were going into an area that you knew a little about because you hadn't actually run a team. Looking back now, was it more difficult than you expected?

JS It was harder than I expected.

MH I was doing a book with you and I remember particularly the 1997 British Grand

Prix was a disaster because you had lots of high-flying guests and the Cosworth engines blowing up left, right and centre.

JS Two of them in the garage! I had the Duke of Kent there and a number of sponsors. When one of the engines went in the garage, you couldn't see a thing for the smoke. Then we had an engine go 20 metres after the car had left the garage. And then a third let go in the garage. Hard to believe now but, in those days, we were taking 12 engines to each race.

MH Would you say it's more difficult than being a driver?

JS Oh yes, it was much more demanding. I was on the shop floor every single day. It was very hard work but we had a fantastic relationship. We had about 250 people and it was very intimate, so we knew everybody. But one of the most important things was that we never had one penny of overdraft the whole time we ran Stewart Grand Prix. Everyone said I was going to lose everything. I'll never forget an English F1 driver saying to me, "You're mad. You're going to destroy your reputation and you're going to end up with no money."

I pre-financed everything with every sponsor. They paid one third in deposit when we did the deal. We made money in our start-up year. And we made a minimum of £5 million every single year. I don't think it's ever happened before and I don't think it will ever happen again.

MH You've been on both sides of the fence: as a team owner and, with the BRDC, as a promoter, dealing with Bernie Ecclestone. Even allowing for CVC taking half the proceeds, does F1 really need the money the race promoters are forced to pay?

JS F1 has become an enormous money machine. Just one man is responsible for that and it's unquestionably Bernie Ecclestone. He has made more money personally than any man in the history of sport. I was one of Bernie's biggest critics when we were fighting to keep the British Grand Prix; the threat of losing it was very real. I don't think Bernie had a real care about the race.

That was one of the most difficult times of my life, actually. Someone said you shouldn't work with children or animals. If you're in a business, then don't work with clubs or memberships. Members are invited to join the club – they can't simply apply – and yet they think they own it. They don't. One of the most important things I did was to separate the business from the club membership. The board, many of whom are not businessmen, were appointed because they were jolly good chaps. It's like being a trustee; it might be flattering to be asked but it will probably be the most taxing thing you've ever done. The same applies to being on a board if it's not done properly. Martin Brundle was a very good chairman when I was president, but it was taking up huge amounts of our time. And the government didn't help very much, unlike other governments around the world, be it China, Malaysia, Singapore, the State of Victoria in Australia, or anywhere else.

MH But you used your contacts to get some government assistance?

Stewart GP: son Paul, Rubens Barrichello, Jan Magnussen, JS

JS The only person who helped was Tony Blair. He gave £8 million to rush through one lane of the Silverstone bypass in time for the Grand Prix because 13 weeks of foot and mouth disease had stopped construction. That was the terrible year, the wet year, in 2000. Why were we given a date for the Grand Prix in April? You don't get Wimbledon or the Summer Olympics in April. I think you know the answer to that.

MH Because the BRDC was being shown who was boss by Mr Ecclestone.

JS Saying all that, I like Bernie very much. We have good times sitting down and talking about Jochen Rindt, who Ecclestone managed, and racing in those days. Today, I get on with Bernie very well and I really like him. He has a fantastic sense of humour. But at that time, he was so tough; wouldn't give an inch. I don't think we could have been friends then because I had to say certain things to support the BRDC and the cause. And he would say some fairly strong things. None of that felt good.

MH So, having been through all that, is F1 too expensive for its own good?

JS The bar has been taken to such a height that it would be unrealistic to bring it down during Bernie's lifetime or that of CVC, given what they have bought into. They have received a huge amount for their investment and it's been a success because of the way Bernie Ecclestone runs it. Whatever we may think about Bernie, F1 is the best presented sport in the world. Bar none. It's global. The Paddock Club has no equal and it's the same standard everywhere we go - with one or two possible exceptions.

MH You say this, having sampled all the right places such as Ascot, Wimbledon and so on?

JS I do. They use the same waiters at every Grand Prix, the same chef, same kitchen equipment. From the moment you arrive at reception and experience the free massage and so on, it's impressive. Okay, it costs between three and four thousand dollars. But the sponsors and their guests get value from that. It's all about the detail - right down to the quality of the credential. The whole thing is very expensively done. Go to Ascot and you don't get a credential like that. Saying that, I'm always in trouble because I tie my F1 credential through my trouser belt loop and keep it in my trouser pocket. If I put it round my neck it crosses out a sponsor's name.

MH Which leads me nicely into asking why do you would want to do things such as work for Genii or RBS or whoever it might be? Do you like being involved and kept busy because, without wishing to be rude, you're not doing it for the money, are you?

JS I can't deny that it's rewarding financially. I've been completely domiciled in Switzerland since 1968; that's my permanent home. I have residency of the United Kingdom because I come in to service relationships, for which I pay British tax. I don't have a mortgage and I don't have any overdrafts. I'm very Scottish in that I believe you can't spend what you don't earn!

MH What I'm trying to say - and what is evident from our conversation - is that you're still as much a fan of the sport as you ever were.

JS Very much. I still love the sport. But I'm proud of F1 and the fact that, for example, all the trailer units are lined up in the paddock within a centimetre of each other. That sort of attention to detail - when you're dyslexic, it's the one thing you're good at. You don't need brains to do that and you also don't need brains to know that everything should be spotless.

And the F1 paddock is spotlessly clean. I bring CEOs, company chairmen, very important people into the paddock and they are hugely impressed by what they see. They cannot duplicate it in their industries. We tend to lose sight of that and take it for granted because we see it every two weeks. Just look inside the garages; absolutely immaculate given the enormous technical work that's going on in there. Where else in the world do you have that?

I still get a buzz going onto the grid. I don't care who the CEO is, or how successful he's been or how much money he's got; if he's not impressed by the F1 paddock and grid, there's something wrong with him. F1 is such a good example of teamwork, of motivation, of the desire to keep that performance at such a high level. And then you see the presentation skills in the Paddock Club and in the motor homes.

MH So how do you see the future for F1?

JS It's simple. Whatever anyone says, there is no viable alternative to the motor vehicle, either for the transportation of people or goods. You can have planes, trains or ships but there has to be wheels to move people and goods at the end of each journey. So why should motor racing not continue for the foreseeable future and, following on from that, why should F1 not continue to be the top level? Why should the next F1 generation not want to do as well as the current generation in the same way that they wanted to emulate people like Alfred Neubauer at Mercedes in the 1930s and 1950s, or Enzo Ferrari for nearly 60 years?

F1 is a great maker of people. It develops that kind of hunger, that kind of need, that kind of delivery. Sport as a whole does that. All the people who won gold medals in the Olympics sacrificed so much to achieve that one performance. It's the same with a racing driver. There's no free lunch.

MH Well, there is today! This one's on *F1 Racing* magazine.

JS An Irishman buys a Scotsman lunch! Someone make a note of the date! I accept. Thank you.

MH Not at all. Thank you. It's been fascinating, as always.

At lunch with **Peter Sauber**

"Schumacher was really good with the Sauber-Mercedes at Le Mans in 1990. He was driving rings around his rivals. You realised he was a big talent. His feeling on tyres, brakes and fuel was special."

Peter Sauber held a reunion to mark an anniversary of his team's success at Le Mans and in the World Sportscar Championship more than 20 years earlier. Of the 87 people invited, only two couldn't manage to come. This is an eloquent testimony to the popularity of a team owner who remains a gentleman through good and difficult times.

More than anything, I wanted his reflections on a varied and fascinated career that has embraced sportscar racing at its highest level and, after several difficult periods, seemed poised to do the same in F1.

Dinner in the Sauber hospitality centre at Monza in 2012 was the perfect environment for a chat with this self-effacing former team principal who has retained the respect of everyone in F1. I expected this to be rather formal, in keeping with the man himself, particularly knowing his reluctance to speak what is actually perfectly acceptable English. We found a solution by having Hanspeter Brack join us at the table. The presence of Sauber's pleasant and efficient communications officer helped the boss to relax.

As it turned out, Peter Sauber spoke remarkably well, requiring assistance with only the occasional turn of phrase. And what he had to say was interesting, entertaining - and, at times, unexpectedly forthright.

Maurice Hamilton I think we have something in common in that early in our careers, we both sold cars for a living.

Peter Sauber Well yes, I did sell cars, but for me it was a necessity I didn't really like. I had no relationship or feeling for cars. I started my own business to build race cars, but it was impossible to survive financially. The mechanic working for me liked Alfa Romeos and, realising how little I seemed to know about the car business, he recommended Alfa Romeos as a car to sell and make some money!

MH I sold VW Beetles, a car I believe you knew well.

PS Very well! The first one I had was maybe in 1966. I didn't want to change it but a friend brought me to a Volkswagen tuner, and this guy was a good salesman! I changed to another Beetle which was a special one, maybe as much as five horsepower more! But I really liked the Beetle.

MH Were you interested in motor racing as a boy?

PS No. The guy who sold me this Beetle convinced me to become a member of a racing club in Switzerland. I started club racing even though it had never been my intention to do it. For me, a car was transport from A to B and the Beetle was a good solution.

MH Was this when you started modifying and tuning the car?

PS I understood nothing about cars. The only possibility to make this Beetle faster was to reduce the weight. That's easy with the Beetle because you change all the metal parts such as mudguards, boot lid and engine cover to Fibreglass. Even the side windows were changed to plastic. I drove in the Swiss championship and had to race in the same class as sportscars. I raced here at Monza in 1968! And also at Hockenheim.

MH That must have been before chicanes were added to both circuits?

PS Yes. Flat out all the way! But I had a better engine - 1.6 litres - by then. For the 1969 season, I took away all of the bodywork, leaving the Beetle platform chassis. I made my own bodywork and it was like a slice of cheese...

MH You mean, like a wedge?

PS Yes, a cheese wedge. And 'Wedge' became the nickname of this car. It was fast, but I still had to race with the sportscars, which was a joke. But it was a nice experience. I met some guys in the Swiss racing scene and I had this crazy idea to build a sportscar because this piece of cheese was actually a two-seater race car. I had a brilliant idea. I bought two old Brabham Formula 3 cars. A BT17 or a BT18, good cars with a spaceframe chassis. But, because I wanted a two-seater, I had to build my own tube-frame.

MH I'm right in saying you were trained as an electrician? So you really had no knowledge of this sort of thing?

PS None. But it wasn't that difficult because, if you look at a crane on a construction site, you get an idea of how to build a spaceframe. I had to educate myself. I understood nothing about geometry, so I used the Brabham suspension and pick-up points and the same point for the steering rack. I won the championship for sportscars in this first year - but it was not so difficult because the car was so fast. I built two of these cars, the C1. The 'C' is from my wife Christiane. I thought that was a bit more romantic than to take the 'P' for Peter or like the BT for Brabham and Tauranac.

MH So, now you really are into motor racing. But that must have been difficult because it was banned in Switzerland following the tragedy at Le Mans in 1955.

PS We drove about 10 races; five hill climbs and five on circuits. The circuits were in Germany, Italy and France because, as you say, racing was not allowed in Switzerland. I stopped after winning the championship because, for me, this was a kind of climax. To drive was nice but it was not a passion for me. I did take part in one or two races each year, just to keep my licence. The last one I drove, a hill climb race close to my home, I won. That was in 1974.

MH How did you live during this time? Were you still an electrician?

PS No, I sold these two cars. Then I was lucky. A driver in the Swiss national championships, who also drove sportscars in international races such as the Targa Florio, ordered a 2.0-litre car for 1971. That was a challenge! My knowledge of suspension was no better than before. So, I did the same thing again, but this time I bought the March F2 car Xavier Perrot drove in the European hill climb championship and I used the suspension as before. This was the C2. It was not a nice car. But it was fast and I built two of them. Even though I sold them, I wasn't able to make money. The interesting part financially was entering these cars and maintaining them. That continued into the C3, the first car for which I made the suspension, the uprights and all these things. I made three of them.

MH Where was all this taking place? You must have needed a bit of space by now?

PS The C1 was built in the cellar of my parents' house, in Zurich. The C2 and C3 were built in a small factory - on the same site where we are today in Hinwil. My father's company had land in Hinwil. There was just me and a colleague. Believe me, the first 10 years were a disaster. Financially, it was a nightmare. I stopped building cars after the C5 because I was running out of money.

MH Was this the period when you switched to BMW M1 Procars, a really great series supporting Grands Prix?

PS Jochen Neerpasch was building up BMW Motorsport and they had this idea for the Procar series. They sold me a BMW M1 for a special price and I had to enter the car for Marc Surer. We were very successful. That's when I met the guy from Seger and Hoffmann, the company building the special bodywork for these M1s. Together, we built a BMW M1 Group 5; it was a very nice car and I still have it. With it we won the 1,000km race at the Nürburgring with Hans Stuck and Nelson Piquet.

"It's so much easier to build a Formula One car than a sportscar"

I'm telling you this because the relationship with Seger and Hoffmann was important for the next step. Group C was born in 1981 and, for this, we built the C6. But the Ford engine was a disaster. The vibrations were so bad they broke the bulkheads! We made everything stronger and entered two cars for Le Mans. But the alternator and the starter were split by the vibrations - even the wiper motor was affected! The engine was fixed by four bolts and, at one stage, the car came back to the pits with just one bolt in place. A disaster. But I was back in the sportscar business - although we had no money.

MH Okay, now we're getting towards the important bit; the connection with Mercedes. First, you built the C7, which ran with the six-cylinder BMW engine. But how did the link with Mercedes come about for the C8 in 1984?

PS The BMW engine was not strong enough and to use the Porsche engine made no sense because they were winning everything and you couldn't beat them with the same engine. I'd had connections since 1981 with a small group of Mercedes engineers in the R&D department - which was separate from the main building. When we were working on the C6 with the Ford engine, I was able to use the big wind tunnel at Mercedes - during the night! For free! Everything was under the table. It was the same with the C7 - with the BMW engine in the Mercedes wind tunnel!

Together, we developed the idea to race the V8 from the S-Class with two turbochargers. But Mercedes had no idea about racing engines. We developed the engine, but the idea was never going to be allowed by the board because, for more than 30 years, motor sport was forbidden after the 1955 Le Mans. But Mercedes were allowed to support customers. So, I took this engine and said, "I'm a customer - please help me." And they did. For appearances, one engine was built by Heini Mader. We raced this engine - but the others were built in Stuttgart. You call it the Salami Tactic, where you cut slice by slice. I brought Mercedes back to motor sport. They know that, but only Norbert Haug doesn't mention it. The C8, C9 and C11 are on display at the Mercedes museum and the text which accompanies them tells the story and is absolutely correct.

MH It was a bit of a shaky start, wasn't it? I'm thinking of the C8 that got airborne at the end of Mulsanne.

PS Yes, we started with a lot of problems. John Nielsen was driving the C8 at Le Mans and the crash was very spectacular. The car was minimum 20 metres high; above the trees. He flew 200 metres - it was easy to measure because there were two white marks where the bodywork touched the ground as he took off - and the landing made a mark in the road. He came with the roof facing forward and then the car turned into one guard rail and then the other. From the take-off to Mulsanne corner, where he finally stopped, was 500 metres.

The engine was still running! Only the front was damaged. The light on the roof was still there. Nielsen switched off the engine and got out. It was like a Mercedes you see in those crash advertisements, he could open the door! The old time-keeping booths were there. John got on the phone and told me: "Peter, I'm sorry, I had an accident on Mulsanne and I don't think it's possible to drive the car!"

MH You were up against Jaguar and Tom Walkinshaw; a tough opponent.

PS It was not so easy because Tom Walkinshaw, he was very clever - sometimes more than clever. Let's say he was very creative! And I was completely naive. Our car was faster, but we had no chance against the Jaguar in 1987.

MH So when did Mercedes officially enter the sportscar championship?

PS We raced in the German sportscar championship. Porsche were stopping with the works team and the last race for them was at the 'Ring on the GP circuit They had a completely new car, especially light, for Stuck. But when Schlesser beat Stuck with the C8, that was the signal for Mercedes to come back officially. In 1988, I had money from Mercedes. I had a good friend there Professor Niefer, who was the chairman and CEO. He told me to bring a model of the C9 to the Geneva Salon motor show - and have it painted silver. Our car at the time was running in blue. I brought this model in a wooden box and Niefer showed it to the board members. There was a lot of discussion and they were saying, "Racing is dangerous. Silver is too official" and so on. Niefer took me to one side and told me, "They're all cowards. Paint it silver. That's an order!" It was only a few weeks before the first race in Suzuka and we removed the blue completely and painted the car silver. We went to Suzuka and scored a one-two. That is the story of the Silver Arrows. It was a beautiful time. But the end was not so nice...

Räikkönen ended 10th for Sauber in the 2001, his first F1 season

MH Before we get to that, I want to talk about your young drivers - Heinz-Harald Frentzen, Michael Schumacher and so on. There were all good, but was Michael a stand-out talent?

PS I don't have a special nose for good drivers. With the first three young guys we had - Karl Wendlinger, Frentzen and Schumacher - we were simply lucky. But Schumacher was really good one year later with the C11. Especially at Le Mans. He was driving rings round his competitors. You realised he was a big talent. His feeling - maybe not on the technical side; it was too early for that - but his feeling on tyres, brakes and fuel consumption was special.

MH And during this period, you win the Le Mans and the World Sportscar Championship. With Mercedes now in sportscar racing, how did the discussions about F1 start?

PS I built the factory in 1992 in Hinwil and I was speaking with Jürgen Huppert and Werner Niefer about F1. It was an on-going process because, officially, it was not possible for Mercedes to return. On the commercial side they were having a difficult time. They had to lay off many people.

I had the budget from Mercedes between 1988 and 92. It was a hand-shake each time. No contract! 1991-92 was a transition year. In 1991, it was the wish of Mercedes to have a little influence, which brought the C291. The engine was a disaster; a sort of flat-12 that looked like a Boxer, but was in two halves with the power coming from the middle. The reason for the flat engine was to have a nice diffuser but it was so complicated, it was impossible. The exhaust was on top; the inlet below. And the engine was one piece, including the cylinder head and the cylinders. You can't believe it. It took so much time to change the spark plugs, it was actually easier to change the engine. The minimum for engine change was four-and-a-half hours.

Mercedes were not sure in which direction to go. In 1992 we built a new sportscar, the C292. It was a beautiful car with full carbon monocoque, integrated roof and absolutely on an F1 level. It never raced. But we knew to step from sportcars to Formula One was not a problem.

MH Are you saying it's perhaps more difficult to build a sportscar?

PS It's so much easier to build a single-seater. Everything is small; the driver's seat instead of being at an angle, is straight and in the middle. Also with a sportscar you have to know how much the wheels travel up and down under the bodywork. All this has to be calculated because the bodywork has to be as close and tight as possible. The windscreen wiper has to work at 400km/h at Le Mans. The doors have to work well. When you have a small driver and a large driver, you have to have the seat adjustment. If you get a small stone in there, you don't finish the race. Then there is the cooling for the driver...

MH This is maybe a good moment to ask you about enclosed cockpits in F1. You've obviously got the experience of that.

PS It's impossible because you have 80 or 90 degrees in the car. So you have to have air-conditioning, or whatever. It's very small in the cockpit; like a fighter plane. The problems are endless when you enclose the car. No way can you do this in F1.

MH Speaking of which, Mercedes talked about F1 but then decided in November 1991 that they were not going to participate. By which time you were some way down the F1 road.

PS Yes, our development was ongoing. In this 1992 transition period we built the car and I visited some races to understand F1. Mercedes gave me financial compensation. Most people would take the money, close the factory and give some money to the employees. During this period, Huppert took over responsibility from Niefer. I remember when I told him it was too risky to continue, he was disappointed. I thought about it when I was in the mountains with my family over Christmas. When I returned to the factory, I spoke with the engineers and with Leo Ress, designer of the sportscars, and we took the decision - we go to F1. It would have been a shame to throw away everything that had been prepared. I called Huppert and said with the money we have, we will take the risk.

MH That decision must have been vindicated when you finished fifth in the 1993 South African Grand Prix - your first race!

PS The first race was fantastic. There was a long pit-stop when we had to change a connection for the gearbox. We had a problem with shifting because everything was

Sauber and his right-hand woman, Monisha, at Bahrain 2012

new and, without this long stop, we would have been on the podium for sure. The cars, if you remember, were black with 'Concept by Mercedes-Benz' written on them. Then Mercedes said "Okay, we can speak about the engine costs, but we have to find sponsors now." That was difficult because over the previous five years or so we had money from Mercedes and now we had to start from zero to find sponsors. It was very difficult.

MH Added to which you were very unfortunate with two sponsors...

PS Yes, two bad experiences; the first was Lighthouse, the second was Broker. Both were a disaster and, without the help of Mercedes, we would have had to close the company. The end of 1994 was a critical time. Mercedes would provide the engine, but I would have to do the rest. It was impossible. I don't really want to say much more about what happened but, when Mercedes signed with McLaren for 1995, I was left with nothing - no engine and no sponsor.

MH Before moving on from 1994, I wanted to ask you about Monaco and Wendlinger's crash during practice. He was rushed unconscious to hospital. And this was a couple of weeks after Senna at Imola. That can't have been easy for you.

PS When you have no money and you're very tired from working very hard, every day, and something happens like that, you get to the point where you just want to give up. I have a good relationship with my drivers - but particularly with Wendlinger. Nice man, nice family.

MH So, Mercedes go but things move on quite quickly because by the start of 1995 you have the deal with Ford engines and sponsorship from Red Bull, followed by Petronas.

PS We got the sponsors, but six months too late. With hindsight, I believe for Mercedes it would have been the better solution to continue the co-operation with Sauber. I think they would have got better value.

MH If you want to talk about value, then signing Kimi Räikkönen must have been one of the best moves you ever made. How on earth did you know about him? He'd only done something like 23 races – in total!

PS It was in 2000. I'd never met David Robertson, his manager, before and he came to see me and explained about his experience with Kimi. All the nice stories: Kimi's go-kart driving; how he was with slicks in wet conditions. David was an excellent salesman! I really don't understand why I gave Kimi a car for three days. We had no money and, normally, when you do a test for young drivers then you make a three-day test with six drivers and make it pay. But Robertson told me this guy is very, very special and he needs a car for three days. And, of course, they paid nothing. I still don't understand why I made this decision!

We made this test in Mugello. It's not an easy track for young drivers. I was only there on the second day and that's when I met Kimi for the first time. He never spoke and it was not possible to speak English with him, maybe two or three words. No more. But one or two things were very, very special. His body language was so impassive and he gave the impression he's so totally focused that if he walks to you, he could walk through you. That's only my personal feeling. I thought this guy is so strange.

The engineer told me they did three, maximum four, timed laps and in. Then they told him to drive eight laps. But, after four laps, he was back in. It was not possible for him to keep his head up. But he never spoke about it. Can you imagine? You get a test with a F1 team and they tell you 'Stay out for 10 laps' And you come back after four.

The steering wheel did not have as many switches as we have now, but it was enough and he managed okay. With the clutch on the steering wheel, he got out of the pit okay; like normal. Late in the day, he knows he's under scrutiny from me. We give him a set of new tyres and reduce the fuel amount. It was clear the new tyres are worth one second and the fuel is another second. But we didn't say anything. On the first lap, he was one second faster. On the second lap he was another second faster. Very impressive! I flew home together with Willy Rampf, our technical director, and we decided, "Let's sign him".

MH And the rest is history. Fantastic. But there was a problem with Red Bull, wasn't there? They preferred Enrique Bernoldi?

PS I had the first big clash with Red Bull because Dr Helmut Marko played a bad role; really bad. Bernoldi was our test driver and he was driving at the same time. He was not good enough. But Helmut Marko was so convinced about his own judgement and Dietrich Mateschitz believed everything he told him. Everything. It was unbelievable.

"Only one person was against Kimi joining F1 – Briatore"

He told Mateschitz that Willy Rampf was cheating and gave Bernoldi more fuel and the wrong tyres to slow him down. So, we have the first disagreement with Dietrich Mateschitz. But I still have a very good relationship with him.

[*At this point, Hanspeter Brack, a touch anxiously, asks Sauber if the previous part of the conversation is on record. Sauber pauses briefly before saying quietly but crisply "Ja".*]

MH But that wasn't the end of the story with Kimi, was it? People were against a driver with so little experience coming into F1. Particularly Max Mosley, then head of the FIA.

PS Mosley was against, but he was fair. I understood what Max was saying because this was not the normal way. We had the Formula One Commission meeting in Monaco and I had to put my case. I had no experience in this and my English was not so good. I had the help of Bernie Ecclestone, Jean Todt, Ron Dennis, Frank Williams and I think, at the end, Eddie Jordan. Everybody helped me - I was surprised. Only one person was against, and that was Flavio Briatore. He said we had the Formula 3000 teams at this time and it made no sense to bring this guy directly into F1. Flavio was protecting his own business and, of course, he had two votes at the time - Minardi as well as his own team. Max didn't vote. He was fair, absolutely fair. For me, it was a miracle to get the licence for Kimi.

MH You've had some interesting drivers, haven't you? I did one of these interviews with Jean Alesi. I went to see him at his home at Avignon.

PS Ah, that's really nice.

MH Absolutely! It was wonderful day. Then I had lunch with Johnny Herbert and the thing that struck most forcibly is that they both spoke with genuine feeling about Sauber. They loved their time with Sauber Formula One - the family, the atmosphere.

PS I think particularly with Johnny, there are lots of funny stories. But also with Jean, even though the second year was sometimes so difficult, but I like him.

MH Johnny said when he's at the races, he comes to find the Sauber guys because he enjoyed his time here so much. Do you let the drivers have their way and just be relaxed? What's the secret?

PS I think when a young driver is starting, the team is very, very important. It's difficult to speak about this because I don't want to make any comparisons with other teams where, sometimes, it doesn't work with young drivers.

MH But what is it that you do?

PS Nothing in particular. I think it's the atmosphere and the way we work as a team; as a family almost. And now Monisha Kaltenborn represents the same values.

MH You could say you have a bit of a reputation for going against the grain. Kimi is a good example. And your business relationship with Monisha is another. She is now your CEO [*later becoming team principal*]. How did this come about?

PS Around 1994-95, Fritz Kaiser was a partner and a shareholder in Sauber. Monisha was born in India, studied in Vienna and London, and worked, I think, for two law firms. She worked for Fritz and one of her projects was taking care of business for Sauber. She made the contract, for example, with Pedro Diniz. She looked after sponsor contracts and the early stages of the engine deal with Ferrari. I bought back the shares from Fritz Kaiser, and Monisha came to us in 2000 to play an important role as we developed the Sauber Petronas Engineering company. During all this time, Monisha showed she had entrepreneurial talent and similar values to me.

When I sold the business to BMW, she basically managed the whole process; it was very complex. When you sell a company to a big manufacturer and all these legal guys are involved, it's a nightmare. During the time with BMW, she also had an important role because they were developing the Concorde Agreement. As a representative of a car manufacturer, she had a lot more power than you would have as a private team. She learned a lot dealing with Bernie and the FIA. She knows the game now. Or, I should say, the game behind the game!

MH I take it Monisha must have played a key role when BMW decided to pull out and you were trying to buy the team back?

PS She did, yes. When BMW decided to pull out, it was exactly when teams were ready to sign the Concorde Agreement after years of negotiation. I submitted a proposal to BMW to buy the company back and they rejected it. At that moment, the team had not signed Concorde, there were no sponsors and no grid slot. Nothing. Absolutely nothing! Monisha played an important role as we solved one problem after another and injected life again into the company.

MH So, just how difficult was that?

PS I don't want to say more about the fight with the FIA and with Bernie, because it was over the limit at times!

MH How did you find that period when you were out of F1? Did you miss it? Did you relax? Did you think "My time in F1 is over"?

PS For me, the important point was to save the company. For a private team, it's still difficult to survive on the commercial side. I sold 80 per cent of the company to BMW at the end of 2005. It was a huge success because it guaranteed the future of the employees. That was much more important for me than losing my personal involvement with F1. I was 62. On the one hand, it was a little bit too early to retire. On the other, I would have more time to relax.

MH And you knew your company would be okay. But you were still involved as a consultant. Did you find it difficult being there but not fully involved as before?

PS I had a contract with BMW as an adviser. I had to go to 10 races and it was my intention to reduce that slowly because, to be honest, it was a bit boring. I had nothing to do. Mario Theissen, BMW's motorsport director, was not so keen to have me around. When you're not welcome, you don't want to be here.

MH So, you're 62, you're very fit. What did you do?

PS My parents had a house in the Swiss Alps for more than 50 years. I decided to build my own house close by. Without this period away from F1, I'd never have done that. It kept me busy.

MH And now? Here you are, 69 in October 2012, back in F1.

PS Finding the financial funding keeps me busy because it is a huge challenge in the current economic environment. But it is a fantastic sport. And this season is incredible. I can say this is the first time we have a really, really good car. And we know why the car is good - because sometimes you don't know why! The daily business is very well organised by Monisha. I'm in Hinwil twice per week, not more.

MH That sounds perfect! Thank you very much for dinner and for your time. You've certainly had a very interesting life.

PS You're welcome. I made a lot of mistakes - but I would do the same again!

At lunch with **Mika Häkkinen**

"I was in such pain that all I wanted was the nurses to keep bringing painkillers. It made me realise I don't just live for motor racing. There is something more important. I can live; I can take care of myself."

Given that he could choose wherever he wished for lunch in Monaco, it was something of a surprise that Mika Häkkinen should pick Stars'N'Bars. If you've been to the Grand Prix, you'll know this is a favourite watering hole, not simply because of the loud music and ready supply of beer and hamburgers, but mainly because it's hard by the paddock fence. In short, it's the last place on earth in which you'd wish to conduct an interview.

But that's during five days in May. For the rest of the year, it's a popular choice across the wide social divides in this unique corner of the world. Stepping inside, it's almost unrecognisable from the bear pit of Grand Prix week.

And there's an immediate clue to the reason behind Mika's choice. There, mounted vertically on one wall, is his McLaren MP4-15 from the 2000 season. He didn't win the championship that year - but he came close after another relentless encounter with Michael Schumacher. And it also serves as an aide memoire of his back-to-back titles the two previous seasons.

Mika walks in, bang on time at midday. He is instantly recognised and well received by staff who are clearly glad to see him - as you would when a racing driver lends you a F1 car for your wall (though in truth, he has nowhere else to put it). We're shown to our upstairs table.

When he was racing, Mika was always polite and smiley. But a man of few words and sometimes a little tense. Now, he looks completely relaxed. And ready to talk. I've been looking forward to this opportunity for a very long time.

Maurice Hamilton Really good to see you.

Mika Häkkinen Yeah, it's been a long time. Welcome to Monaco!

MH I have to say, living here is such a huge difference from when you started racing and travelled around Europe in a converted bus. Were you living hand-to-mouth? How do you remember those early days?

Mika It was challenging, yes. Financing the go-kart or Formula Ford was really tough but we always found a way. We never did think that money was the issue; it was more about the passion that was taking us forward all the time. We saved here and spent more there - but we were still racing. It was really important to get the right connections; the right people in the programme. I had certain powerful companies helping but that didn't mean they were throwing money at our project; it was calculated and finely tuned. But it gave a lot of confidence in the programme. It felt strong.

MH From what I've read, you had a lot of inner confidence. Was it always within you?

Mika It's not just me. I've learned with my son, Hugo - he's 12 years old - when we go testing and racing. I have understood that kids need confidence but it doesn't come automatically. It's about giving them security. If you can do that, the confidence comes up. It's not just saying, "Oh, you drive really well." They need to learn to trust you. That's what my parents gave me when I was a kid. I felt "I can survive, I can do this." And that means you can try extreme things when you're driving.

MH You're saying if you saw a gap, you had the confidence to go for it?

Mika Yes, but that didn't happen automatically, it took practice. It was the push from my father. He was teaching me "When you see a gap, just go for it. C'mon, go for it!" As soon as you have this confidence, you'll do aggressive overtaking - and it works. You feel "Oh, I did it!" My son is experiencing the same thing. When he doesn't believe it will work out, I tell him, "Just do it. Trust me." For a young boy there are a lot of reasons in his mind why he can't do this. But once they do it, they come out of there and think "Whoa! This is easy." But nothing is automatic.

MH But you were naturally quick, too.

Mika Yes, you have a gift for driving - but more comes from learning. If you're good at writing, that's fantastic. But if you want to be really good, you have to practice and polish your talent to make it perfect. You need someone to tell you "Why did you do it like that? Try it this way." You need someone to give direction.

MH It's nice that you remember this from your childhood and can pass it on to Hugo.

Mika I really enjoy it, but it's a long process. It doesn't happen overnight. When you're working with a young kid, they change all the time. It's fine-tuning.

MH During your early days in Europe, a key moment was a Marlboro test at Donington in late 1987. How did that come about?

Mika I wasn't yet managed by Keke Rosberg. I don't know who they contacted. It was an invitation for drivers who had won categories in Formula Ford like me, but also winners from F3 and F3000 or Formula Ford. We were on a sort of European tour with this bus; we were already four weeks on the road; just having a shower where we could - not many places! So when Philip Morris said they had organised a hotel, it was great. Wow! A warm room and you could have a hot shower. It was a great experience, brilliant to go there; I'd never in my life seen something like that.

Of course, I was nervous like no tomorrow but yet I had this inner confidence that when I sit in a car, I'm gonna go for it. I didn't care who was there. I didn't have worries about who was going to kick my ass because I knew I was just going to go faster than anybody else. It worked out really brilliantly. Of course, it was a bit complicated because my English wasn't so good. So the communication with the likes of James Hunt wasn't so brilliant. But I think James saw something in me. At the end of the day, what mattered was the clock. Good lap times, lap after lap. They said, "We'll take this guy. Even if his English is not so good, he will learn. But the driving we don't have to teach him; he can do that well."

MH Had you been to Donington before? It's a tricky circuit and I guess it was cold?

Mika Hadn't seen it before and, yes, a really tricky circuit. And, yes, bloody cold. But when I went to the test I said, "Come on. Four weeks in a bus." I was so happy to be there. I was just so proud to be doing that and show them what I could do.

MH Okay, so this gets you into F3. I want to ask about your first meeting with Michael Schumacher, which was at Hockenheim in 1990 - and you beat him.

Mika It was German F3. We were coming from England and they underestimated us quite a lot. In free practice, we had a misfire, and I was halfway down the list of times. But they didn't know we had a misfire and didn't pay any attention to us. We were able to fix the problem for qualifying.

As you know, Hockenheim then was massive straights that in an F3 car seemed to last for ever. At the start of a lap, I came round the first corner flat out and there was a car not far away, so I got a tow for the first straight and I knew that was an improvement of maybe two-tenths on that bit alone. I was about to overtake this car before the first chicane, but then I thought, "I'm not going to do that. It may cost a tiny bit of time but I'm going to follow this car on the next straight." So I gained maybe half a second on those two straights and I banged in a time which was one second quicker than anybody else. It was an incredible time.

You could see mechanics dropping their tools on the floor and thinking, 'What! Where are these guys coming from?' They didn't know I was just so lucky to get the tow. We would have got the pole position anyway, but that margin just made the German F3 teams and drivers look really crappy. And when the race happened, I just went flat out. I led the race from the start.

On the podium there was a mix of feelings. Michael was standing there and, of course, he was disappointed. I was spraying the champagne everywhere.

It was nearly three titles in a row following his 2000 Schumi dice

MH But then, at the end of the year, in Macau...

Mika Next question?

MH Yes, well, you win the first heat and then...

Mika When you go back in time and something negative happens, you don't really want to talk about it. But, of course, fans are reading about it and people like you remember what happened! It was an awful, awful situation for me because we had really great preparation for this race.

We qualified one second quicker than anybody else. I got a perfect lap in qualifying; the car was just flying. Michael was improving his car all the way through the weekend, so he was closing the gap. I won the first heat, by maybe four or five seconds, so a comfortable victory.

MH Because it's on aggregate, isn't it?

Mika Yeah, the two races together. At the second start, okay, I made a slight mistake and Michael was able to overtake. I thought, 'No stress. I just have to follow him'. I did that, lap after lap. And then he was slowing down. The performance was going down in his car and I'm trying to stay behind him.

Of course, when I had to slow down, my tyre temperatures drop and my car becomes difficult to drive. It was not the same car any more and I started struggling. At the start of the last lap, or second-last lap, we were coming past the start/finish line and Michael missed the apex of the next very fast right-hander. With the speed and the sort of power we had in F3, a mistake like that means you slow down in a big way. I knew I had to overtake him. I started to do that - and he moved across at the same time. Of course, that's it. I remember thinking, 'I don't believe this'.

So, who to blame? Myself. Afterwards, you think, "Racing is racing and it's always tough," But when you see in your mirror or you know somebody is moving so quickly behind you, and you move across - well, you don't have to think twice about what's going to happen. But, as I say, this is motor racing; no point being negative. But, obviously, the team wasn't very happy. They lost a lot of money because the prize money was big. For me, it was a massive learning curve.

MH Your first year with Lotus, that was a huge learning curve too, wasn't it? Learning about F1; communicating with the team. How important was that year with Lotus?

Mika The problem was, it was also a learning curve for the team as well as myself, so that makes everything even more difficult. At the end of the day, driving the car was my job. But, of course, there was the media, more travelling, taking more physical challenges. It was more complicated. It was hard, very hard.

MH In 1992, when you had the Ford HB engine, you actually had a pretty good season, considering the circumstances of the team. You got a couple of fourth places.

Mika We had a different chassis by then. We'd started with the same chassis that Martin Donnelly had the accident with in Jerez in 1990. We had to make that chassis really strong because we didn't want it to break in half. So, the car was very heavy and we knew there was no way we could perform.

When we went from the Judd to the Ford engine for 1992, that was a big help. Financially, it was a big decision for the team because it was a very expensive package. A new chassis definitely helped us a lot and as you say, a couple of fourth places.

So, we had better performances, but there was something wrong. Success is important - you obviously need to win - but you have to be realistic and that was sometimes difficult for everyone to understand. It's like, "Guys! I'm not superman; I cannot make magic. If you give me this machine, it's impossible to race against the Ferraris or McLarens that have gearshifts on the steering wheel; they have this and that. It's no chance."

So, sometimes there was too much pushing for the drivers to perform. Okay, like I said, you do your job - but don't push all the time in this direction. Otherwise, I lose my motivation because we have to be realistic. The pressure was high. We needed a lot of money to change things.

MH Well, the big change for you came in 1993 when you were a test driver for McLaren. Michael Andretti goes home for good after the Italian Grand Prix in September and, suddenly, there you are, race driver and No2 to Ayrton Senna.

Mika Yeah. That was nice...

Senna was not amused when Mika out-qualified him

MH Um, well Senna didn't think it was nice when you out-qualified him for your first race at Estoril. Is it true that Ayrton hadn't really been talking to you much during the weekend? And when you finished qualifying, when he asked how you did this, you simply smiled and said, "Big balls". Is that true?

Mika Yes, that's true.

MH He wasn't very pleased, was he?

Mika Ayrton was not very pleased. At all. The thing about Ayrton in 1993 is when he started the season, he was already somewhere else. He knew the performance of the car was not matching the Williams and he was definitely not happy because Alain Prost was winning. When I came to Estoril, Ayrton knew that the performance of the McLaren was okay. But he never expected me to beat him in qualifying. Okay, the time difference was hardly anything but, you know, I don't think anyone had beaten him in qualifying in his whole career. I mean, he was a god. It was a real shock for him. But when he was very kindly asking how I did this, I cracked a joke and said, "Big balls".

At first, he didn't get it; he didn't understand. When he realised, he said, "Okay, I'll give you a lesson. You want to play a game with me? Okay, let's do it that way." So, he didn't give any information, no sharing, nothing. It made my life difficult. Of course, there were things I could see; things I knew that he was doing. But little things make the difference when you're on the edge of the performance, and some of the things he didn't share with us basically helped him perform better.

I don't think it was only because of what I said in that joke. I think he realised I was a big threat. So he put all his experience, all his power to just kick my ass and to show the world that, hold on, this young bloke is not going to beat me. And he did that. He kicked my ass, definitely in Adelaide. But Suzuka wasn't so clear. I could have been quicker than him in qualifying in Japan, but I had a problem with the brakes and I spun off in the chicane. But, hey, that's if... if... if...

MH You always seemed to have a very good relationship with Ron Dennis. How much of an impact did your accident at Adelaide in 1995 have on him, because that was a shocking thing for you, and for him too? [*Three laps into qualifying on the street circuit, Mika suffered a left-rear puncture just as he approached a 110mph fourth-gear right-hander. The McLaren-Mercedes snapped out of control and was launched over a kerb before slamming sideways into a one-layer tyre barrier in front of a concrete wall. Häkkinen hit his head on the steering wheel after the safety belts stretched - such as was force of the impact. Had it not been for an emergency tracheotomy performed on the spot by the medical team led by Professor Sid Watkins, Mika would not have survived.*]

Mika I had a good relationship with Ron from the first day we met. Did the accident made the relationship stronger? I don't think so. But I think it changed the way he saw that I don't give up; I'm the fighter. I was loyal to the team all that way and I think that helped Ron fight even harder; to make sure we had a car with which we could win.

MH Tell me a little bit about your actual recovery from that accident. I didn't realise, until reading about it just recently, that you went through a very bad time indeed. I mean, really terrible.

Mika If you look at the accident, it looks nasty - but it doesn't look like, "Wow, that's really bad." But when you hurt your head, it's always dangerous; it's always painful. I cracked my skull and that gave me huge headaches, which aren't fun at all. The doctors had to check everything because you have a lot of elements in your head that make us operate. I went through the hell.

I went through so many different tests to help understand that everything was functioning correctly in my body. After the accident the doctors fixed things, not completely, but did the very best they can do. And, of course, the nerves got a little bit damaged, so my face was not operating exactly like it should.

In the first month, I was in such pain that I didn't even think about motor racing. All I wanted was the nurses to keep bringing me painkiller tablets. Everything was calculated. Whatever I was doing, it was written down as well as the measure of this and that. To let me sleep at night, they had to put tape on my eyes because the nerves didn't work and the eyes wouldn't close. It was horrible, but when I thought about it all and that terrible moment, it really made me realise, "Okay, this is what life is really all about. I don't just live for motor racing or for something else. There is something more important than that. I can live; I can take care of myself.'

I was in Australia for five weeks or something and I wanted to come back home; I didn't want to stay there any more. So they did all kind of tests to find out if I could

Happy and relaxed: these days Mika is still a busy man

fly, because there were worries about the effect of the pressure in the airplane. Finally, yeah, Ron and Mansour Ojjeh organised a private plane and I was able to come back. I was so happy.

Straightaway, I went to Sid Watkins' London Hospital, and I thought they were just going to do a little bit of a check up. But no; I was there for, I don't know, a week or two, going through the same tests again, just like I did in Australia. I went crazy. When I saw the nurse coming with the needle, I said, "Get out of here!" I was so fed up with the hospitals and the needles and the tablets. I just wanted to get out of there.

Finally, I went back to Monaco. After a few days, I realised that everything was a bit different. I think it was because the headaches and pain didn't really let me enjoy life. I flew to Finland, where I had a good Christmas. I was enjoying it and getting rid of racing and the accident.

MH So, when did you start thinking about driving again? You had a test pretty soon after that, didn't you?

Mika It was when I went back to Monaco. That's when I felt it was time to start talking about motor racing. McLaren organised a test at Paul Ricard. One side of my head was shaved because they put some bloody things through my head in hospital. When I went to the test, the mechanics looked at me and I could see them thinking "Okay, what's going to happen now? What's this guy going to do?" But when I jumped in the car, I immediately felt, "This is it. I'm back home." Everything was good and

I experienced again the quality of the McLaren, how fantastic it was. It was so comfortable; the car was made for me and I remember thinking, 'This is amazing'. I went flat out immediately and I didn't think about this corner or that corner or what if something happens. I wanted to show the mechanics, "Okay guys, let's go back to business."

And then I started training, but that was very difficult to get back into. I had lost a lot of weight - I wish I could do that now! - but the problem was the general fitness had dropped in a big way, which made it challenging to come back. But I did it in the end.

MH You had to wait a while, though, before the results started to come through. You didn't score your first win until the end of 1997. But then it really took off.

Mika Yeah, Adrian Newey, Neil Oatley and the whole team designed a brilliant car in 1998. It was just perfect. We were 1.5 to 2.0 seconds ahead which, as you know, is light years in F1.

MH And all the time, you're racing against your old friend, Schuey.

Mika I have to say, it was a pleasure to race against him. He already had great confidence and a good knowledge of winning races and championships. In 1998, it was tough racing against him but, really, for me, it was more about David Coulthard. He also had great confidence and he was really quick. But I knew his weaknesses and strengths. Which was just as well because I knew that unless I put myself on the super edge, he was going to beat me. When we had a car like this, it was quite easy to make a great lap time. But if I didn't do the super lap, David would beat me. So it was difficult because you were more or less racing against your own team-mate.

MH I'm sure DC would be pleased to hear you say that. But I have to return to Schumacher and ask you about that incredible moment at Spa as the pair of you went either side of poor [*Ricardo*] Zonta at the top of the hill. Actually, can I start with the lap before when Michael edged you onto the grass at the same place. You had a chat with him in parc fermé, I remember.

Mika Yeah... but the race was over and I had won. I said, "Hey, come on, this is not correct", and tried to make him realise this. The team was really upset; they took the wing end-plate [*damaged by the rear wheel of the Ferrari*] to let the stewards have a look at it. Martin Whitmarsh was not happy and tried to make the stewards accept that you can't continue like this.

MH When you pulled the move past Zonta, can you remember how you felt?

Mika Yeah, yeah, absolutely I remember. When you follow an F1 car at that speed, it is an incredible experience simply because you have no air. The steering is light and when braking the whole car feels light and feels like it's going to explode. When Michael moved on the left and I moved on the right, I got the tow from Zonta. So, even though we were going very fast, I suddenly had extra speed.

Of course, there has to be a little bit of luck there. There is no one saying to Zonta "Slow down so that Mika can overtake." Michael went to the left because the circuit was

Häkkinen's first F1 win was in the GP of Europe, Jerez 1997

still a little bit wet on the right so he knew if he went on the right and I went left, I was going to have the drier line. So he took the safe option. I went on the right. It was wet but I knew he would not have a chance. After what had happened before, he knew that now he has to give up because of what he had done to me. Otherwise the both of us would go off the road. It was a great experience. A really great victory.

MH I want to move on towards the end of your F1 career. You had a couple of failures. You'd had an accident...

Mika I'd had quite a few of those!

MH Mmm, yes. But one in particular, during testing at Monza, had quite an effect. Was that the one where you thought, 'Sod this. I'm off'?

Mika Monza... when my steering wheel came off?

MH That would be the one...

Mika On the straight there is this little bump; just by the start-finish line. You're flat out but you know it's coming. It's very unpleasant, actually. For once I was a bit more relaxed; sixth gear, 330 or whatever km/h. I hit the bump, my left leg bounced up - and it touched the steering wheel's quick release. The wheel came off. I'm doing 330km/h with the steering wheel in my hand. Oh shit! I couldn't believe it. I'm thinking 'What can I do?' The car started pulling slightly on the left. The only thing to do was slam on the brakes; all four wheels locked. The car is sliding halfway down the straight all the way to the first corner. I touched the barrier a little bit on the left side. Then I saw the marker boards coming, but luckily they were made of light material. I came to a stop. Then that accident in 1995 came to mind. I thought this could have been a really big one.

I walked back to the pits and explained what had happened. I said, "Guys, give me the rest of the day off." I went back to the hotel and had a think. I probably should have got back in the car and continued driving. But things started going through my mind at these speeds and things like this can happen. It's too much.

MH I remember here in Monaco - actually, a few metres from the front door of this building, where the McLaren motorhome was situated in the paddock - there was talk of you maybe coming back to F1. We all had a chat with you. Was this a bit of a publicity exercise or were you really interested?

Mika I was very much interested, actually. I was fit and I was feeling energy. I could see the mistakes other people - the drivers and teams - were making and I had time to think about all the mistakes I had made. And I'm thinking, "I'm going to fix all these mistakes. I'm smarter now. I can do this!" I contacted my manager, Didier Coton, and said, "Let's go back and start talking to teams about how we could do this." But all the meetings about coming back were actually very complicated.

I was expecting people to say, "Yeah! Welcome back. Let's go for it!" I knew how ready I was but I realised that this is F1 and I'm not going to go through all that pain again to get the success. If people are not ready to make decisions and move, I'm not going to wait another seven years until I'm going to win again. It came to the point where I said, "Okay, let's stop this." But my passion for racing was still there, and I did DTM.

MH Which you enjoyed?

Mika I did. It's not club racing. It's proper cars and young guys who are serious and want to be F1 drivers. So they'll do anything - and try to beat me.

MH Which brings us up to date. You seem really happy and contented. How are you filling your time?

Mika I've been an ambassador for Hermes, a logistics company in Germany since 2008. And, of course, I've been working with Johnnie Walker. I have a long-term contract with them, which we announced in Monza last year. They're doing great work globally to make people aware of the dangers of drinking and driving.

MH Do you find that satisfying?

Mika I do. It's been a great journey. Such motivating work because racing and driving are my business; so, for me to enter new areas of work in my life is brilliant. It's very challenging. You cannot live in the past; you have to find new things in your life to motivate you. I'm also an ambassador for Mercedes-Benz, doing work in China for AMG. They are very successful over there. I've seen a lot of changes in the market; the potential in China is just incredible because of the way it's moving forward.

I watch all the Grands Prix, of course, but especially because I'm writing a column for a Finnish newspaper. And also because I'm taking part with Didier in the management of drivers. That's also really challenging for me because I'm having to learn about how to write contracts; about how do I explain this and that; about putting everything together and being in the right place at the right time.

This became important, especially when Valtteri Bottas signed for Williams. It's been a multi-year programme we've had with Valtteri which has worked out - but it's been a very difficult road. Luckily, Valtteri is a brilliant racing driver, a great talent. He works really well with the people. It doesn't mean you have to like him, but you can communicate with him and build up the relationship with him to do something good. That's why the people at Williams, the mechanics and so on, they like him a lot.

MH Well, from what you've told me today, you've plenty of fantastic experience to draw on. Thanks for your time.

Mika Not at all. Like I said, it's been a long time...

At lunch with **Flavio Briatore**

"It's official! There was no proof I was involved in Singapore. Which is why I won in court. If what people said was true, then why did I fire Piquet in the middle of the next season? Why take that risk?"

I returned to Monaco for this interview in March 2013, but the venue was a complete contrast to lunch with Mika Häkkinen a few weeks before. We had moved from one side of the Principality to the other; from pub food to haute cuisine; from Rascasse to Portier; from a quiet and modest man with winning ways to an extrovert character with form of a different kind. Both had claimed world championships in the best possible way. But, for Flavio Briatore, his track history had been both trumpeted and tainted in equal measure.

Briatore won double championships with Michael Schumacher at Benetton and Fernando Alonso at Renault, marking each with the flamboyance to be expected of a hugely successful marketing man from a knitwear company finding himself in the very different world of Formula 1 ceremony and finery.

But his reputation was to be blemished by 'Crashgate', a scandal surrounding Nelson Piquet Junior crashing his car in order to assist Alonso to win the 2008 Singapore Grand Prix. Briatore was banned from F1 for life by the FIA, a penalty that was subsequently overthrown by a French high court. The FIA threatened to appeal but an out-of-court agreement was reached.

Briatore had not spoken about this or, indeed, much else in F1 for three years. He not only agreed to talk to me, but he also suggested we meet in Cipriani, his high-end restaurant in Avenue Princess Grace. The immaculate interior has a nautical theme, but far from sinking without trace, Briatore was swimming as strongly as ever and not averse to making waves.

Maurice Hamilton I hear you're a TV star now, doing *The Apprentice* in Italy. How's it going?

Flavio Briatore Very well. We're doing another series in September. You can lose your grip with the new generation very easily because you're talking always with the old guys. So this has been a fantastic experience for me.

MH Is this the first time *The Apprentice* has been run in Italy?

FB Yes. When we started, no one knew what it was but, after two or three weeks, we had an audience of more than five million. The success of the show depends very much on the quality of the people, and that worked very well for us.

MH When I watched the British series with Lord Sugar, I was often amazed by how stupid some of the contestants were. Did you find that?

FB Yes. But you fire them as soon as possible. The people in the end were very strong, very competitive, very good people. The winner is working with us here in Monaco. He's a nice guy.

MH How does it work? Do you think up the tests that the contestants have to do?

FB No, we are not involved so much in that. It's when we get to the boardroom that we [*Briatore points to his long-suffering assistant, Patrizia Spinelli*] really get going. It's just like normal business. This was the really interesting part because the right people were coming through. When we fired someone, it was not because the television people asked me to. The TV people wanted more girls, but we fired the girls immediately because they were no good at all. In the end it was very close. Everyone was trying to guess who would win. It was very popular in Italy. People were having dinner parties and inviting friends to come and watch the show.

MH So, it was good for your profile?

FB Very good, yes. We got nominated for the Oscars of Italian TV - and we finished second. The winner was a comedian who has been doing this for 20 years. Sky cancelled most of their shows and all that's left is *Master Chef*, *X Factor* and *The Apprentice*. All the other shows are gone. I enjoyed it but, in the end, it was tiring because you are filming all day.

MH So, what else are you doing?

FB Cipriani, Billionaire nightclubs and Billionaire clothing. We have 25 stores for Billionaire clothing. In the next six months it will go up to 35. The turnover is around €60 million. The shops are very successful. But only the clients decide if you are successful. We have two shops in London, in Sloane Street and Harrods. We are in Rome Airport, Dubai, Abu Dhabi, Russia, St Moritz, St Tropez, and Las Vegas.

MH When you're doing all this, do you get time to keep in touch with F1?

FB Yes, I'm speaking to Bernie a lot. Every day I'm talking to somebody from F1. I keep contact all the time, I never miss anything.

MH Did you find last year exciting? I know we've had discussions in the past about how you feel F1 should entertain above all else.

FB Exciting, yes. But I think the problem F1 has at this moment is that three or four teams pay for their drivers and, with the rest, it is the driver who pays to race. We've talked about this many times and the problem is same, the cost of running a team is astronomical. Whatever money the team takes from Bernie, they spend. I believe it is split 60 per cent for the team and 40 per cent to FOM but, whichever way you split the money, it makes no difference; the money is spent. And when you have the driver paying, I'm not sure you have the best drivers in F1.

MH But the way things are now, it is so competitive that the driver with money has to be quick as well.

FB I know, but I have never seen a pay driver who is really quick. For the majority of the field, the driver is part of the budget. It never happened like this before. We paid our drivers at Benetton, maybe not so much, but we paid them. A team like Jordan paid at least one driver. Now it is very different.

MH But is that not due to the global economic climate these days?

FB Okay, it is a big crisis worldwide, but I don't think F1 ever really felt that. Or, they forgot that there is a crisis. From what I understand, a lot of teams are struggling - a lot of teams. To have a healthy F1, you need to have healthy teams. During my time at Benetton, we produced a profit every year. And we invested that profit in the factory and the team. There was a waiting list of teams trying to get into F1; we had pre-qualifying at 6am in the morning; it was a business.

If you want to develop anything in your business, you make a profit. The bigger the team, the bigger the profit. The team needs to run with the money from the promoter and from Bernie. The sponsor is the plus, the sponsor brings the profit. This is the reason why the driver is now part of the budget. In our budget, the driver was a cost. Now, excluding the top four teams, he is the income.

MH I know you have always been keen on cutting costs. So what is your view on the change of the engine formula from the 2014 season, which, initially anyway, is going to be hugely expensive?

FB I was fighting for ages to have the frozen engine spec. It was my idea; I pushed for it with Max Mosley and it went through. It was an incredible saving for everybody. I do not understand what is wrong with the present engine. F1 is incredibly close and competitive now. Why do we need to change the engine?

MH Well, the argument is F1 needs to be seen to be relating to road cars because of the need to show green credentials. Do you think motor racing should be doing that?

Peter Sauber: "I had big clashes with Red Bull over Räikkönen"

Launch of the 2004 Sauber, with Massa and Fisichella

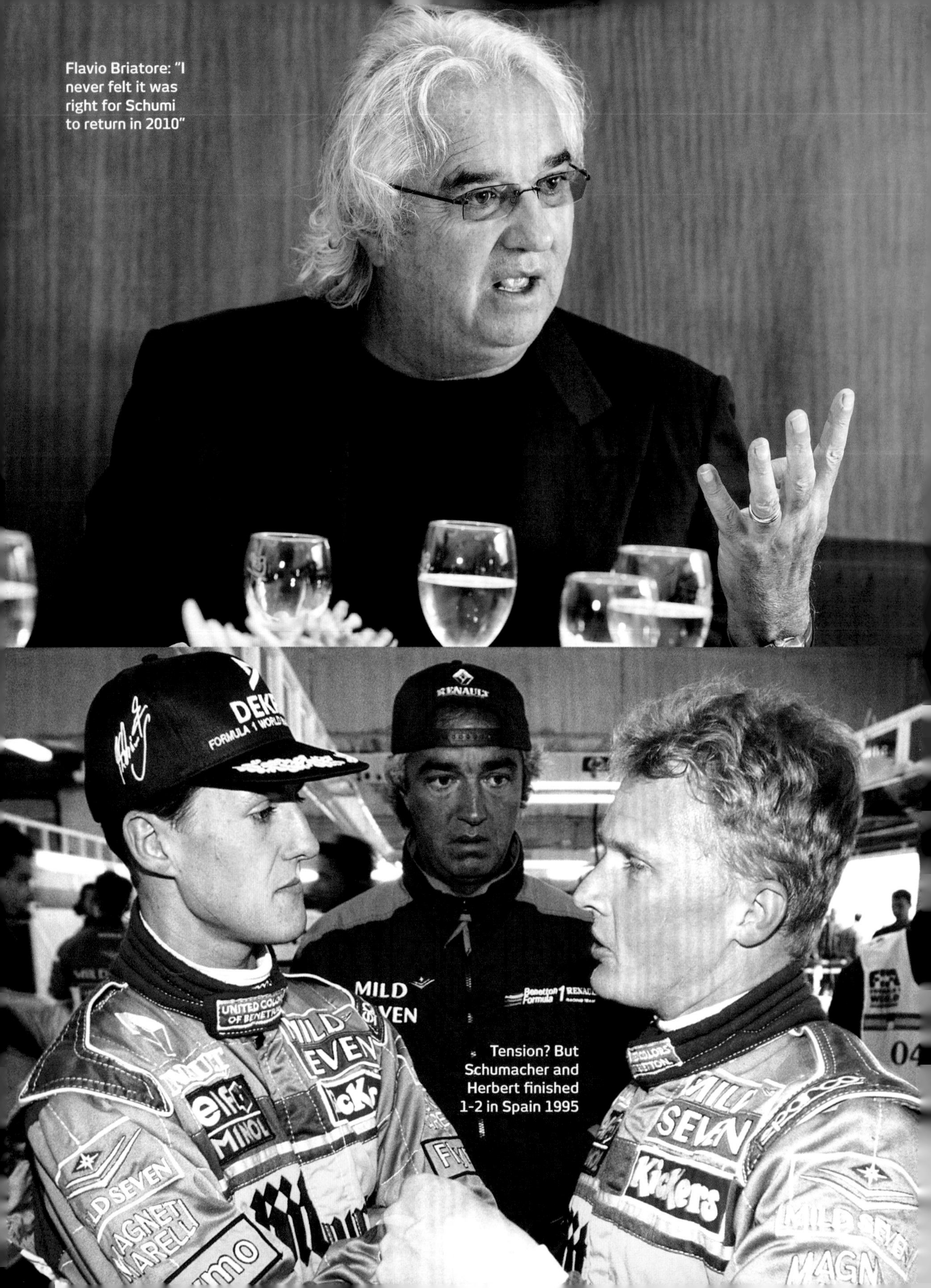

Flavio Briatore: "I never felt it was right for Schumi to return in 2010"

Tension? But Schumacher and Herbert finished 1-2 in Spain 1995

Mika Häkkinen: the Spa 2000 win was "a great experience"

Mika had a good relationship with Ron Dennis fom the day they met

Sun

Reigning World Champ Häkkinen claimed four wins in 2000

Martin Brundle, the same open, quick-witted guy MH met in 1984

Brundle overdid it in qualifying, Monaco 1984, but walked away

Hamilton recalls, "Prost would slip past, unnoticed, to win by stealth"

Prost and Senna in 1988 – a spirit of co-operation that did not last

Marlboro
Marlboro
BOSS
MEN'S FASHION
Marlboro

Eddie Irvine, living life to the full, and getting richer and richer

Irvine wins in Germany, 1999. He misses the title by 2pts

Gerhard Berger, always a joker and always a major F1 talent

Hungary 1992: Senna wins, Mansell is 2nd and Berger 3rd

Patrick Head: as robust and forthright today as in his heyday

Williams with his warring drivers, Mansell and Piquet in 1986

"Oh, bugger it, I'll sign anything." Alan Jones, as relaxed as ever

Canada 1980: Jones wins and is interviewed by Jackie Stewart

FLY saudia
saudia
saudia
Mobil
MICHELIN
Techniques
d' Avant Garde
TAG
saudia
Leyland
TAG
1

Monaco 1981: Jones holds off eventual winner, Gilles Villeneuve

Charlie Whiting's Ferrari favours? "It's completely ludicrous"

Hockenheim 1980: Piquet wins the German GP for Brabham

"Changing the engines in F1 for 2014 will be completely mad"

FB If you watch DTM, you recognise the Audi from the Mercedes and so on. If you paint all the F1 cars black, you can't tell the McLaren from the Ferrari or the Force India. F1 is an event, a race. If you want to talk about the engine when marketing F1, maybe it is possible to do something. But, to be honest, I really don't see why the engine in F1 should be linked to the road car.

The spectators don't care about road cars when they're watching F1. They care about the drivers and the fighting between them whatever engine you have. I believe that of 99.9 per cent of the spectators - excluding some old journalists like you, Maurizio. Actually, there used to be about six or seven of the old British journalists and now everyone's gone - there just seems to be you!

MH Yeah, thanks for that Flav...

FB No, is good to have you here. But the point is nobody cares. When we won a championship, nobody asked how many cylinders we had. All they wanted to talk about was the *speculari* (mirrors) through the race. If it costs a team $50,000 or $100m, the spectator doesn't care. If Ferrari spend $200m, do you think the people care? For me, changing the engine is completely mad. There is nothing wrong with the engine we have now.

MH I take it you feel as strongly as ever about the costs even though there is supposed to be a restriction on spending?

FB You have Ferrari, Red Bull, McLaren and Mercedes with very important budgets. Then a few times last year you saw Lotus, with a very small budget, beat the big teams. And sometimes Sauber and Force India were in among the top four teams as well. I don't understand how engineers with a budget of 200 million must feel when a team with 90 million is faster. They should be devastated. That was the story with Benetton - we won the championship with much less money than other top teams.

MH You would be in favour of a budget cap?

FB Of course. Why is it not possible to have a cap? The top teams already have an incredible amount of money. And then they talk about 170 people doing aerodynamics. It's not the drivers' world championship, it's the wind tunnel world championship. Okay, the income the team has is very important. But however much money you get, you spend. It makes no difference. The worst word to put in F1 is 'budget'. The moment you tell people your budget is 10, the next day it's already spent.

MH People complain that CVC Capital Partners take too much money out of the sport. Are you saying that isn't the argument because the teams get enough in any case?

FB Absolutely. FOTA put some discipline into wind tunnel use. So, if you do 300 hours or 50 hours in the wind tunnel, what's the difference if it's the same for everybody? You are saving a lot of money. Nobody in F1 thinks about the spectator; nobody cares about the people watching TV.

MH I remember when you came into F1, you were amazed to find the teams were building cars just for qualifying.

FB It was completely mad. When I arrived in F1, I had come from the business world; I had not served an apprenticeship in racing and looked at F1 in a different way. Everyone was building a qualifying car, so there was no performance advantage any more. So, what was the point? Then, when we brought in parc fermé, people were saying: 'Ah, you ruin it'. But it was fantastic for the mechanics. Everything we did was orientated towards what the spectator and the show didn't need. Do you remember, teams started to put screens across the front of the garages? That has to be the stupidest thing I ever saw in F1. You come to see racing cars - and we put a screen in front of the car. All this changed with FOTA.

MH Talking about FOTA, do you remember in 2009, there was a meeting at Enstone...

FB Two o'clock in the morning.

MH Yes, and FOTA suddenly looked incredibly strong and there was talk of a breakaway championship. How close did that come to happening?

FB Very close. But we did not want to split with Bernie because we didn't have any problems with him; no problems with the commercial side. There was a lot of confusion. At the time we were complaining more about Max because we wanted more say in the running of the teams. We wanted to be part of the rule-making and not to be

Cheers all round: Alonso wins the inaugural Singapore GP

told this is the rule, take it or leave it. I think FOTA did an amazing job. It was the first time we had controlled the costs, and it was unanimous.

MH Why do you think it didn't work out for FOTA? What happened?

FB For me it was Singapore [*Crashgate in 2008/09*] and for Luca di Montezemolo, it was when he resigned. And then Ron Dennis was gone. All the strong characters had moved on and the FIA and Bernie were back in charge. There was no problem with the commercial side because we had a contract. The problem was more with Max and the FIA because we wanted to be part of our destiny; we wanted to be part of the rule making. This was the reason we had the big fight with Max.

The worst was when he said we had to enter the next year's World Championship before or after Silverstone - normally you have until November. Nobody applied and this was when Max made up an entry with strange team names. This made F1 look completely crazy. It was a pity because we had been working closely with Max on cost cutting and, as I said, we had no problems with Bernie commercially. But you have to say, because of the interference of the FIA, teams such as BMW and Toyota stopped. We could have done a lot of good in F1, especially with the costs.

MH Do we need to bring in more manufacturers, such as Honda?

FB Yes, but only if the cost of F1 is sensible. For me, that is about €120-150 million a year for a big team. F1 has been improving the show, making the races more spectacular and entertaining. So, there is a good possibility the constructors will come back if the business is profitable - like it was when Benetton bought Toleman and you could do business. But if you spend €60 or €70m to finish last all the time, you do stuff like that only if you're completely nuts. If there is no chance to be a top team or to win, the only certainty you will have is that you'll have the worst drivers.

MH You mentioned Singapore 2008. The Tribunal de Grande Instance in Paris in early 2010 rejected the FIA's life-time ban on you. How do you look back on all that?

FB I feel the same. The court in Paris was very clear: I was not involved at all. That is what the letter said.

MH Did they actually say that? Did they put it in writing?

FB Yes, it's official. There was no proof that I was involved in Singapore. Which is the reason I won in court. I've nothing more to say; I say it already at the time. If what people claimed about Singapore was true, then why did I fire Piquet in the middle of the next season? Why take that risk? Why not renew the contract because it would be 30 or 40 per cent less money and there would be no trouble if all this was true. I had Fernando back and, for me, the second driver was not important.

I respect exactly what was said in the court. After that, I have an agreement with Jean Todt that the FIA will not appeal. I stay away with no problem at all. I had the moral responsibility because I was in charge of the team. But now it is gone.

MH Was that a very difficult time for you?

FB Yes, but this was the time when I wanted to stop anyway. The year before I had wanted to stop but Fernando came back from McLaren, so it would not have been right for me to finish then. But I was happy to stop. F1 was finished for me at the time. For sure, it was hard because people treat you like a criminal. It was unfair. In the FIA investigation, they had this Witness X but nobody knows who he was. Mr X was the proof, basically, but he never signed the statement. The FIA signed the statement, but he didn't. For me it was much easier to say I respect exactly what the appeal court says and leave it at that.

These things make you stronger. I had a fantastic time in F1. Now I have a fantastic time with my family. I'm very lucky because I have very good health. I'm not jealous. I don't have a vendetta with anyone; there is no drama. I enjoy myself and this is the most important thing.

MH You certainly seem very happy. I know you had cancer a few years ago. How is your health now?

FB It's good because the cancer is gone.

MH Did that change your view on life and what is important?

FB For one week! It's human that you move on and forget. When you are in the hospital and before you go to surgery, you don't care about anything else; you just think you're

Briatore was hurt by Alonso's unexpected McLaren move

going to die. Then after the recovery and one week, I tell you, everything changes and you go back to the way you were.

MH So, would you like to come back to F1?

FB No, I don't think so. Now I have a son, three years old; I'm working 20 hours a day for different businesses, different investments, different situations, here and in America; I'm very happy. This restaurant, for example, is the most popular in Monte Carlo. I was in F1 for 20 years, won seven championships with two different teams, discovered the two big stars after Ayrton Senna - Schumi and Fernando. I know everything that's going on and I know to have a team at this moment makes no sense financially. So, there is no reason for me to come back to F1.

MH I take it you watch the races on television?

FB I still enjoy watching F1 and I think Sky have done an amazing job. But my belief is that we're losing a lot of viewers.

MH Why do you think that is?

FB Because when you had free-to-air RAI or BBC, then I think the BBC was about six million viewers and Sky has a lot less. I think Bernie is doing the best he can under the circumstances because pay-tv has the money and the others don't. Bernie is doing a fantastic job because the income is very good when the financial circumstances worldwide are not so good. Look at the US Grand Prix, he did an incredible job there. And now we have India, Abu Dhabi - a new world.

MH But at the expense of losing traditional races.

FB Yes, fewer races in Europe; that is not good.

MH Agreed, but these race promoters can't afford the high F1 costs.

FB Yes, but if the teams spent less, they would need less and the promoter would not have to pay so much. Then the promoter would have more money to actually promote the race; these are difficult times for the promoters as well. It's simple; if the teams are spending 40 per cent less, everything else goes down by 40 per cent. Plus, the more the cars are similar, the better the racing.

Look, we call it the Drivers' World Championship. If you took 10 cars from GP2, painted them all yellow and put in the top 10 drivers, you would have an amazing race and you would see who is the best driver.

MH People will argue that F1 shouldn't be about everyone having the same car.

FB But the chassis is not performance, so why not let everyone have the same chassis? Why are they spending a fortune channelling the air up and down, and this and that? Okay, if you want to play around, you play around with the wings - like in our time. Now you have telemetry from the factory. This is ridiculous. You need to have 30 people in the factory supporting the race. Completely mad!

MH I have to say I agree with that. Particularly as F1 is supposed to be containing costs.

FB But they're not. Some teams are spending lots of money and, as I said, you have Kimi Räikkönen in a Lotus winning a race. Actually, I believe last year Lotus had the best car in F1.

MH You may be right. Speaking of Räikkönen, do you think Michael should have come back in 2010?

FB No. Everyone was very excited in the beginning but I never felt it was right. The world has changed from when, say Alain Prost came back in 1993. He had a very strong car, the Williams, but when Michael came back it was very difficult because you had Fernando, you had Lewis Hamilton, you had Jenson Button. And the Mercedes was not the best. I prefer to remember Schumi as a winner and not struggling to qualify and finish ninth. It was not the image of somebody exceptional like Michael.

MH You said earlier that Fernando was the other driver you brought to F1. How long do you think he will be prepared to wait for Ferrari to give him a car capable of winning the championship?

FB This is interesting because Fernando is driving better now than in my time. Last year, in 2012, he did an amazing job. It's important for Ferrari to remember that the performance of the car was not good and it needed Fernando to do these things with it.

Schumacher wins for Briatore (second right) in Adelaide in 1994

I believe he is very involved with Ferrari. He loves it. And he loves winning the championship. Ferrari have the technical capability and the finance to provide a good car. But they remember that, for a driver, the time is very short between when you start racing and stop. So, if the technical side is still the same, I don't see a big difference; I don't see what's going to change and make it better. It's like you go to the bakery every day and take the bread; there is no change because they provide the same bread. It's very difficult to make the big jump in performance. Red Bull are on top and can keep going. Mercedes were able to develop this year's car because they were not having the results last year. Ferrari need to make a step. Fernando cannot wait for ever.

MH When Fernando left Renault to go to McLaren in 2007, did that upset you? Was it a surprise?

FB Yes, because he didn't tell me immediately. I was disappointed because Fernando started with me from the beginning. I supported him always, through the difficult times, like when I put him in the car in place of Jenson. You guys thought I was mad. Jenson was an exceptional driver but, at the time, I believed Fernando was more special. I had nothing against the British or anyone else. This was the fact at the time. People said I did it because I was managing Fernando, but my job was to find the best available for Renault. It was the same with all the teams I had.

MH Mention of that reminds me of the late Tom Walkinshaw, who ran the Ligier team for you. You were also together at Benetton, of course. What's your memory of Tom?

FB We were partners for a long time in various ways over many years. He was a very tough guy but at no time did I have a problem with Tom. Never. He was always correct, a super guy. And he wanted to win; a guy from the same time as Ron Dennis, Frank Williams and Ken Tyrrell. If you are like them, you want to win.

MH The first memory I have of you and Tom working together is when you took Michael Schumacher away from Eddie Jordan after Schumi made his F1 debut at Spa in 1991. What exactly happened there?

FB We knew about Michael already because a friend of mine had been telling me about three drivers who were very quick: Karl Wendlinger, Heinz-Harald Frentzen and Michael Schumacher. At the time, it looked like Frentzen was the quickest. So, why did I pick Schumi? Because, you will remember, Bertrand Gachot was put in jail and Eddie was looking for a driver for Belgium and he chose Schumacher. I was very interested to see if this guy was as good as my friend believed.

After qualifying at Spa, when Schumacher was seventh on the grid, I spoke to Willi Weber, Schumacher's manager. He was very happy to talk with Benetton because Michael was on the way up. He told me Eddie wanted - I don't remember how much money - for the next race, the Italian Grand Prix. His sponsor was Tic-Tac. I said: "Don't worry. If Tic-Tac don't pay, you can race with me - for no money." The day the money did not arrive from Tic-Tac, we signed the deal. We did not steal anybody. We just signed a contract with a driver who was free to sign. There was a lot of bullshit in the newspapers. I signed the contract and, if it was wrong, then I would have been taken to court.

This was important for Benetton because we did not have the budget to pay top drivers. We thought our car was very good but, if you don't have the right driver, you never know. So I had to find somebody young with enormous potential or pay someone like Gerhard Berger or Riccardo Patrese. But if I talk to people like that, they are laughing because they are saying, "You are Benetton, a T-shirt maker." So, this was the best way because we could have this guy, maybe growing with the team, and it cost me nothing.

MH Bringing us up-to-date, tell me about your association with English football and owning Queens Park Rangers. Did you enjoy that?

FB Not at all! It was a disaster. But there was a lot of talk and people writing things which were not correct. We took QPR when they were bottom of the championship. There was the four-year plan and we took them into the Premier League. I don't understand why there was all the fuss. We did it with not very much money. After Bernie and I went away, leaving Mr Mital and Mr Tony Fernandes to run the show and spend a lot of money, it's funny to see they still have six or seven players who were with us in the championship.

I believe we did it quite well but, I tell you, it was no fun at all. You need to treat football like a full-time job and not like an investor. There were too many people; the manager, the assistant manager and, always, you are dealing with the agents. In the end, we sold it. *Basta!* Enough!

MH You had a reputation for getting through managers.

FB If you don't fire these coaches, you never go up. When you understand someone is not good enough to do the job, it's better you fire them immediately rather than waste another six months. I felt we were going nowhere with these guys. In the end, we made it. The most important thing in sport is the result.

MH Which more or less brings us full circle. The very first time I ever spoke to you was after you had fired Johnny Herbert from Benetton halfway through 1989 because you felt he couldn't do the job. I rang you to ask why. You said: "Because he's sick!" The British media were indignant, but you were right. And Johnny agrees because he had not recovered properly from terrible ankle and feet injuries sustained in a Formula 3000 accident in August 1988.

FB Look, as I said before, I had no experience of motor racing. I see that every driver in F1 has two legs. Johnny has only one... if you know what I mean. So what do you do? Do you keep him? No, because it was a danger for him as well. It was not a question of being nice or not nice. I maybe saved him from another accident. That's the way it is.

MH Indeed. You were never one to mince your words, Flavio. Good to see that hasn't changed. Thanks very much for your time. And for a superb dinner.

FB You're welcome, Maurizio. I like to look after the old guys...

At lunch with **Martin Brundle**

"They were going to take my foot off, until Sid said "I'm getting you out of here". I still have a lot of pain in my ankle, but when I look at Johnny's feet, I think there's nothing wrong with mine. His are in a terrible mess."

I first made the journey to see Martin Brundle in King's Lynn in March 1984. He had just been announced as a Tyrrell F1 driver after taking Ayrton Senna to the wire at the end of one of the best F3 championships of all time. The roads and countryside in Norfolk have scarcely changed. And neither has Martin, despite the massive rise in his profile, due more, it has to be said, to his career as a TV presenter than as an extremely competent racing driver.

He remains the same open, quick-witted guy, his eloquence making interviews just as pleasurable now as they were when he was this fresh-faced kid pushed before the F1 media nearly 30 years ago. The one thing we've got right this time, in December 2012, is the choice of venue. Instead of chatting in a car showroom, we're meeting for lunch in the Dabbling Duck, a classic country pub in the village of Great Massingham. Once I've sorted a glitch with my digital recorder, it's a perfect place to reflect on the extensive and fascinating past of a Norfolk boy made good.

Maurice Hamilton The F1 landscape has changed so much since 1984, hasn't it? Tyrrell's normally aspirated Ford DFV was up against the turbo Ferraris, McLarens, Brabhams and just about everyone else. But, unlike the back of the grid teams today, you were able to do things like produce a stonking performance on the streets of Detroit, where you crossed the line in second place. It's so competitive now throughout the grid that it's impossible to gain any sort of advantage whereas, in 1984, when a tight circuit like Detroit suited the DFV, you were right up there.

Martin Brundle Yes, absolutely. If you got through pre-qualifying, you had a very good chance of being in the top 10 on the grid and then an outside chance of a top-six finish. But it's so much more complex now. With CFD, the wind tunnel, simulators and all sorts of things, you can't get close to the top teams. In those days, on certain occasions, you could walk around the McLarens and think "Right, I'm going to beat this lot." Now? Forget it...

MH In 1984, we didn't have TV monitors in the media centre. We had to go trackside to watch and keep a lap chart. It was actually a much healthier thing to do and you could see what was going on. In Detroit, I stood on the inside of the final chicane and you were really nailing that little Tyrrell through there. It was mighty. Was that one of the most enjoyable races you had in F1?

MB It was, yes. But I got a royal bollocking from Ken for daring to overtake Elio de Angelis in that very chicane. And Jackie Stewart said it was risky too. I got such a ripping from Ken that night.

MH Why?

MB Ken was trying to keep my feet on the ground. But I knew Elio's Lotus had lost third gear - which neither Ken nor Jackie knew. You used to lose gears left, right and centre in those days. You then had to miss them out with the H-pattern gearshift; you couldn't do that now. There was a little left-hander coming past Cobo Hall and then a short run to that fast chicane. I knew he was missing a gear because he would come out of there really slowly. I thought 'I can have him now. I can have him'. And sure enough, I did. Ken thought it was outrageous to take that risk.

MH But you didn't take a risk coming out of the chicane for the last time, did you? If you had, you might have won because Piquet was struggling just ahead of you in the Brabham.

MB Yeah, I was about the width of this table behind Piquet on the run to the line, only to meet Charlie Whiting and the Brabham team jumping up and down on the pit straight. Charlie was their chief mechanic and he was right in the middle!

MH That's the irony isn't it? Charlie, of all people [*now the FIA's F1 race director and safety delegate*]. If you did that now, he'd have you sent off to Siberia or somewhere.

MB You're barely allowed to stand on the pit wall now.

MH We went to Dallas straight after Detroit. I remember having dinner with you and Liz [*Martin's wife*] on the night before the accident and you were very...

MB ...pumped up? Which is why Ken was trying to knock me back. This was another street circuit. We were quick from the start of practice and, in my mind, I was going to be on pole position. Then I hit the wall.

MH Were you just pushing too hard?

MB No, I got a rear puncture. There was a chicane lined with concrete walls. Maybe in the run-off areas there were some tyres but, everywhere else, it was concrete walls. I turned in and the left-rear came round on me a little bit. My right-front tagged the wall; didn't really hit it but this kicked me left, which is what took the front off the car. Then I hit the right. So, the third time I hit the wall, my feet were sticking out the front. I'd never broken a bone before and I've never broken a bone since.

It was one of those disbelief things. I can definitely remember, I got out the car and tried to walk off because I wanted to prove to myself I was fine. But I knew I wasn't because my leg wasn't attached to my foot at the time; only held together by skin. I knew I'd hurt myself but I didn't want to believe it was that serious because I was on an absolute roll. They put me in an ambulance with no air-conditioning and I passed out.

MH I remember it was stinking hot all weekend.

MB It was. The next time I woke up, my foot was caught in the catch fencing. That's the sort of detail Sid Watkins had to sort out in the intervening years because there wasn't enough room to get a stretcher round the debris fencing into this medical unit. I remember they finally got my foot out of the fence, got me into this hut where they more or less said there's nothing we can do for him here, he's going to have to go to hospital. Back into the ambulance, no air-conditioning, passed out again.

And the final pain was when I could hear the race from my hospital room. Bernie had ensured there was a blackout on local TV and I couldn't see what was going on.

Every hour this big, big nurse would come and stick a pin in my foot. "Can you feel this?" "Can you feel this?" I began to work out what was going on so I did an impression of feeling a bit of pain. My foot was just swelling, swelling, swelling and obviously I wasn't getting any feeling to it. Then I heard the doctors talking about it.

MH Amputation?

MB They were going to take the foot off, yeah. Sid said "I'm getting you out of here" and we headed home. But I was like a space cadet. Funny, I went through Dallas on my way to Austin in November and, as I walked through the airport, it suddenly dawned on me it was the first time I'd been back since 1984. And under very different circumstances.

We bought three first class seats. I was comatose with pain killers and Sid sat beside me. These were the old-style first class seats and we had to buy three so that the seat in front of us was down and my legs dragged over the back. I was in a hell of a mess.

"I think I'm a lot luckier than those that got hit on the head"

MH I shouldn't make light of this but I often have a smile to myself when I see you, Johnny Herbert, Marc Surer and Jacques Laffite hobbling back from the TV compound. Quiz question: "How would you know these TV presenters used to be racing drivers in the 1980s?" Bleedin' obvious when you see your various flat-footed styles of walking because you've all had serious foot injuries of some sort, haven't you?

MB Yes, all waddling along. That was the era when we used to sit right at the front of the car to kind of balance the weight of the engine. I was one of the lucky ones who survived all that, relatively speaking. I have a lot of pain now from my ankle but when I look at Johnny, I think there's nothing wrong with my feet. His are in a terrible mess.

MH In the mornings are your ankles seized up and sore?

MB Yes, you limp. There's no cartilage. I spent thousands of pounds having it opened up and thoroughly examined; there's nothing you can do. It's done for. But then I think, well I'm a lot luckier than those that got hit on the head or didn't come through it.

MH Saying that, looking back at your career, how pivotal a moment was that accident?

MB Totally. First of all, it stopped my flow; like I said, I was on a roll. Then Tyrrell got banned because of the weight thing they had going on while trying to beat the turbos. I had absolutely no idea about that. First I heard was at 10 o'clock one night in hospital when a journalist rang and asked me for a comment on being chucked out of the championship. I've been in hospital a month, my career is in tatters and now I hear this. It turned out Ken hadn't quite got round to telling me about it. [*Tyrrell was alleged to have been adding ballast in the form of small lead balls when replenishing a water tank in the latter stages of each race*].

That accident did two things; it compromised me on some of the fitness levels I needed - although I found ways around that. But where it absolutely stuffed me was left-foot braking.

MH But left-foot braking didn't come in until quite a bit later, surely?

MB The early 90s, I guess. It's quite an advantage but the only time I ever left-foot brake is when driving a kart or doing TV features for Sky F1. I have no choice then.

The good thing about the F1 cars now is they are very much stop and go. What really helps me in modern F1 cars is having your feet so high, you don't use your ankle. You don't swivel your feet like before. You're pushing your whole leg forward, braking with your thigh and your gluts. I did 40 laps in the Ferrari. When Mark Webber asked me how it went, I said I loved it. Then he asked what hurt the next morning. I said "Funny you should ask that. My arse really hurt." And he says "Exactly, mate!"

MH All things considered, you had a pretty good season keeping up with, and occasionally beating, Schuey when you were Benetton team-mates in 1992. The last dozen races that year were really strong with four or five podiums. You would have won Canada had something not broken.

MB Yeah, the diff went. It was interesting racing against Michael because, in the end, I was faster than him sometimes through places like 130R at Suzuka - because I had to be! He was quicker on the slow corners so you just try to get better in other areas. I didn't have that finesse with my left foot and I could never live with people like Michael in slow corners. They had this way of keeping the car rotating; keeping a little bit more apex speed but straightening the car. We'd be comparing slow corners and Michael would have less throttle, but more wheel spin. But he wouldn't have the steering angle I had because he could use his left foot.

My son Alex does it; all kids all do it now. Your left foot on the brake is nearly as powerful as your steering wheel in situations like that to release the car and move it around. I never had that facility. I'm not saying it's absolutely a road block in that respect; it's just that little bit of finesse you can sometimes do with. There's some corners that were not quite flat out where you really want a touch of left-foot brake. You want the throttle flat open but you just want to put the nose of the car down; you want to load the front tyre.

You're basically driving four contact patches. It's very simple in that respect and if you ask contact patches to support the car, turn the car, slow the car down or accelerate the car all at the same time, they can't. That's where you need a bit of left-foot finesse. I sometimes try left-foot braking on the road - and everyone's nose is against the windscreen. No finesse! In an F1 car, ironically, it's not an issue any more because your feet are so high.

Brundle and Schumi were team-mates at Benetton

MH You mentioned Alex, which brings me to you sharing an LMP2 car at Le Mans in 2012. You've always enjoyed racing sportscars, haven't you? You did some amazing things, particularly with Jaguar and, specifically, the purple one - what was the type?

MB The XJR14. The best racing car I've ever driven. I was on pole at Le Mans, even after I finished F1. I had loads of poles in sports car racing but it was more about the two-and-a-half hour stints. You get into a rhythm and a flow that just suited me. Maybe the sportscar had a touch more understeer than suited my driving style, but I think, more than anything else, it was psychological.

I raced for Tom Walkinshaw and he thought whatever I did was right. I had incredible support from him and felt invincible in a sportscar. I see my son doing exactly the same thing; he's been awesome in 2012. I have to say I didn't feel unbeatable last year because I was 53 years old and Alex was 21 and, pleasingly, he was quicker than me.

I was the lead driver through just about all of my sportscar career, which meant I had the Schumacher advantage. Things were developed around me. For instance, I remember sitting in a wooden buck with Ross Brawn in a freezing cold workshop at Kidlington. "Okay, I want the gearlever here" and there would be, literally, bits of wood with nails. It was perfect in every respect. The psychological advantage was huge.

I was consistent and economical on fuel and tyres. The other thing was, I had the stamina. I did eight-and-a-half hours at Le Mans last year. I was having one of the busiest years of my life so I can't pretend I was in peak condition at my age, but I wasn't in bad nick and I found that quite easy, actually. I have the stamina my old man had.

MH You're a very slight build; where does this come from?

MB I don't know, but I can drive hours and hours. I can come out of the commentary box at, say, the Nürburgring, get on my BMW K1600 GT bike and ride 500 miles home. I've done it several times. At the end of a busy weekend, I put on my leathers and ride through Germany, Belgium, France and Britain to Norfolk, get home and feel absolutely fine.

MH I talked to you prior to Le Mans and I remember thinking then how hectic your life was. You were going to Canada for the Grand Prix then straight into Le Mans.

MB I made signing on at Le Mans by five minutes. It was that close.

MH Were there any periods during Le Mans where you thought "Oh Christ, have I asked too much of myself?"

MB Yes, on the Tuesday after Canada I was pretty battered - but you don't have to perform until the Wednesday night. Why I loved it was sharing with Alex and driving the LMP2 cars, which are great. They're not that far behind that XJR14 in terms of driveability; great little cars. I wasn't part of a works programme, so the expectation on me was virtually zero. I was just enjoying myself.

If you want to talk about hard years, then 1988 was the toughest of my life because I was doing IMSA and the World Sports Car Championship for Jag, which I won. I started off by winning Daytona and finishing in Fuji in October. Somewhere in the middle of all of that I became Williams test driver for their active car when Nigel Mansell said he wasn't driving that car any more. "Put a monkey in it," he said, I was the monkey. I'd be testing the active car, then I ended up driving the Belgian GP for Williams when Nigel had chicken pox. I went to America 14 times that year and I thought I'll never ever be busier than that in my life again. 2012 came close. It's been mad moving to Sky, 20 grands prix, Silverstone, Le Mans test, Le Mans, Goodwood, Alex racing. It's been great.

MH Do you have a lot to do for Sky; stuff in between races that we don't know about?

MB Sky have really gone for it, which I love. There's quite a lot going on, filming features and so on. We've got a lot of air time to fill. I don't know about you, but several times a day I stop and read what's going on. You've got to be up to date, haven't you? Twitter, internet, Autosport.com, everything.

MH But did you enjoy 2012?

MB I've never been happier since the very early years of ITV. I really enjoyed the days with Murray Walker and Neil Duncanson running it. I'm definitely the happiest I've been in TV thanks to the resources and creative energy at Sky.

MH It's taken me three-and-a-half hours to get up here from Surrey and I was thinking, as I was driving up "Martin, how do you do this?" Particularly at the end of a long weekend, all you want to do is grab your bag from the carousel at the airport, jump in the car and go home as fast as possible. And you face that drive.

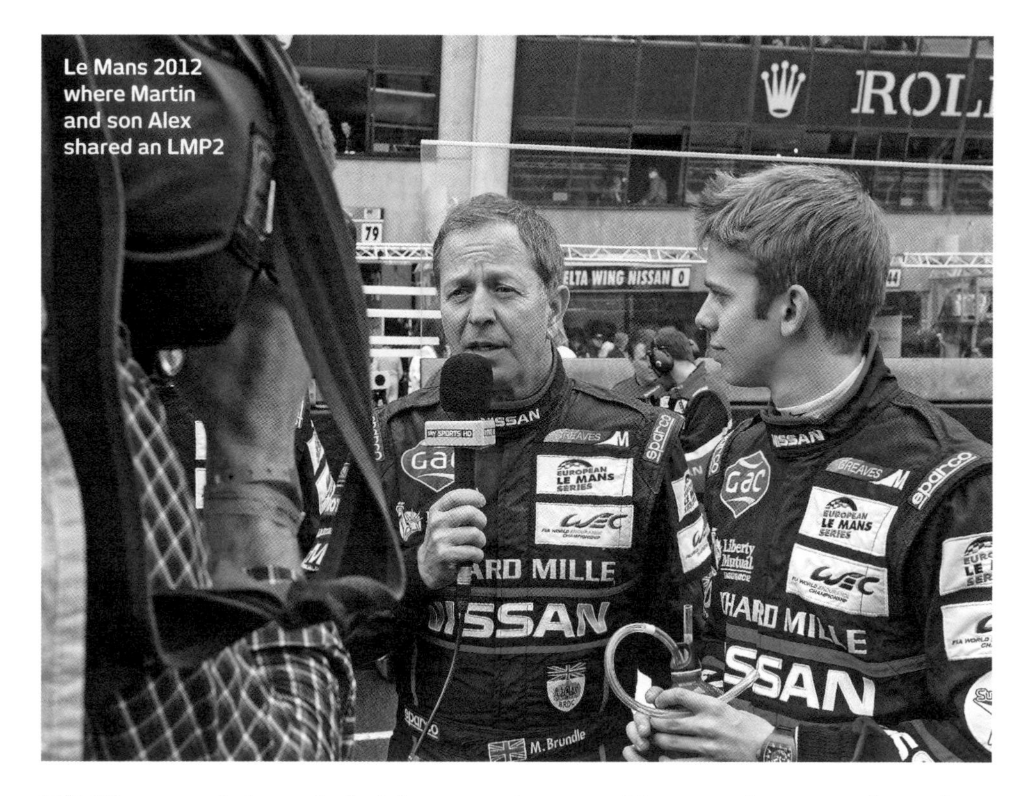

Le Mans 2012 where Martin and son Alex shared an LMP2

MB When you do it regularly, it becomes the norm. It's two-and-a-quarter hours from Heathrow to my house. Yeah, if I could find time, we should move but there's lots of memories up here. We've got a nice house and the family is all around.

MH You're in your 50s now, so you don't want to move now, do you?

MB Do you know what I'll do? I'll stop, retire and then move. I'll get it completely back to front.

MH As your friend and commentator 'Crofty' would say, "Trust me on this. You won't be able to stop, mate."

MB [*laughs*] No, I know. You're probably right. It's lovely up here. There's not a mile of motorway in Norfolk and that's why it's so hard to get to - but also why it's so special when you get here. You can't pass through this place; you either come or you don't come. I'm a Norfolk kid. It's very easy to think that the whole world revolves around F1 but, when you come back here, you realise it doesn't. It keeps your feet on the ground.

MH What are you driving on the road?

MB Jaguars mostly - an XFR at the moment. The thing is, you can drive them quite fast and they don't seem to upset people as much as other brands. The XFR is a stunning car. And then I've got my E-type. It's a '65 4.2 Coupé, Series 1, but it's nicely sorted.

MH I saw you in a helicopter at Goodwood. Do you actually own one?

MB I share one with a mate. It's hangered about seven minutes away. Obviously, it's no good for London but it's brilliant for somewhere like Goodwood, which is an hour and 15 from here, instead of four hours by road. But wherever you live, it's not quite the right place, is it? How long does it take you to get to Silverstone, for example?

MH At least two hours from Surrey.

MB You see, I'm much nearer to Silverstone. And I'm an hour and 15 from my front door to checking in at Stansted; so it's not quite as bad as some places. The guys who really impressed me in the early days were people like David Leslie who lived in Carlisle, or the Coulthards in Scotland. Every weekend in their motorhome, they'd do eight hours each way for a 10-minute kart race somewhere, or a 10-lap Formula Ford race. Can you imagine coming from Carlisle to Thruxton to do a 10-lap race and get taken out in the first corner? Now that's hardcore. I don't think I'm hardcore at all.

MH When I came up here to interview you back in 1984, we went to your family's car showroom in King's Lynn. I had to do a recording for British Forces Broadcasting Service and we sat inside a show car to do it because it was nice and quiet. I was pretty pleased with myself but, when I took the recording back to the studio in London, the engineer said, "You were sitting in a car when you did that, weren't you? It's not much good, mate, because I can hear your voices bouncing off the windscreen."

MB And you still can't bloody work the things after all this time, Maurice...

MH Yeah, okay! Talking about things not working, what did you make of McLaren in 2012? Is it fair to say that they should have won the championship but for strange and sometimes silly things going wrong?

MB I'll never forget when I drove for McLaren in 1994, going to the factory and looking around this room that had a lot of white-coated gentlemen in it. It was all about radiators and ducting. Nothing else. There was another room where they were shooting pellets at suspension. I was just blown away.

But the car never ran to temperature the whole year; it was always too hot. And I remember Monaco where we ended up with no oil and no water in the car when I finished second. I was lucky I got that one over the line. I thought about that room during the last two or three laps when all the alarm bells were going off and asked myself how this keeps happening.

If I think back through the days when David Coulthard was there and in Kimi's time; they've always had reliability issues. They're really great people but you can't get away from the fact that McLaren won the 2008 drivers' championship and the last time they won the constructors' was in 1998. How does that happen? When you see the excellence that they have and the facilities and the resource and the drivers, you wonder why.

MH Is there any connection with McLaren insisting on sticking to a policy of equality among their drivers?

Monaco 1994: Brundle finished second for McLaren

MB Yes, that's another contributory factor. But there's a disconnect in there somewhere. If you were starting up in F1 now, four people would be on your 'must have' list: Sebastian Vettel, Fernando Alonso, Lewis Hamilton and Adrian Newey. Three of those four have passed through McLaren in recent years. So something doesn't quite work.

MH I don't understand why that thing isn't utterly bullet proof, because, if you look at Ferrari and Red Bull, they're a lot more reliable, aren't they?

MB I did a feature at Ferrari earlier in the year and they were fantastic. They let us right into the inner sanctum; we sat in the rooms people had never been allowed in before with a camera. They were building the 2012 cars either side - so don't point your cameras that way. Yeah, all right, we won't do that then. Incredible access and I'm looking around at this facility and thinking, "This is quite old; this is small. They've not wasted a lot of resource on fancy bits, have they?"

MH In some ways, it's what you'd imagine a racing team to be like in the old days.

MB Like most of the ones I drove for! I mean, it wasn't quite Tyrrell but it's very old-fashioned. I'm thinking, "Is this it?" Ferrari are not always as fast as they should be, but they have some bullet proof material.

MH Look at the reliability Michael Schumacher had with Ferrari. Something like 58 races. Unbelievable!

MB But then, interestingly, McLaren currently hold the longest run of points scoring. Okay, everybody gets a prize these days, rather like a lucky dip, but to have a run like that is quite something. But then that doesn't fit, does it? What we're saying is you've got a team that doesn't have good enough reliability and yet it currently holds the record for consistent points finishes. I think what that tells you is that McLaren, unlike the other teams, have equal number ones. If you did a forensic analysis, would McLaren be more unreliable than the other top teams? My gut feeling is they would be because they seem to have key mistakes, key problems.

MH Based on 2012, they seem to have different things go wrong. With Red Bull, it was the alternator all the time, probably an overheating issue given the way Adrian Newey shrink-wraps his cars. But with McLaren it's "We don't understand it. Where did that come from? In 50 years, that's never happened before." At the time you were with McLaren, your family was still running the car dealerships. Are you still involved?

MB No, we sold up in 2007.

MH There was a neat tie-up at one point because you were selling Toyotas and, in 1999, we both did Rally GB; me as a co-driver with Louise Goodman in a Ford and you in a works Celica with the legendary Arne Hertz as your co-driver. It was your second Rally GB, if I remember correctly. How do you look back on your rallying experience?

MB I really enjoyed it. I'd go rallying again if I got the chance, but I'd do it in a lesser car. Quite why I thought I could get in a four-wheel drive, full house world rally car and not crash it, I don't know. How arrogant is that? But I loved it. Especially in the Toyota. That was great. Both times I crashed because I stopped listening to my co-driver.

MH Co-drivers are not sitting there for the ride, Martin! What did you enjoy? The ability to use car control, reaction and reflex?

MB I think, more than anything else, it was the challenge. In my mind, rally drivers are the greatest drivers in the world. I'm absolutely clear on that because they have to cope with changeable conditions on an unpredictable course that we in the racing world just can't even begin to comprehend. A little bit of dirt on a race track and we go flying off the road. It's so intensely difficult to do what they do. The top guys get to know the stages quite well but, even so, it's no wonder they crash quite frequently. It's so hard to do.

MH You're being a bit hard on yourself because you were very quick, once you got into it and listened to the co-driver. The point I was making is that the sideways stuff wasn't really new to you because of your background when racing as a youngster. Right?

MB That's right. I started off in grass track racing, banger racing; three miles from here. So I was sliding around in autocross, rallycross, autotest and all that sort of thing. I did hot rod racing, banger racing and stock car racing. I also did a couple of stage rallies up here in a little Celica GT. Then, in 1996, I suddenly decided to do the RAC Rally in a Ford Escort Cosworth, which was the rallying equivalent of jumping into an F1 car and doing the Monaco Grand Prix.

MH That's true. But you did a bit of testing beforehand, didn't you? Although testing in rallying and the event itself are two very different things. The gulf is much bigger than testing in motor racing.

MB Absolutely right. I remember testing with Didier Auriol and Carlos Sainz in Wales and getting within half-a-second a mile of them. Everybody was, like, "Wow, that's incredible!"

MH It was.

MB But as you know, it was because we were going up and down the same piece of forest road. Which is what I was used to - you know, going round and round the same piece of race track all day. So, we come to the rally itself and the first proper forest stage was early in the morning, foggy and wet - somewhere in Wales.

MH It was at a place called Radnor, one of the British classics. A fast and steely place on a good day but truly bloody awful on a day like that. I think I know what you're going to say...

MB I was 15 seconds-a-mile slower; 15 bloody seconds over one mile. I couldn't see where I was going. I couldn't get my head round how they did that.

MH Because they rely totally on the notes. They believe in them.

MB Exactly. And, with the best will in the world, I couldn't do that. Carlos told me that the course just appears in his mind when the notes are being read. Total trust, flat out into the fog on a slippery road. Absolutely amazing.

MH Hmm. Well, I won't tell you how much slower than you Louise and I were. Mind you, we did finish third in class. But, getting back to F1, you're quite an experienced old hand now, one way or another.

MB I think I do my 500th Grand Prix sometime in 2013, although I'm told that doesn't count because some of those races were as a fan when I was four years old or something. Let's say I will attend my 500th Grand Prix towards the end of 2013.

MH You can't buy experience, Martin. It stands you in good stead, as has become obvious during our chat today. Thanks for sharing it with us.

MB Good fun, as always. See you up here in another 30 years...

At lunch with **Alain Prost**

"Senna was a fantastic story in sport, one that happens only four or five times in 50 years. Even if it finished badly for Ayrton, it is really a nice story at the end. But this did not come across in the film – it's very sad."

Talk to engineers who worked with Alain Prost and they'll go out of their way to tell you just how good the Frenchman was. They feel you need to know that Prost's manner of driving belied one of the most canny and economic styles in the history of the World Championship - quite some claim! The respect from key people at Renault, McLaren, Ferrari and Williams, teams he drove for in more than 200 Grands Prix, leaves no doubt about the diminutive Frenchman's place in the pantheon of F1 greats.

Prost's one drawback, from his point of view, was a need to say what he thought in the face of injustice. It got him into trouble with the FIA and, more famously, during his ferocious battle with Ayrton Senna in their two years together at McLaren. Never mind the details, the fact that Senna singled out Prost, to an almost obsessive degree, as the man he had to beat says everything about Alain's prodigious talent.

While Senna was succeeding by throttle-blipping, opposite locking, delivering totally thrilling visions of blinding speed, Prost would slip past, almost unnoticed, to win by stealth. That goes hand-in-hand with the way he appears in the paddock; a diminutive figure merging into the background, but seeing all, understanding it and not being afraid to quietly pass comment if he feels the need.

His relationship with the British media has always been pleasant and functional, more so in the later years, and so it was when we met in Abu Dhabi 2012 for lunch at Renault and to reflect on a career which was exceptional by anyone's standards.

Maurice Hamilton Nice to see you. I see you're here as an ambassador for Renault. Your association with them goes back a very long way. Thirty years, I guess?

Alain Prost Longer than that, actually. You're thinking of Formula One, but it started with the racing school in 1975. Then it was Formula Renault, Formula Renault Europe, F3 and F1. And don't forget, I came back in 1993 to win the championship with Williams-Renault. After that, a-year-and-a-half in communication, doing a few things for Renault, especially outside Europe. Even when I was in F1 as a team owner, I always had the link and a possibility to be back with them on the engine side, but that didn't work out. Recently, I've been involved with the Andros Trophy on ice with the Dacia. So, we have always been close. More than 35 years, different periods, different things, but the connection with Renault has always been there. I'm pleased to be doing this now.

MH Part of that pleasure must be getting to drive the Red Bull RB6 recently. How did that feel?

AP The funny thing is that I drove my Renault F1 car from 1983 at Dijon and Le Castellet... [*the Renault chef appears with a choice of roast lamb and couscous salad or monk fish with green salad and balsamic vinaigrette. Alain chooses the lamb, I opt for the fish. It's a working day for us both, so we go for sparkling mineral water rather than the tempting choice of chilled white wine in this heat*].

MH You were saying you drove the turbo from 1983. You had three poles and won four races with that car. Did it bring back nice memories when you climbed on board?

AP No, actually, it didn't. Maybe with the small exception of the French Grand Prix because the car was exceptional there when I won that race at Paul Ricard. But, other than that, I really didn't remember much about driving this car. In fact, I found myself asking how were we able to drive these cars at all, especially on street circuits such as Monaco and Detroit?

MH Because the car was big and heavy?

AP Big is okay. But heavy, yes. It was difficult to brake and I needed to push the clutch very hard. This, combined with the engine response and the gearbox; it was really awful. When I drove the Red Bull, it was more like what I was used to in 1993 with the Williams. I could remember how that was. It's almost 20 years since I drove the Williams and there were similarities, but there was a huge difference in the 10 years between the 1983 Renault and the Williams.

I could drive the Red Bull easily, but you cannot push and go to the edge. First of all, I did not have my seat. I was not fitting the car very well, so the more you push, the less comfort you have. So the last tenths of second, the last second, you can't judge. But what you can say is it feels... nothing spectacular.

Nothing has changed that much, unlike the difference between the 1980s and the beginning of the 1990s. Everything with the Red Bull was perfect and optimised. The engine was not a surprise at all because it was the same sort of thing that we had a long time ago - not more power because that's been reduced, but quite progressive. The Renault has always been a good engine for that. And the gearbox and brakes are exceptional; really good. Previously, when you braked, you could feel the pitch. Now it's stiff, like a go-kart. But I could not get used to braking with the left foot; I'd never done that before. The biggest difference is maybe the driving position.

MH Is it more comfortable?

AP You are really surprised in the beginning because you are lying back completely. Visibility is very bad; this was never a problem with the old cars. Now, the engineers think much more about the ergonomics of the car for the driver. Before, you were told to just get in and drive. At Williams in 1993, I was given Nigel Mansell's seat - modified, obviously! The philosophy was focused more on the technology and improving the car, the driver was almost an afterthought. I think it's easier to drive the cars today.

MH Even with the higher *g*-forces?

AP Yes. You are more together with the car and it's easier.

MH In 1983, you sat very upright in the Renault and close to the wheel. And close to the front of the car as well, so your legs and feet were very much lower than the drivers experience today.

AP That's true. I remember in about 1989, when I was working with the big company Rhône Poulenc in France to do some tests in the car for the heart and so on, I asked them to monitor the blood pressure in the legs. Because the legs were going down, we were having less and less blood pressure as the race went on. We knew a guy from downhill skiing who was working on the flow of blood. He had adapted what everyone now has in sport, *bandes de contention.*

MH A sort of elasticised full-length sock?

AP Yes, I wore these socks and I didn't show this to many people. I always wanted to try and improve things like that and have less problems.

MH Before moving on to your championships with McLaren, I want to go back to your first experience in 1979, when the team was very different and run by Teddy Mayer. It was quite an important time for you because you needed to establish your reputation.

AP This was a time when F1 was changing a lot. I liked Teddy very much because he was like a father to me. In many ways it was like a family team. Teddy was very passionate about motor racing, in the tradition, I'd say, of Bruce McLaren.

MH Did Teddy engineer your car?

AP Yeah, he liked to do that and, for me, that was okay, especially in the beginning because you really learned a lot with these guys. You learned from the qualities and the faults. If you want to progress, you need to see everything. The first problem I had, and I'll always remember this story, was when they brought the McLaren with

"Compared with 1983 the view is lousy, but the car is easier to drive"

new front suspension to Jarama in Spain. I did not know very much about suspension but I looked at it and I think, "Shit, something looks strange. I really don't like that." Jean-Pierre Jabouille was driving at Renault at the time and I said, "Please can you come discreetly and see what you think about this front suspension." He said it was difficult to say because obviously he could not go very close and have a really good look. But he said, "Be careful. It really doesn't look very good. Go slowly for a few laps and see what happens." I do a slow lap, then two more. Then I go a bit faster and, going downhill, I start to push, and I lost two front wheels!

I was very lucky because, a week before, we had a meeting of the Grand Prix Drivers Association and Jean-Pierre was already pushing to have catch fences at the bottom of the hill. I lost the right-front wheel, then I turned and lost the left one. If the catch fence had not been there, I would have been in the paddock!

MH I remember you broke your arm at Kyalami when the rear suspension broke.

AP Yes. And I had a rear suspension break at Donington during a private test and I finished up in hospital. I lost also the front suspension in Canada, but I had a shunt with Riccardo Patrese a few laps before, so you cannot say if that contributed. But then I had a very bad suspension failure at Watkins Glen. I was not very happy after that.

MH I think, by then, Ron Dennis was on the point of taking over. Things were about to become very different at McLaren.

AP Yes. Ron Dennis had the same passion as Teddy, but with a different vision of the future. I must say I was really impressed when I saw Ron for the first time when he was running a BMW Procar team in 1980. You could almost not trust him or believe him because the vision he had was so... big! In all the years I've been with Ron, apart from 1989 when we had some difficult moments, he has always impressed me with his vision for the long-term. He kept thinking and looking at the details. It was very impressive. Teddy was not like this. He was more short-term and full of passion for each race and very happy with each good result. But he did not have Ron's vision for the future. I don't think many people do, to be honest.

MH You became champion with McLaren in 1985, having lost out to your team-mate Niki Lauda the year before. Niki was telling me a story concerning you both at the last race of 1984 in Estoril when you were fighting for the title.

AP There are so many stories... which one?

MH Well, Niki says he had been, shall we say, staying out late on the night before the race. He was annoyed on race morning because he was not feeling great and knew that meant you would probably win the championship. Then he says he saw you on race morning and heard you'd been up to no good as well! Is that true?

AP It's possible! But that's not why I lost the championship.

MH I know. You did all you could by winning the race and Niki finished second to win by half-a-point.

AP But I have to tell you that the evening after Niki won was quite... memorable. I remember Elio de Angelis, it was five o'clock in the morning and we'd had quite a bit to drink. He asked me to bring him back to his hotel. I stopped in front of the hotel and he asked, "Why don't you bring me closer to the door?" So I said, "Okay, you want to get closer?" I reversed the car. Then first gear, there was a big glass door, I went through – and down into the lobby. I said, "Okay, now ask for the key to your room." I had to go back to my hotel in a taxi because the car was stuck there, in the lobby. Marlboro was very, very nice because they took care of the damage.

MH Great story! I really don't think that would happen today.

AP I think you're right. It's a pity.

MH Talking about damage to cars, reminds me of Spa 1986. There was an incident at the first corner and you had to make a pit stop for a new nose. You came from the back to finish sixth and score one point, as it was in those days. You said that could be vital in the championship, and it was! But the thing I remember is John Barnard telling me some time later, and with some amazement, that your car was bent like a banana. The front suspension was damaged and there was damage at the rear. He said he had no idea how you not only drove the car like that, but how you also managed to finish and score a point.

Prost and Senna in 1988 – a spirit of co-operation that did not last

AP That's why 1986 was my best season, that and 1990 at Ferrari. In 1986, I always thought that we could be world champions even though the Williams cars of Nigel Mansell and Nelson Piquet were much better and much quicker. I really wanted to get this point at Spa. But I was young. Every time going into Eau Rouge, I was thinking, "You don't know what can happen." I had a car for right corners and a different car for left corners! But I got a point. When racing and fighting for a championship, you know that sometimes you have to take risks, but even so, this was a big risk.

MH It certainly was. On the other hand, the 1988 British Grand Prix saw you pull out because the conditions were so bad. Tell me about your thoughts behind that decision. Was any of this to do with having been right there in the rain when Didier Pironi had that terrible accident during practice at Hockenheim in 1982?

AP A few months before the accident you're talking about with Didier, we'd had the fatal accident with Gilles Villeneuve at Zolder. You need to remember that, in between, we'd also had the accident in Canada when Ricardo Paletti was killed when he hit Didier's stalled Ferrari on the grid. I don't want to go into all the detail except to say we'd had a lot of bad accidents. While we're talking about this, we mentioned Elio earlier. When you think about the accident he had during testing at Paul Ricard in 1986, that was terrible and should never have happened, because of the lack of proper attention to deal with this. It shows how much the safety has improved. But Didier's accident in 1982 really horrified me. [*Pironi, lapping quickly, had caught Prost, who had* *just been overtaken by Derek Daly's Williams. Thinking Daly was moving off line to get out of the Ferrari's way, Pironi powered into the spray and straight into the back of the Renault. The Ferrari took off, landed on its nose and did terrible damage to Pironi's ankles and feet. He never raced again in motorsport*]. I had stopped, of course, and seeing Didier was awful, really awful. I went straight to the Renault motor home. There was only myself and Gerard Larrousse, the team boss. He said I should try and get back in the car as soon as possible. I said, "I'm going to go in the car but I'm going to tell you, from today, I'm going to do what I want to do when it's wet. I want to be the only judge of the best thing to do." I always kept this philosophy even though you cannot do it all the time.

In 1988 at Silverstone, I can't remember if there was a shunt at the first corner or whatever, but the car was not correct and I didn't understand why. Neil Oatley told me afterwards that the car was bad, which was why I could not drive it. I was really nowhere. I decided to stop because you know how it is when it's wet like this; it's fifth gear and you need confidence. I was losing confidence and the car was going nowhere, so I stopped.

People said I couldn't drive in the wet. But I was really good - okay, that's my opinion - when it was wet or slippery. No problem. In fact, I like it very much when it's like that. But when it was very wet and you have the combination of aquaplaning and visibility, I never wanted to take the risk. I was always thinking of Didier. But how do you say that to the press? It's difficult, but I lived with that even though you are losing a little bit of credibility with the press, but not really with the team.

MH The team may have understood this but your relationship with Ron Dennis was quite difficult at times. Particularly that moment at Monza in 1989 when you were on the podium and handed the winner's cup to the crowd below. You knew Ron had a big thing about the team keeping the trophies, and yet here you were, not just not keeping the cup, but giving it to the fans.

AP It was not premeditated. I had just signed with Ferrari, I had won the race with thousands of people in front of me. To be honest, I don't know what happened. It was like a sort of present for the *Tifosi*, but Ron was so upset. I could understand later on. You know, when you have these kind of tough years, tough relations, you lose your judgement - I'm talking about myself, not anybody else. You have people like Jo Ramirez or your engineers trying to keep the stability, otherwise you do things from your heart but you don't know what you're doing. The trophies for Ron are very important for the history of the company. So, there was that and the fact we were in Italy, I had won and he was losing his driver who was now becoming a Ferrari driver. So I can understand that. I did not do it on purpose at all.

I said okay I am going to make a copy of this trophy - because we could not get the original back, that's for sure! When I was doing things with McLaren in 1995, we had a nice evening for the whole factory, a Christmas party. That's when I gave him the trophy for that race. But, you know, nothing was done to hurt anyone. We were losing some spontaneity at the time, because you are so stressed every day.

"I had one car for right corners, and a different car for the left"

MH You were coming to the end of a pretty tense time with Ayrton. Have you seen the film *Senna*?

AP I have seen a big part of it. I did not want to talk about the film before but now I'd like to give my opinion. It can be a bit long, but I want to be precise.

MH No problem. Please go ahead.

AP Obviously I do not like the film, from what I have seen and heard. And I do not want to see it completely because I know what it is like. When they first talked to me about the film, they asked if I wanted to be part of it. I said "Sure, why not?" The only condition, well, it's not a condition but you need to understand I told them, "It would be fantastic if you could show Ayrton before he arrived in F1, what he was like in F1, fighting with me or against me, and the Ayrton after I retired. If you do that, a mix of the nice stories and sport, the fight and the human side, then it's going to be a good film." Because it is really something unbelievable. In my opinion it was a fantastic story. But you need to mention a lot of things that happened after I retired.

So I did almost eight hours of interviews. Eight hours! Talking much more on the human side so that you could understand how he was before, because he also told me, after I retired, how he had been when we were racing. But I also wanted to make the point that when I retired we saw a new Ayrton Senna. It is a fantastic story in sport, one that only happens, I don't know, four or five times in 50 years. Even if it finished badly for Ayrton, it is really a nice story at the end.

But what I do not like at all in the film at all, is that this did not come across. You only have one chance to do a film like this because if you have done it, you're not going to do it again. I find it very sad. If they wanted to do a commercial film with the bad guy and the good guy, then do not make any interviews; do not ask me anything.

MH But the film does suggest that there had been some kind of rapprochement between you and Ayrton.

AP Yes, but I was trying to explain what happened a week before Imola when Ayrton called me, not every day, but almost. There's a few things he told me that I would never tell anyone. I would never tell anything about what he said during this week. When you hear that Ayrton said, "Alain we miss you", that was organised and arranged by TF1 and it completely misses the point. I cannot be happy about that.

The reason why I cannot be happy is not because I look the bad guy; I don't care much about that because... I'm alive, I'm okay. But I would like everyone to know who Ayrton Senna was, what exactly our fight was about and also, what happened at the end. If you want to tell a story, tell the true story; not something arranged like this "Alain, we miss you" clip. Our story did not end in 1994. Our story will last until... for ever. And you want it to tell the truth and I'm very upset. I'm more upset now than I was when the film came out. That is only the reason why.

MH I saw the film three times. I enjoyed it very much but I did say "If you're a fan of Alain Prost, don't watch this film." It wasn't balanced in that respect.

AP It has to be balanced; that would be much better. Obviously it is not very good for Ayrton, but it is not bad either. At least you understand the personality or the character at the time. Especially when he was against me. He was a different person then. Not like when he was fighting against Michael or Nigel or whoever. Fighting against me, he was different. You need to explain that.

MH A lot of your problems with Ayrton emanated from when you had your sabbatical in 1992 and then came back to drive for Williams in 1993. There was talk of Ayrton joining you for 1994. What's your view on that? Did you refuse to stay if Ayrton came?

AP In the middle of 1993 when we had discussions about Ayrton, it was difficult for me. Never, at any time, did I ask to be a number 1 or a number 2. The only thing I said to Frank Williams was you are not going to have Ayrton in the same team as me. Then in mid-1993, Frank called me. I knew already from a few weeks before that Williams were having some pressure from Renault to have Ayrton. I was in the southwest of France and Frank said he would come to see me. I always remember this day. He said I have pressure, what can you do, how do you see these things? What do you think?

I said, "If you want to take Ayrton, you choose. I want to compete against Ayrton, but not in the same team. I want to have the best chance possible to beat him on the track." So he had to make a decision. I said to Renault, "Okay, you are pushing for Ayrton and you gave me aggravation this year because it is not easy. I have a two-year contract; you pay me the second year of my contract and I leave." And that's what happened.

Prost takes his No1 status to Ferrari in 1990 to win in Brazil

MH Apart from the Senna business at the end of 1993, you actually had quite a tricky year for various reasons, starting with the FIA giving you problems over your licence.

AP Yes, it was a difficult year. I felt very well inside the team but outside the team it was a very strange ambience with the press. When you looked at the press in France, when I was winning it was absolutely normal because I had the best car and I was with the best team, more horsepower than Ayrton's car, and things like this. Always, always a polemic. It is very difficult to motivate yourself when it is like this.

It was day and night all the time. When you lose a race like Donington, people do not realise there are many, many reasons for this. Ayrton's car, when it was wet, technically, it was a different car. For sure Ayrton was very fast but in these conditions his car was much better. But there is no point that the French press attack me in this way. Winning is one thing but you need to win in a good ambience.

MH You won at Imola with a sticking throttle. Was that one of the best wins in 1993?

AP I don't know if it was one of the best, but it was a good one. I realised at Imola that there was no objectivity because I'd had a good win and nothing was said, yet they had criticised me after not winning at Donington.

MH What was your happiest period at McLaren? 1985, 86 and 87?

AP Even 1988 was not that bad, although I felt the difference at the beginning of that year when Ayrton came. But I was not unhappy. I think it was the way to go; to have a new start in the team with Ayrton and Honda engines. I had the meeting with Honda at the end of the year in Geneva. I remember like if it was yesterday, meeting Mr Kawamoto and three other people from Honda. We said we had a tough year in 1988 but we did not have any problems with Ayrton that year. There were tough moments like Portugal, but that happens. He won one more race, eight to my seven, but, if you remember, I could have won Hungary when I overtook him and then went a bit wide. I started from seventh, he was on pole. That's part of the game.

But at this meeting at the end of the year, I said to Honda, "I don't want to enter into any technical consideration, but when you see an engine arriving at the track that is specially for Ayrton, then psychologically, that is not easy. He has won the championship and I have come second and we had a good year, but I want to have the same treatment for 1989."

But the fight from the beginning of 1989 was much, much worse. I don't want to go too much into details now. That year was really a disaster and I felt very bad.

MH You've seen things from both sides of the fence. Having been a driver, you ran your own team from 1997 to 2001, and it was difficult. How do you reflect on that now?

AP Very simple I didn't want to do it. I knew it would be very, very difficult in France, but I was being pushed by the French *politique* to do it. But, considering all the aspects, I think we have not done so bad. Reflecting on everything, if you think about the relationship with Peugeot which was bad because they did not want to put in any money. Then I had signed a very good contract with Yahoo, but we could not do it because of the internet crisis. I had also signed a contract with Prince Al Waleed for his son – then we had September 11.

I don't want to go too much into details but we were paying $28 million for the engine; we were supposed to pay $32 million the year after. If you look at what happened to Brabham and Jaguar and other teams and what's happening today in France, what can you do? At the end of the day, it was not bad. I really suffered because, again, the image was not that good. In fact, I thought it was a good experience. The only thing I regret is that I think we missed one year. We needed one more year to prove that we were much better. In any case, finding the right money to continue would have been very, very difficult.

MH Is that the most stressful time you've ever had?

AP By a long way. No question. I was very happy when we stopped because you cannot do that for ever; work with no consideration for anything else and just attack. My telephone was red hot. I was leaving the factory at 11 o'clock every night. We had some unbelievable stories about people who wanted to buy the team. One day I'm going to write a book about that.

MH I'll look forward to it. Based on our chat today, it should be a best-seller! Thanks for your time.

AP No problem.

Reigning world champion, Prost wins at Imola 86 for McLaren

At lunch with **Eddie Irvine**

"The fact that I drove for Ferrari is more important than having been in F1, because Ferrari is a world brand. I mean, who gives a f*** about an ex-Williams driver?"

It had been a couple of years since Eddie Irvine and I had had a decent chat when we met at Monza in 2011. Both being from Northern Ireland, we used to be in regular touch. But, typical 'Irv', as soon as he was done with F1, he was gone, into a world of dealing and money that would leave Eddie Jordan standing.

EJ, of course, gave Irvine his big break, first in F3000 and then that infamous drive at Suzuka in 1993 when Eddie outraged Ayrton Senna. National bias aside, I've always rated Irvine as a more than useful driver; certainly one of the cleverest I've ever met. And one of the most direct. He was only in Europe briefly, so we snatched an hour in the Ferrari motor home on race day; not ideal for this sort of interview chat - and, yet, in many ways, an absolutely perfect location given the character and background of the man in question.

Maurice Hamilton You still seem popular here; people recognise you. Do you like that?

Eddie Irvine What I don't like is when I don't know if they're going to recognise me. What I'm saying is I hate walking in where I think I'm not going to be recognised - and then someone does. And I hate thinking I might get recognised - and they don't, because you just don't know how to deal with that. That's why I like America because I'm not recognised anywhere. I'm a free person. In Italy, it's usually "Ah, Eeeddeee! Eeeeeddee..." You know they're going to be okay.

MH What about in Ireland?

EI That's the worst because you never know which way it's going to go; you don't know which reaction you'll get. When I'm there, I just keep my head down and keep walking. The trouble is, if you ignore the tossers they start the "Who the fuck d'you think you are?" bit. That's why I don't go out when I'm in Ireland. I stay home. I go to my sports centre, I go to my bar sometimes.

MH Where's that?

EI O'Reilly's in Dublin, under Tara Street railway station. It's doing well.

MH A night club?

EI No, just a bar. I dropped the prices to the minimum. Now you can't get in through the door. The economy being what it is in the Republic of Ireland, everyone is looking for value. Northern Ireland, meanwhile, is coming back because the pound is low. The problem for the south is they have the euro wrapped around their neck; they can't set interest rates as they would like. America is printing money and stimulating and stimulating, but the ECB is tightening, tightening. It's daft.

MH What are you doing, businesswise, in the North?

EI Buying land; if you've got cash, you've got to buy land. I've bought your old school!

MH Bangor Grammar? You're kidding!

EI Yep! I'm going to knock it down!

MH I always felt someone should do that! They're moving to a new site on the edge of town. But you surely can't knock all of it down?

EI Not the original old building. But the rest of it will go. Do you want to buy an apartment there? You'll be wanting to retire back home!

MH Sorry, no. It hasn't got a view of the sea! But it's a prime site.

EI It is. I took a look the other day. It's falling down. So is my old school, Regent House. You'll remember the rivalry between our two schools? Well, now a Regent guy has got you stuck-up Bangor Grammar c***s in the end! I'm buying as much as I can in Northern Ireland. And Miami is going crazy.

MH How much time do you spend in the States?

EI I'm in Exuma all the time. In the Bahamas. Bought a marina there as well.

MH Hold on! One thing at a time. What do you do in Miami?

EI Buy, sell and build houses. I used to live there, but now I'm in the Bahamas. I always wanted an island. I used to watch *Robinson Crusoe* and I always wanted an island! I just love the freedom. There's Great Exuma; 3,000 people live on it. There's probably a few hundred on Little Exuma. And I'm south of there. On a freehold virgin island; nothing on it at all. A kilometre long; 25 acres. I can pretty much do what I want.

MH Is this is the place where I read you're going green?

EI Yes. But there's different ways of doing it. A guy has bought an island up from me and he's put in five or six huge wind turbines and a million dollars worth of batteries. For me, that's not fully green. And he's built a 35,000sq ft house. That's missing the whole point. If you want to do that, why not just stay in America? I've designed three pods to make one house. They're being built in Bali and it's going to be very simple technology. The water is going to be heated by the sun.

MH Where does the water come from?

EI You have to make it. I've got a solar-powered water maker. All you need is salt water and you pump it through a filter at 800psi and fresh water comes out the other side because the salt can't get through the filter. I drink it, straight out of the other end of the filter. It's a very simple process.

MH This is such a contrast to the life you used to lead; to the image you had created previously of the party animal, 'Fast Eddie' and all that stuff. Are you saying now you like peace and tranquillity?

EI I like the silence. I've built a shed that I live in. It's got a fridge and cooker and all that sort of stuff. The point is, I'm free. My boat is there; my airplane is sitting at the airport. I just walk out, get in the plane and take off. I don't need to call air traffic control; we're free in the Bahamas. The airport is eight miles from the marina, which is on Great Exuma.

MH And this is the marina you were saying you've bought?

EI Yes. The first time I saw the marina, I thought this could be amazing. I found out that the place had been running down ever since one of the owners had died. I said I didn't want to insult them with the figure I'd offer. A year later I got it for the figure I wanted. It was an amazing deal. I had some Americans come in and offer me double what I paid for it, but I don't want to sell because it suits me perfectly. It's a lifestyle thing.

MH I take it you can go swimming in the sea?

EI You've never seen water like it... well, you've probably seen pictures. It's like Bombay Sapphire, that pale blue gin. It's a sand bar which goes about a mile out to sea.

Irvine is more of an action man now than he was in Formula One

MH What do you eat?

EI Catch fish. There's everything in restaurants in Great Exuma; the supermarket is a boat ride away, right across the street from the marina.

MH What do you do to keep fit?

EI Walk round an island with no roads; cut down paths to get to the various places where you want to build. That keeps you fit.

MH Are you doing all the building yourself?

EI I do a lot of the loading, the physical stuff, because I want to stay in shape. I'm not that good at putting things together - I'm better at taking them apart.

MH Like in your Grandad's scrap yard?

EI Exactly! I'm much better at that.

MH How do you communicate?

EI Skype. Pick up a signal from Little Exuma. I've got high-speed internet at the marina. I'm in touch all the time with the bar, Eddie Irvine Sports in Northern Ireland and Miami. I'm much more involved than I was. I break balls now and keep on top of it. You have to because I'm involved in other businesses with good businessmen. It's raised my game and allowed me to see where I need to be at with some of my other stuff.

MH So, if you're not there, where do you go?

EI I have to go to Miami because I'm building houses there. I have to go to Boston sometimes for board meetings with the software company I have there. I go to Ireland.

MH Do you still enjoy coming to Italy? You used to be passionate about it.

EI I love Italy. I love the food and the wine. I've just been to Portofino, had lunch with my friends there in a little place you go to by boat. Italy is amazing.

MH Talking of boats, do you still have *Anaconda*?

EI Yes, I was on it all week in Italy. But I'm sending it to the island; it's going to be the headquarters for the pylon build. Then it's going to stay in New York as my house boat.

MH Is that the way to live in New York now? I thought you had an apartment there.

EI I have, but I've rented it out and get so much rent that I can't justify keeping it for myself. Anyway, I'm not there that often and I don't particularly like living in an apartment. And, to be honest, *Anaconda* is too big for me now; for the way I live. It's a perfect house. But when it comes to a boat, I want a quick in and out. I just bought a Sunseeker for that. *Anaconda* will be a perfect house in New York.

MH It's getting pretty old?

EI It will still be around in 50 years. It's steel and aluminium; a Dutch-built boat that weighs twice as much as a normal boat that size because of the quality. So long as I paint it every seven years or so, it will last for ever.

MH Is your sports centre in your home town in Northern Ireland doing okay?

EI It washes its face, let's say. The soccer pitches do well. We're looking at doing more stuff, such as a Northern Ireland Experience. I think Northern Ireland massively underestimates its potential as a tourist attraction. We've got great golf courses, great scenery, Strangford Lough, the Antrim Coast Road, Lough Erne. The problem is most Americans don't even know there is a direct flight into Belfast. They all go to Dublin. The Irish Tourist Board does something with Northern Ireland but the reality is the emphasis is on south of the border.

So, we're looking to promote Northern Ireland. You've got Clandeboye Golf Club the Ava Course - which is amazing. I just love that course. We've got one of the biggest brands in the world in the *Titanic* - which was built in Belfast - and they haven't done a great job using it. I have a house overlooking Strangford Lough; it's a stunning location. Business people come over and they can't believe the life they can have in Northern Ireland. £15 for a round of golf; join a club for £250. Go fishing.

The only problem I've ever had with Northern Ireland is the weather. Saying that, it's perfect for playing golf. If you choose a nice day, it's the ultimate golfing experience. And now Northern Ireland is producing all these golfers who are doing so well.

MH Do you get to any of the golf majors?

At Suzuka 1993 Irvine diced with Senna, much to Senna's outrage

EI No, I can't be bothered with the fuss. Coming back to being in Italy, that's why I like it here. I have an apartment in the centre of Milan. But I'm going to give it up because I don't want the distraction of having something in Italy while I'm working on the island. I want to get it perfect because so many people have made a mess of their islands in Exuma. I want to set an example of how it should be done.

MH But you're quite gregarious. I can't see you being there on your own.

EI I fly people out. But, saying that, I need my solitude. I don't party that much now. I just like my freedom. I'm a freedom freak; it's the number one thing in the world for me.

MH So, you'd never thinking of settling down? Does the greying hair attract women?

EI Yeah! The ones I don't want.

MH You can send them to me!

EI I think they like the false perception that I'm ready to settle down. And they like the idea of the planes, the boats, the island, the marina. I like hanging out with women. But you do earn these grey hairs, don't you? I'm a lot wiser now than I was five years ago, and I will be a lot wiser in 10 years than I am now.

MH When you worked in your grandfather's scrap yard and someone said to you, "Look, in 2011 you'll have been a Ferrari driver and you'll be very well off." Which of the two would have surprised you most?

EI Ferrari driver.

MH You said that without hesitation. Is that because you always had an eye for a deal? You were always going to make something of yourself?

EI Yes, I was always up to something. The fact that I drove for Ferrari is more important than having been in F1. By a mile. Part of that is what the Italians feel a Ferrari driver should be. I live my life the way Italians like to live theirs. I like the food, the wine, the women. In a way, it probably wasn't good for my career because I came up against Schumacher who was at the peak of his power. But no other team-mate beat me in F1. And I wouldn't have been that much better off at somewhere like Williams.

MH Does being an ex-Ferrari driver meant a lot to the outside world? Is it still good for you now?

EI For sure. I mean, who gives a fuck about an ex-Williams driver? Ferrari is a world brand.

MH You say that, but does it mean much in North America?

EI Not really, because they don't know that much about Ferrari and F1. Formula One is nothing in America. No one cares. No one gives a damn about Ferrari either.

MH Going back to 1999, you could have won the championship, but I guess Ferrari wanted Michael to win it for the first time since 1979.

EI For sure they wanted Michael to win it; they had invested so much in him. What happened was they took the car out of the wind tunnel as soon as he crashed and suffered that broken leg at the British GP, so there was no development.

MH One of the things I could never understand was how you didn't go well at Suzuka. Here was a track you knew like the back of your hand; the place where you made a stunning debut in 1993, and yet you were nowhere in 1999. In fact, you spun going through that right before the hairpin. I remember looking at the TV pictures in amazement because you just didn't do that sort of thing - and certainly not at Suzuka. What the hell was going on?

EH I had aero, but I had no grip. None at all. We could measure the aero, so we knew how much I had. But there was no grip. I qualified closer to Michael the next year in a Jaguar! I drove though the first corner on the first day and it was just like driving on ice. If you look at the races there, every year Michael would be fastest and I would be second or third quickest within a couple of laps. But in 1999, I just couldn't drive the car. It was like that for the whole weekend.

MH So, what was happening?

EI Dunno. I had the same aero as Michael, the same downforce.

MH But no grip. So, what was it? Tyres?

Eddie gets testy when marshalls damage his car at Suzuka 1999

EI I really don't know. You'd need to ask Bridgestone. At the second corner, I had to take a chance to get through. Michael, he was in, round and out so much faster. It was ridiculous.

MH You mentioned Jaguar. You made a bit of money out of that.

EI I did very well. It's a shame because I think it was a great idea - but badly executed. Jaguar paid way too much for Stewart. They bought a shell, which is funny, because Jacques Nasser has bought a couple of houses in Miami and he's paid way too much for them as well! I remember this deal went through and I thought, "Who paid *that* for that?" It was Jacques Nasser. "Ah, that explains it!" Unbelievable. He paid nearly double what the house was worth. That tells you a lot about how he ran Ford [Jaguar].

They paid too much for everything, and it wasn't quality. Then they realised they had to have a wind tunnel - they were using a wind tunnel in California. I can't remember who said this as a sort of joke, but it was true. It went: Jaguar were asking, "Do we have advertising organised in the newspapers? Advertising in the magazines? Signs all round the place saying Jaguar is coming back? Do we have the girls lined up? Drivers with their overalls? Have we got all that?" "Yeah, yeah, we've got all that?" "Oh shit! We don't have a car." That was the problem. They didn't realise it's a technical exercise.

The problem was Jackie Stewart had sold them this piece of junk. You can't knock Jackie for that! They were the suckers. There was no way they realised they then had to spend more money to make a proper team. Ford didn't know any better. It was a mess from the beginning. It only started to get sorted out when they got Mark Gillan on board. He was fantastic. I loved working with him. And the Greek guy was very good.

MH What about Niki Lauda?

EI He did a sensible job but I don't think he was focused enough. He made some good decisions and it was going forward – and then they got rid of him. I was probably the only person who got paid a lot of money, but I fulfilled my contract 100 per cent. I didn't bullshit them at any point. I got them podiums. I told them exactly what I thought. And 99 per cent of the time, I was right.

MH Do you think you stopped racing at the right time.

EI At 37, yes I did. I would have missed out on a couple of deals outside motor sport if I'd still been racing. It was time to get on with it, otherwise it's delaying your progress in the business world.

MH How do you learn about these business things, get a feel for what is going on? Do you read all the financial papers?

EI I do read them but I read most things on the Internet. I don't follow the market. Okay, the stock market I watch a little bit because it's more about people's mood than anything. Business is all about fundamentals. Mood is everything, as it is with most things.

MH When you were racing F3000 in Japan, you were making money then – outside racing, I mean.

EI I was. I was buying shares because everything was going up at the time. Even in a hurricane, a turkey flies. You couldn't not make money at the time. If you were in, you were doing well. It was pretty much gambling because if you're buying a share, you need to look at it as if you're buying the whole company; go through the books, know the people. Otherwise, you're gambling.

MH Talking about gambles, do you think that's what Michael did when deciding about his comeback?

EI I thought it was a good idea at the time. But he should have quit after the first year because he's been useless compared to before. So, what's the point?

MH He missed the buzz, I suppose. Sitting at home not doing very much and suddenly he has to organise his life, mundane stuff and so on. Do you think that was an issue?

EI It's an issue for most retired drivers because some of them are one-trick ponies.

MH Can I take you back to the end of 2009 and comments you made about Jenson Button moving to McLaren? You said he was going to get slaughtered.

EI I said he would be slaughtered on speed, but I also said he was the best No 2 McLaren could have wished for. And, effectively, that's what's happened. Lewis has beaten him 95 per cent of the time, but Lewis has made so many mistakes he hasn't progressed to

"Lauda did a sensible job at Jaguar – mostly" reckons Irvine

be the driver he should be at this stage. He's still quick, but that's it. And now that everyone can overtake because they press a button, his amazing ability has been negated.

That's what pissed me off with launch control. I was really good at starts and all of a sudden every wanker was good at starts. Lewis used to be brilliant at overtaking - but now anyone can overtake. I think Jenson definitely made the right move and it's been perfect for McLaren because, when Lewis has fucked up, Jenson's there.

MH Do I take it you're not in favour of DRS?

EI I think it's ridiculous. It's like a line I used years ago that I see *Social Network* stole in the movie. You don't get your photograph taken with a load of little fish; you want your photograph taken with a marlin. So watching F1, you see overtaking all the time - which is the little fish. You want to see a move where you go "Holy shit! How did he do that?" It's been dumbed down to the lowest common denominator. For me, the whole thing is a joke: press the button to overtake, little tiny engines, tiny tyres, kerbs and run-offs. There's nothing to hit. That was an advantage I had - I very seldom went off the road on my own. And the other thing now is that no one ever breaks down, so the small guys don't get a chance to score points. Now, everyone gets a point; it's almost like you turn up and you get a point. It negates the history of the sport.

MH Okay, but surely you must think that managing tyres in the race should be part of what a driver does?

EI That's what Jenson is doing better because, back in the day, it was: murder the tyres, pit, murder the tyres, pit. Sprint, sprint, sprint. The only problem is, I hate the start of the race because the cars are so damned slow.

MH What's your thought on qualifying, with the three parts and dropping the slowest cars? It's a bit different from when you had four sets of tyres, an hour to set your time – so just get on with it.

EI I don't see what was wrong with the way we used to do it. You have four sets of tyres. Okay, nothing happens at the start. So what? A movie doesn't start with 18 guys getting killed. So you get a bit of action, it builds up and all of a sudden, everyone goes nuts in the last two minutes. It's bang, bang, bang, bang, bang. The times come down. That third lap used to be nuts. And if you got it really good then your fourth lap was even more nuts. And if you screwed up... that's the way it was. I can't help but think it's been designed without understanding human emotion. It's designed for television. It's all about the corporate; all about looking lovely and perfect.

MH You came into F1 just as refuelling came back in 1994. Actually, you did two races at the end of 1993 without...

EI It was one-and-a-bit races! The final one in Australia didn't last long... I crashed. Saying that, it definitely makes sense to carry fuel for the whole race.

MH Do people still talk about the Senna incident at Suzuka?

EI Yes, but I can't be bothered talking about it, to be honest.

MH Have you see the *Senna* film?

EI Amazing! I think it's a bit unfair to Prost, but then this is all about Senna. The execution of that film... it's a piece of art.

MH Do you keep in touch with Bernie; do you see him much?

EI No, I don't see him. I get the impression he's purely driven by money now. The problem is, they've got a big debt and that has to be paid. I don't think we should be at places like Bahrain and Abu Dhabi; places that don't bring anything to F1 except money. It's like a night club; you let a load of ugly rich guys in there because no one else will go. And then they won't go because there's only ugly rich guys – and they don't want to be seen as the ugly rich guy! I don't even know what Bahrain looks like; I don't think I've even watched a race from there.

MH Have you seen BBC TV coverage with our friend EJ?

EI I have! I love EJ, but I can't listen to him. I think DC is doing an amazing job. He pretty much gets everything right except when it comes to overtaking. Like the Jenson thing in Canada. That's not a corner, that's a straight. So, if Lewis went to the left-hand side and DC says Jenson went there because that's the racing line, it's not the racing line. It's a straight! You can drive down the inside you can drive down the outside.

So, once Lewis is there, he's there! I don't agree with what DC says about overtaking stuff. Martin Brundle is fantastic. But as for EJ! He waffles and waffles and doesn't say anything. He goes round and round and hopes by the end you've forgotten what the question was - because he has, for sure!

MH Have you done any TV?

EI I've done bits and pieces. The BBC talked to me about this a while ago, but I only wanted to do Canada, Monaco, Monza, maybe the British... and that's it. I wouldn't mind going to Australia, but I can't do it. It's too far, now that I'm on the island. It would eat into my life too much.

MH This island really has become a major part of your life, hasn't it? Been lucky to catch you before you disappear. Thanks for the chat.

EI Okay. I'll send details of the apartments at your old school. I'll do you a deal. You'll love being there!

MH That'll be the day - on both counts!

At lunch with **Gerhard Berger**

"At Toro Rosso, Franz Tost and I were criticised for being too hard on the young drivers, for wanting too much. Then Sebastian arrived. Immediately, we realised this is what we had always hoped for."

As soon as I mentioned the idea of lunch and a chat, Gerhard was full of enthusiasm. He promised that he'd be in touch when he was next in London. A couple of months went by and I hadn't heard from him, but he hadn't forgotten. Racing in the 2011 Goodwood Revival provided the perfect opportunity for a lunchtime meeting in London's Soho Hotel on the following Monday.

The only problem would be deciding what to leave out when rewinding through a career spanning 210 races, five teams (including Ferrari and McLaren), 10 wins - and an awful lot of laughs along the way.

Maurice Hamilton Good to see you. I thought this might be called off when I heard about the big shunt you'd had at Goodwood in the Cobra Daytona.

Gerhard Berger I just lost it, braking at the end of the back straight. I'd been driving the Jaguar E-type I shared with Adrian Newey. I had a good lap with the Jaguar, so I just tried to do the same with the Cobra - but it doesn't take to braking like the Jaguar! The rear axle is quite tricky; it doesn't like weight transfer as much as the Jaguar. I lost it, put two wheels on the grass and couldn't bring it back. It was head-on into the wall.

MH But you're okay?

GB I'm okay; the car was a bit hurt. I have no problem with accidents, that's racing. I was just disappointed for the team because everybody puts a lot of love into the car and you don't like to destroy it. It's part of the Goodwood Festival of Speed. I don't think there's anywhere else in the world you see such a high quality of race car and drivers.

But the thing for me is the public really lifts it. I looked at that very carefully last weekend. If you would transfer this event to another country, it wouldn't work. It works in England because of the way people get dressed. It looks real. Out of 10 people, you have eight where you don't think they've dressed up especially for this event. You think it's normal. You feel like you are back in the 1960s. It's their culture but if you went to another country, you would feel everyone was just dressed for this event.

MH Are you into old racing cars?

GB No, not at all.

MH If, by some miracle, somebody had your first F1 car, the 1984 ATS, at Goodwood, would you go and look?

GB I have to say, when it comes to my old cars, I feel something; I'd feel attracted by it.

MH That shunt at Goodwood was actually quite rare for you because haven't had that many accidents, have you? There was the big one at Imola in 1989, but what I'm trying to say is that you had a pretty spectacular style of driving, particularly in the early days, and got away with it.

GB My attitude changed a lot after that accident with the Ferrari at Tamburello. After that, I would say I never could do what I did before. It slowed me down a bit.

MH Can't say I ever noticed you being slow!

GB I was never able to take the kind of risk that had been okay before. If I go back when I was with Arrows in 1985, Benetton in 1986 and then with Ferrari for the first time, everything I did was on the limit. It had to be, otherwise I was bored. I always was looking for an extra kick. I remember the long straights at Hockenheim where you were doing over 300km/h. The track was narrow and in traffic you either lift off or, to overtake, I found putting two wheels on the grass worked fine. You are flat out, just steer it and the car comes back in. That was the kick.

MH I'll take your word for that!

GB I remember on one occasion, I think it was Patrick Tambay and Eddie Cheever who were ahead of me, and I think, "Let's try all four wheels." It was maybe 320km/h and I start to pass them on the grass, but it didn't work and I started spinning between these two cars. I didn't touch anybody but they came to me afterwards and went mad. But I felt great!

But after Imola in 1989, I thought, "Wait a moment; if it was 300km/h and you kissed the wall, you could be dead. So, forget all this bullshit. You want to kill yourself? Then it's just a question of time." That's when I realised how much it hurts going into a wall. Okay, I would still drive at a risky level when I had to, but I stopped all the nonsense.

MH Talking about nonsense stuff... going through all my old notes and your columns and so on, I noticed in 1987, when you were with Ferrari, you started left-foot braking, but you had some rather strange experiences beforehand.

GB I was always looking for good ideas to improve my driving and I had been trying left-foot braking from time to time before F1. I started left-foot braking in the F1 car in the 1980s because with the turbo lag, I couldn't keep the turbo running at speed.

I didn't do it in every corner. I just did it in corners where I didn't shift gears. It kept everything much smoother. It worked quite well. But the problem was, I didn't have the feeling or the power in the left foot. When I have to brake hard, I need the right foot.

What I should have done was go to Fiorano for three or four days, just doing left-foot braking until I built up the sensitivity in the left foot and strength in the leg. But the mistake I made was having the right idea but the wrong approach. I thought about switching the pedals around, so I would still be braking with my right foot but building up the sensitivity with my left on the throttle.

MH Are you serious?

GB Yes. Obviously, the right approach would have been preparing your left foot by getting a very small clutch pedal, move the brake pedal more to the left instead of the right, like we do it today, and get used to it that way. But my idea was maybe switch the pedals. And this didn't work out.

MH Did you actually have the Ferrari fitted with the throttle and the brake the wrong way round?

GB No, much worse. I had a Lancia Integrale road car and I had my mechanic switch the pedals so I could practice. It was unbelievable. I was in my home town and there was traffic. I nearly crashed into everybody because my brain can't handle it. I was on full throttle and not braking, then braking too much. It ended up a nightmare.

MH My God! I'm not surprised!

GB Good idea. Wrong approach.

MH Sorry, we got a bit side-tracked there. Going back to the shunt at Imola 1989, this

"Tambay and Cheever came up to me later, and they went mad"

was the first race I did as a summariser, working with Simon Taylor for BBC Radio. So, I'm really nervous and then, bang! You're into the wall and the Ferrari catches fire. I'm thinking: 'What the hell am I going to say now?' Because there was no movement, no sign of you emerging from the flames. And it was a big fire. You had to be dead.

GB Yeah, from the outside it looks like no way someone is going to get out of there.

MH The fuel tank on that car was a sort of U-shape, coming from behind the driver and alongside. You only had burns on your hands and minor injuries compared to what it could have been. Yet, saying that, it made you aware of the danger of having the wall there and you later went to look at it with Ayrton Senna. I think you have regrets about what happened, or didn't happen, after that.

GB Yes, that was a sad story. A really sad story. I remember Ayrton called me in hospital at the time and asked how I was. I said: "I'm okay but, Ayrton, I think if you have a technical problem at this corner, you're in the shit. The wall is much too close." We agreed the next time we were at Imola, we would take a look to see how we can move this wall.

We had a test there and Ayrton and I walked to Tamburello. We looked over the wall and said: "Look, we cannot remove the wall because there is the river behind." Instead of looking at the bigger picture and thinking about adding a chicane, we were just thinking how we could move the wall. I remember we talked about this at the exact place where Ayrton died. I think about this a lot.

MH You were clearly very close to Ayrton even though he was obviously very quick and gave you a hard time on the track.

GB In my career, I faced a number of good drivers like Michele Alboreto, Nigel Mansell and Thierry Boutsen. I never really had a problem with the speed, you know; not even with Mansell. Okay, my heavy accident put me back but, until then, I was always there in qualifying. With Nigel, the race was different because the Ferrari was so heavy to steer. I was complaining about the steering and he kept saying it was not a problem. Of course it wasn't because he had so much power in his arms and he had the advantage! But the point is, I never faced anybody that worried me about speed.

So I go to McLaren in 1990 and I think Ayrton's just another driver; no problem. I remember the first day of the first race at Phoenix and I was quickest and I started from pole. So I say: "Okay, another one, no problem." In the race, I was ahead of Ayrton but then after nine laps, I hit the brake pedal too hard, my foot caught the throttle and I went into the barrier. Ayrton went home to Brazil and thought about it.

MH And he was quicker from then on. What did he do in particular to beat you?

GB Ayrton played the game in a perfect way. I began to realise he was so much more experienced than me. I had started racing very late but he had been karting and doing all these things as a kid. He was able to understand details quicker than me. He had seen them before, whereas I still was in a learning period even though we were the same age. I could see from the telemetry that my disadvantage was not the speed; I was losing out to him because of all things he could put together.

MH Are we talking politics here?

GB Everything, from setting up the car, politics, concentration, physical condition. As a package, he was a little bit ahead everywhere. But I had no reason to complain to him or the team. I had to do my homework. I learned about discipline and the concentration capability he had; the attention to detail that made him the way he was. Of course, he had unbelievable natural speed. But then I think we all had. The difference was he could put everything together. Out of 100 per cent, he would have 98 per cent right.

MH I know you've been asked this question before, but you did help him to relax, didn't you? He'd never thought about that before, certainly in relation to going motor racing. How did that work?

GB I think he enjoyed my way of life, and he took something from it. But at the end of the day, he just played a game because day and night he was thinking about how he can fuck your racing.

MH So he applied everything to that as well?

GB Look, I really liked him a lot. But Ayrton was extremely selfish. He'd be a bastard, all of those things, but in a sympathetic way. That's how it should be. You're not going to be World Champion and win races just being the nice guy. But people did not criticise

Imola 1990: Berger (left) takes second, Senna retires

him. They did not realise it because he'd been such a nice guy at the same time. Very clever. He was the same as Michael Schumacher in this sense, but he did it in a much better way.

MH But is it true you did a lot of crazy things that he did not expect, such as throwing his briefcase from a helicopter?

GB Yeah, it's true. Flying into Monza, I just opened the door of the helicopter and threw it out, hoping it would fall into the trees at Lesmo. But I missed it by a moment and it fell where there were some marshals, so he got it back.

MH I still can't believe you did that! What's the story about throwing away the car keys when you were both driving through the middle of Milan?

GB Ha! Ayrton was driving. We were in huge traffic and people started to realise it was us. Suddenly there's hundreds of people around. The light goes green and I just reached over, took the key out and threw it out of the window. Ayrton was underneath the car, looking everywhere for this key and people are surrounding him; dancing round him. So now there is a big, big traffic jam and the police arrive. They're going mad. Then they see it's Ayrton and start helping him to find the key! Big guy in a uniform looking everywhere on the ground.

We had a lot of fun together and I really liked being with him. He was a great team-mate. The only problem was, he was too fast!

MH When Ayrton died in 1994, you were a pallbearer at the funeral. I've only seen the pictures and film clips, but it looked a highly charged occasion. I believe when you went back to Brazil for the first race of 1995, you went up to the grave at six o'clock in the morning and had a quiet moment of reflection.

GB I did. I'm not someone who goes to church all the time but I was taught that when somebody dies, we take a certain approach to it. For example, whenever I'm in Austria, I go to the grave of my parents, make sure there are fresh flowers there; always put a candle on. It's our way to do this and you do it best when you are alone. You can use the time to think a little bit and remember them. When you're younger, you don't think about these things. But we are coming to the age when we see things differently. Now, for me, it's a very nice place to be for a moment because it calms you down in a big way. It just has... something.

MH The thing that surprised me about Ayrton's grave is how simple it is. Because of who he was, I expected something elaborate, and yet there is just a little plaque in the ground. There are no tombstones anywhere in the cemetery. It's like a park; very peaceful, really beautiful. Did you feel that?

GB I agree. Absolutely. It's very interesting, the way they do this in Brazil.

MH When you look back on your F1 career, you've had a lot of team-mates. Was Ayrton the best you had? I'm talking overall, not just as a driver.

GB As I said, I liked Ayrton a lot, but my favourite was Jean Alesi. He is such a lovely person, such a big heart. He's outstanding.

MH Ah, I was going to ask you about Jean because I had a wonderful lunch with him in Avignon. What a character!

GB Yeah, he's an interesting combination because he can seem very naïve but, at the same time, he's very switched on. When you think you can use his naivety, you get caught. And when you think he's very switched on, you think, "Shit! What were you thinking, Jean?" He is so unpredictable.

MH He told me about you catching him out during testing at Silverstone by coming in, saying the track was dry when it was really wet out the back.

GB That was so typical of Jean. He never warmed up anything. His quickest lap was usually the first lap of the day. It was unbelievable; I don't know how he did it. So I knew what would happen when he went straight out on slicks. We waited to hear the big spin! Did he tell you about Estoril, because that was even better?

MH Funnily enough, no!

GB The Portuguese Grand Prix and we were driving our balls off in second and third places. He was just ahead of me and I could not go quicker. I had to think of a way to get by him. I radioed the Ferrari pit and told Jean Todt that I could go a second quicker

Was any victory more sweet? Berger wins the German GP in '97

but I couldn't pass Jean and they had to tell him to let me through. So one lap later, going down the straight, I can see Jean's head shaking from side to side! I know they're telling him to let me through and he's going mad. He was so pissed off, he slowed down to show everyone that it was a team order.

I didn't say anything and, a couple of races later, I did exactly the same thing! Again, he was so pissed off. After the race he said to me: "These bastards in the team, they always help you." Then he looked at me for a moment and said, "You didn't ask them, did you?" I replied, "Of course I did!" He went mad! It was so funny. But what a really super guy. And he's got such a nice family. Jean is still one of my best friends.

MH Talking about family, tell me what happened to the Berger haulage business. Do you still run it?

GB Yes. I have the logistic business. It's now a 50 per cent partnership with Red Bull. I have a trailer production company and I also have a truck service station.

MH How do you spend your time these days?

GB Roughly 25 per cent of my time is on business. Twenty-five per cent is wheeling and dealing like I always have. The other 50 per cent is spent taking care of myself and having fun; motorbikes, helicopter, skiing. I'm very lucky to have the privilege to enjoy 50 per cent of my life this way. It's a very nice balance.

MH You've always seemed balanced in your approach to racing, to everything you do.

GB Yeah, but don't underestimate the daily pressure you're under when racing. You have to deliver, and it doesn't matter which side of the pit wall you are. It's highly, highly competitive in a pool of sharks. I enjoyed it very much, but it wears you out.

MH When did you feel the most pressure?

GB At the end of my career in 1997, back with Benetton. I knew my time was over. The team was collapsing because Ross Brawn was going to Ferrari, Rory Byrne – a brilliant guy – was gone and Flavio Briatore was into the political scene. I was worn out. Then I lost my father. And then I was sick and missed three races. I knew that would be it for me at the end of the season. It was a high-pressure situation.

MH And yet you had your last win, an incredible drive at Hockenheim.

GB I'll never forget that. I said to myself, "I have to show my capability once more and then I can forget it." That showed me how much of this is in the head because I really shouldn't have done this race. I had just come out of hospital, Flavio didn't want me in this race and tried everything to stop me. People were very nice, but with a kind of Chinese smile that said, "What you are doing back here again?" The Renault wasn't a winning car but I knew I had to prove myself. That win came because I somehow put all my forces together. I was full of antibiotics from a sinus operation; I was physically not fit at all. To win that race was an incredible feeling.

MH You moved into management with BMW and Williams; how did you enjoy that?

GB Very much. I'd grown up in a family business and I've always been involved in running things. That's why I did all my contracts myself, I never had a manager. So I was very happy when BMW asked if I would like to run their motorsport department. It was a great experience to understand how a big manufacturer works and, on the other side, to deal with Williams. I've always had great respect for Patrick Head and Frank Williams.

MH Did you get to realise there's a lot more to this business than just driving the car?

GB Yes, you get a much bigger picture; you see so many more tools you could work with as a driver to get success. You learn it's not just about braking late! You could sort out your game before you even get into the car. That's what some people understand at a very early stage. That's what Ayrton understood.

MH Actually, talking about just being a driver, this reminds me of a story from when you were with Benetton-BMW, so this would have been 1986. We were in Detroit for the Grand Prix and there was a party by Ford at their museum in Dearborn. I was getting a lift in a car with you and Benetton's team manager, Peter Collins, who was driving. There was a woman in another car driving alongside going home from work. You were talking to her through the window and there was a conversation when we got to some lights, do you remember?

GB I don't remember exactly, but I believe you.

Monza 2008: Toro Rosso boss Berger and Vettel celebrate the win

MH We got to another set of traffic lights and you said to Peter, "Watch this" and you got out and started walking towards this woman's car. The lights changed and she floored the throttle. And so did we! You were left standing in the middle of the road. We disappeared, but then did a U-turn and went back to get you.

GB [*laughing*] Yeah, that sounds about right.

MH Okay, coming back to more responsible times, how different was the period with Toro Rosso compared to Williams?

GB That was another great experience. More of an entrepreneur exercise compared to BMW-Williams. A killer responsibility at Toro Rosso was finding budgets. If you're BMW Motorsport, you have all the responsibilities and all the pressure. But once the budgets are agreed, you go to sleep and you don't think about that. At Toro Rosso, it was very different. But it was nice to take over Minardi and try to put together a new team and find success. Obviously, to win a race with Toro Rosso, at Monza 2008, was a big moment.

MH So, you saw Sebastian Vettel coming through, you saw what the kid could do.

GB Sebastian was brilliant straight away. We could see this guy is really special. We had difficult times with Scott Speed and Tonio Liuzzi. Franz Tost and I were criticised for being too hard on the drivers, for wanting too much from them. I didn't agree. When a driver cannot deliver, you get all the excuses. And when, like me, you've been a driver for a long time, you know all the excuses, all the bullshit. But you start to think that maybe things are different, maybe the young guys need more these days. And then Sebastian arrived.

Immediately, Franz and I realised this is what we had always hoped for. Sebastian asked questions all day long. Speed would never ask you anything. He thought he knew everything but he was the most stupid driver I have ever seen. He was not talented. So, here is a guy like Vettel, very intelligent, very fast, and yet still asking lots of questions, wanting to know everything. Franz and I could not understand why BMW had let this guy go! We knew we could do something with Vettel and it worked out fantastically.

The only weakness Sebastian had was putting himself under so much pressure because he was so hungry. It was clear that, when he won the championship, he was going to make another big step because this pressure would be released. And that's what's happened in 2011. That's why Webber has struggled against Vettel because Mark cannot make the same big step forward by releasing the pressure of the world championship.

Sebastian has started to remind me a little bit of Ayrton. You can see it in his starts; you can see it in qualifying when the maximum pressure comes. You have to put your forces in a very narrow window and you have to deliver. Sebastian has the special capacity to do this. Just like Ayrton had.

MH Do you think Sebastian has changed as a person?

GB No. He's a lovely guy. But when you work with him, you find he's a complete killer. He's a guy who you think couldn't do anything to anybody, but when it comes to competition, he has the killer instinct. He doesn't show it; that's the great thing about him. That's why we all like him so much.

MH Talking about liking people, I want to backtrack for a moment. To 1988 or 1989, you were having dinner on your own in Budapest. you saw me and a couple of my colleagues come into the hotel restaurant and you invited us to join you.

GB The British mafia!

MH That's what you called us. It was a brilliant evening. You made us laugh with the stories about your childhood; the things you were doing behind cars on skis, in the snow.

GB Not on skis! Just our shoes! We had heavy snow in the winter and the walk home was quite long. So, we put one guy lying on the road like he'd had an accident. The cars come and stop, the guy stands up and says he's okay. But we've been hiding at the side of the road and, when the driver gets back in his car, we are hanging onto the back. Volkswagens were the best because they had a big bumper, but the Fords were bloody dangerous because the bumper was very narrow.

You would hang on, and that was okay until there was no snow. We would be doing maybe 80km/h, with just your shoes on the road. With the Ford, you could lose your fingers when you came off! These Ford drivers must have wondered what was going on when they'd find gloves frozen onto their back bumper! The other problem was you didn't want to be the guy who got onto the bumper and found he was by the exhaust!

MH I remember you also told us about your road accident around the time you entered F1 in 1984. You were so, so lucky, weren't you? It was a massive shunt and, if I remember, the guys who came along next were doctors.

GB I broke my first and second vertebrae. I was lying in a river, halfway in the water, halfway out. There is no traffic on this road at night. But these guys had been on the motorway, coming from a holiday and were just passing through Austria. They were hungry, so they came off the motorway to see if they could find somewhere to eat.

I was having the crash and this was the first car behind me. They jumped down to the river to save me. I was half conscious and I complained about my neck. They realised immediately they cannot touch me. The ambulance came and wanted to put me onto the stretcher but this guy said: "Listen, he's going to die if you put him onto the bed in a normal ambulance. Looks like he has a neck injury. You need an airbed."

The other thing was, these guys were helicopter emergency doctors and they had infusions and everything in the back of their car. So, when the ambulance arrived, I was already on infusions! Without these two guys, I'm sure I would be dead.

MH Do you ever see them now?

GB Not for a while. They came to a race once.

MH So they knew you went on to do okay in F1? They must have been delighted. But just how lucky was that?

GB It really makes you think about circumstance; about the things that can happen in life. When you look at this accident, here were doctors off the motorway because they're hungry. They came at the exact moment I had my crash, they knew I had a neck injury and they had infusions in their car.

You think about Tamburello and my accident: big crash, big fire and I'm okay. And then you think about Ayrton - same place and he hits the wall in exactly the same way. He has no broken bones but the front wheel comes off, a bit of suspension hits him at that critical place on his head, and he's dead.

MH If it's going to happen, it's going to happen. Is that what you're saying?

GB That's it, yes. You have to enjoy life while you can.

MH You've certainly done your fair share of that, Gerhard. Thanks for sharing it with us.

GB It's been nice. Good to catch up again with the British mafia!

At lunch with **Patrick Head**

"When a driver puts more weight behind his dislike of the other driver than the furtherance of the team, it's incredibly self-indulgent and counter-productive. We don't want to employ drivers like that"

The trick about chatting to Patrick is to remove him, however briefly, from the distractions of a job he continues to love. That way, you get the full benefit of an extraordinary recall peppered with an honest and frequently amusing interpretation. Invariably, it will be delivered in the robust and forthright manner that quickly became his hallmark when he arrived in F1 in the 1970s.

When we spoke, back in March 2011, Patrick was in the process of relinquishing technical control of the team he, along with Frank Williams, shaped into the pace-setting, championship-winning organisation loved and respected throughout the motor sport world. His enquiring mind has switched to the intricacies of hybrid power. But he continues to have plenty of opinion and memories as a true 'racer', and it's these I want to tap into over lunch in the Boar's Head in Ardington, a typical country pub in rural Oxfordshire.

Patrick chooses the scallops to start, followed by Dover Sole. But, first, our photographer Glenn Dunbar needs to explain he would like a portrait at some stage...

Patrick Head I'm getting a bit long in the tooth for this close-up photography.

Maurice Hamilton You say that, but I see you're still a keen biker. I watched you arrive on the BMW, whatever it is. Do you still keep one of those in London and one at this end to go from Didcot station to the factory at Grove?

PH Yes, but it's not because I'm mad about biking. It's because I live very close to the river in Chelsea, so if I was to go by car, I wouldn't have anywhere to park at Paddington station. And another thing, if you were to try to drive from London to here, there is no way of knowing whether it's going to be three hours or an hour-and-a-half. With the scooter, you just don't get held up. Even from Didcot to Grove, if you're in a car it can take 40 minutes; on the scooter it takes 15 minutes.

MH I'm surprised by how you were belted into it. It's quite an elaborate system.

PH Yes, it's a lap and diagonal from one side and then a diagonal from the other. So you have an X across the middle of you and a single lap-strap. But it's gone through all the 30mph frontal impact tests.

MH So they want to keep you in it and basically prevent you from falling off?

PH It's got a metal tube frame and it's also quite good at keeping the weather off you. On a bright summer's day, you'd think, "Why have I got all this stuff above me?" but in the winter, you're very pleased to have it there, particularly when it's snow and ice. You can actually do tail slides in the snow!

MH Can you lean that thing over?

PH Yes, you can... don't call it 'that thing', Maurice!

MH Okay, okay! What is 'that thing's' official title?

PH It's a BMW C1. They don't make them any more; they only made them for a year or two. It's a very good idea that should have been allowed longer to gain acceptance. But I think it cost more to make than they could sell them for. So they chose to withdraw it. You get people who are C1 devotees. They're good machines.

MH You still have another, dare I say, proper bike, don't you?

PH I've got a Ducati and a BMW R1100S. I used to ride the bike to the French GP. I'm looking to go to the Nürburgring this year, and somehow I'll find a way of going via Beaune! Which is pretty indirect but, if you look at the direct route, they're all motorways and very dull and very boring. So I'd like to try and go a couple of days early and find a way of going via Burgundy country.

MH So, you've come by bike and train today. To do what at the factory? Would you have come here hot from the drawing board, and I say that because I believe you still have a drawing board.

PH I do, yes.

MH When was the last time you used it?

PH I was on the drawing board a lot during the Formula 2 project [*announced in 2008 and subsequently abandoned in 2012*] because I would draw out the layout of the car and the installation and so on. I would then take it upstairs to a three-man office where they turned it into a CAD [*Computer Aided Design software*] layout and produced the detailed drawings. It's actually rare these days that I'm on the drawing board. I should do more, but I don't.

MH Do you miss that?

PH Umm... yes, I do miss it. But it just doesn't fit in with the process now. I know it's slightly different for Adrian Newey because he's leading the geometric design of the car whereas I'm not in that position. Adrian doesn't do many of the other things I would do in the company. Horses for courses.

MH Is it the creative side that you would miss? The solving of a design problem. That sort of thing?

PH I think solving whatever the problem is in front you as you work it through on a design is challenging and interesting. I'm 65 this year, it's sort of rushed up on me...

MH I know the feeling...

PH Yes, well, I think I've got to get into sorting out how to drive a CAD terminal, which is all about time needed to learn it. It's just like learning another language. I think that, ultimately, even if I wanted to get in and design... I don't know, wheelchairs or something like that, it's much easier to do if I could do it through CAD. It's a tool - but a very precise and useful one.

And now, with the way we build the whole assembly of the car, pretty much everything is created through solid modelling, which means you've got all the defined surfaces and geometry. If I produce a drawing on paper and it's considered to be anything that could be integrated into the car, it would have to be turned into a CAD drawing anyway. And that's pretty wasteful.

MH So, when you leave here, you're going back for a board meeting. Are you finding that you have to do a lot of admin - if that's the right word - and so on in your present role? How does that work?

PH As a director, I play a part in the admin but I wouldn't say it occupies a huge amount of my time. I'm a director of Williams Hybrid Power as well and I keep a close eye on their challenges and how they're dealing with them. If I think I can help in any area, I will sit down and discuss things.

MH From what you're saying, you're still very much hands on. The impression one gets, perhaps wrongly, from the floatation and sale of shares is that perhaps you're paving the way to withdrawing. As you say, you're 65 this year, so what's the story behind this from your point of view?

Mansell in the FW11, 1986, which won the Constructors'

PH In modern lingo, 65 is the new 40!

MH I'm with you on that because I'm actually older than you.

PH Really? Ah... you don't look it!

MH And the same yourself! Here... keep taking this stuff. Cheers!

PH Cheers! This is quite nice. What is it?

MH It's a Bourgogne.

PH Excellent. As for the floatation, obviously it wouldn't have happened unless Frank and I had agreed with it as a process. For me, there was no great master plan to extract myself from Williams. But, as a minority shareholder, you'd have to be a bit of an idiot not to see that an IPO gives a minority shareholder the chance of getting equal value for their shareholding, which is very unusual in a private company. Normally the minority shareholder has at least a 50 per cent mark down in the value of their shares.

MH Okay, I understand what you're saying, but I wondered if this was a way for you to ease out, given your close relationship with Frank. When Frank talks about you and his respect for you, one gets the impression that if you weren't there, he would really miss you. So, I was wondering if you felt you needed to be there for that reason - perhaps not solely for that reason, but that the emotional tie would stop you pushing off even if you wanted to.

PH It's true that Frank and I have operated together for a long time, but we're individuals; we're not joined at the hip. We've certainly worked closely but we don't go on holiday together; I wouldn't say there is heavy social interaction away from work. I hadn't looked upon the floatation and the fact that I was about to become 65 as a marker that says, "Patrick you're going to have to retire now."

MH It's interesting that you mention 65. It's an age that people latch onto when thinking of slowing down, retiring, whatever. But I'll bet, if you're like me, when you were 55, you said, "Christ, when I get to 65, there's no way I'll be doing this. I'll want to have stopped travelling or whatever" and yet it comes up so fast, you're 65 before you know it and have no intention of stopping. It catches you by surprise, doesn't it?

PH It does, yes!

MH So, you still want to keep doing it, don't you?

PH I'm not claiming for one moment, inside Williams or without, that I'm centrally on line, but I participate in a lot of what goes on at Williams and it keeps me pretty busy.

MH KERS took up a lot of your thinking in the past. Where does KERS sit in F1? Are you glad to see it? Do we need it so that F1 can be showing green credentials?

PH Well, there's a sort of basic truth behind motor racing that you want the cars to be extremely powerful, difficult to drive, safe in the fact that they should offer the driver as much sensible protection as possible on the circuit, should there be an accident.

It does strike me that there's quite a lot of public interest in technology. For instance, if I'm picked up by a black cab from my house in London, I'm not suggesting that every taxi driver recognises me and I'm not sure they going round saying, "I've had that Patrick Head in the back of my cab." But every so often they'll turn round and say, "When you off to Melbourne, then?" Or "what about this KERS, then?" They don't really know what it is but they are interested in the technology side.

Meanwhile, does it make the racing more interesting? I'm not sure. I rather doubt it. Yes, the commentators will be saying, "He's pushed his KERS button." Does that make it exciting to watch? I'm not sure. I'm not against it. As an engineer it's very interesting technology and has relevance for road vehicles - not just cars, but buses and any sort of transport system. I think being involved with it in F1 brings acceptance that it can be part of a performance vehicle, so there's a sort of physiological acceptance of it.

Mine's the Dover Sole. Ah, the liver and bacon. That looks a good choice, Maurice.

MH Always the way, isn't it? You see someone else's choice and it looks better than yours.

PH So, to finish the question is KERS valuable to F1? Overall as an engineer, I would say yes. As a spectator, not sure.

MH How important is it for F1 to be seen to be doing something along the lines you've said - feeding back into the motoring business, covering green issues?

Head, still involved during 2011 testing with Barrichello

PH I think from an image and a marketing point of view, it's pretty important. From actually saving the amount of thermal energy we put into the atmosphere due to F1, it's absolutely insignificant. But you have to put into perspective the fact that if you take all the fuel that all the F1 cars use all of the season and put it all together, it wouldn't take a jumbo jet across the Atlantic once. It's important to acknowledge that.

MH Although you're doing far fewer races, do you still enjoy it as much? Forget the travel, which bores us all to death, but when you get there, do you still feel a buzz when you walk into the paddock?

PH Yes. You're there knowing that there are 11 other teams. Their job is to beat you and your job is to go out and beat them. So it's a challenge and if you don't rise to the challenge, then don't do it.

MH Talking about challenges, the period just before a car runs for the first time must be the worst for a F1 designer. All that waiting to get a measure of how good your car is. You must have been through it, going back to the FW6 and so on. You've done all you can do and now you're waiting for it to appear in the metal, as it were, and find out if the car is any good.

PH It is a very tense time. I think for the design chiefs responsible, it's a time when they need to be supported rather than attacked. You have the end of the team that's dealing with marketing and sponsors, and it's great if you go out every day at the test and put in a quick time. You're at the top of the list and everybody thinks everything's hunky-dory. But it might not be like that. And I suppose it's inevitable but some magazines regard testing almost as if it were a GP practice and they put in who's at the top and who's at the bottom.

I mean, you get a bit of an idea. You can certainly tell that, say, Red Bull's preparation has been better than McLaren's, without mentioning our own. Then we go to Melbourne, which is a great track but it's mostly slowish corners and any of the quicker corners are just in-out; they're not long, sustained corners, so you can't tell a great deal.

In 2004, for instance, with our rather ugly tusked F1 car, Juan-Pablo Montoya, had he not spun at Turn 2, would have won that race, and I think at Malaysia a couple of weeks later, he was 12th or 14th on the grid. Melbourne doesn't really show up the characteristics of the car that will carry it to race wins and championships. So after Malaysia, if it's the second race, you need to take a careful look at the relative performance.

MH Looking back at all the cars you've done, was there any particular one that you were concerned about - a car that was, not a risk, but you'd gone out on a limb a little bit. The FW14B for example?

PH It's interesting that you put your finger on that one. I was certainly very concerned about the FW14B, the active-ride car. The 1991 car, the FW14, had been a very good car. It had the first sequential, semi-automatic 'box. John Barnard had done a semi-automatic box on the Ferrari, but it was the classic, three-rail box, and the sequential one was slightly different, in terms of how it operated. Nigel went out in the first four races, when in good positions, with gearbox failure. It turned out it was the most trivial of problems that could have been fixed in 30 seconds, but it just took us a long time.

There were so many odd contradicting bits of information and the problem was, when the gearbox did itself an injury, there tended to be a load of stuff coming out of the inside, so it was very difficult to establish exactly what was going on. After the first four races, I think Ayrton had 40 points and Nigel had zero. By the time we went to Japan at the end of the year, they were fighting for the championship. It so happened it went to Ayrton. But, had we got our act together earlier in the year, FW14 could - and should - have easily won the 1991 championship.

So, it was clear that the car was very good and I'm sure that with further development of the aerodynamics, the 14 could have won the championship as a non-active-ride car. But we'd been running the active ride programme in parallel for quite a time. And, depending on the type of circuit, it was clearly up to a second-and-a-half a lap quicker.

The problem was, you then took on the potential for huge unreliability. It was a car completely suspended via its hydraulics circuitry. Even now, I think hydraulics is, if not top of the list, then pretty close to top of the list of why F1 cars go out of races, even today. This is going back 18 or 19 years with a lot less surety behind the hydraulics side.

So it was certainly a big concern over the winter, but the only way to deal with concerns is to list all of the potential problems and make sure you've dealt with them. That's what we did. In fact, the 14B was not that different from the 14 from an aerodynamic point of view. It was the trick suspension that was so different.

"If I make a mess
I prefer someone
to tell me rather
than just seethe"

MH Going right back to your first car, the FW06 in 1978, what sort of buzz did you get when you went to Brazil and suddenly, with a simple car you were doing lap times that meant you were getting the better tyres from Goodyear for the first time? That must have been a nice feeling right at the start.

PH Yes, it was. This was at the time when Goodyear were getting the beginnings of a challenge from Michelin. There were certain contracted Goodyear teams and I think we were paying for our tyres, I can't remember. Frank would know - ask him!

If you weren't among the top Goodyear teams after the first practice, you just took a second, or three-quarters-of-a-second step back, because you didn't get the latest tyres. So, yes, that first practice was pretty important to make sure that you made your mark.

MH It was simpler then, wasn't it? Just look at the structure of the team. There was just one engineer per car, a couple of mechanics, yourself, Frank. But look at it now. There's a host of people.

PH It is a host of people. The cars were a lot simpler then. I would say the knowledge about what was going on with the cars was a lot less. It was a case of however much time Alan Jones would give you before he went off partying.

So you might have a 10- or 15-minute debrief, if you were lucky, and that was the data you had. We didn't have any on-board data recording, so you were then reading the tyres, you were looking at the brake wear, you were putting together the picture to try and help yourself make decisions about what to do with the car. The driver would turn up the next day and you'd go out for the first practice on Saturday morning and you knew from the lap times and from what the driver said after the first run whether or not you'd made the right guesses the night before.

But it was good and you did feel very connected to what was going on. Whereas now, I think that's one of the... I wouldn't say problems because the whole style of it is completely different now. But it's true to say that any one of the people on the race team will only have part of the information or part of the picture. There's no point in old boys like me going round, saying, "Oh, it was so much better in the old days", because they don't have the old days, they've got it as it is now. I'm sure there are maybe some other compensations.

MH Is there too much information coming at you now?

PH You don't have to look at it. It's a bit like somebody with a Blackberry, you know. You do get some people the moment their Blackberry goes 'Buzz', they have to pick it up and look at it, and there are other people who are more disciplined about when they decide they're going to access their mail or not.

MH Do you find, given our age, that experience does bring this ability to stand back and look at things and see the bigger picture, whereas young guys, as we were once, you're almost too close to it?

PH Because of the nature of their jobs, in that they've got individual tasks, they're bound to be very close to what goes on. Certainly, when you design the car yourself, you've got a certain protective or defensive approach to either the car being criticised or it being off the pace. Now that I'm involved in the development of the company, I don't psychologically have ownership of the design and therefore I can take a very detached and dispassionate view. I think that's quite useful, and useful for the company.

It lets you be fairly tough about why you're off the pace, and your knowledge will help you to make judgements. Saying that, it doesn't help you make the changes. But maybe you can participate with the people who are at the white heat of the design of the car. Maybe you can help them understand what they've got to do.

MH You used the word 'tough' in connection with dealing with team members. Can I move that across to drivers. You mentioned Alan Jones earlier. You are roughly the same age, you grew up together, you were mates, as it were. But, as time has gone on, the drivers get younger. You have to have a different approach, don't you?

PH It's like running previous drivers' sons, that really makes the point.

MH Yes, and now you find the fathers are younger than you, which is a bit worrying, isn't it? Have you almost looked upon drivers, forgetting perhaps Alan, as employees? They're there to do a job and you deal with them and that's it. If they don't do what they're supposed to do, if they make a mistake and it's clear that they weren't thinking properly, how do you view that? Do you have a word with them?

PH They are there to do a job. But the F1 racing drivers I come across now are

The active ride in the FW14B made it absolutely the car to beat

extraordinarily professional, not only in their driving but in the way they manage themselves and generally in the way they work to optimise the capability of the team.

But every now and then you get somebody doing something stupid, like going out and sliding into a barrier at Monaco on the third lap of first practice, as happened to us once. You've got to sit down with them and say, "Look, you just did not have your brain in gear because the lap times you'll be doing by the time you get to qualifying will be four or five seconds quicker than that, so you're not impressing yourself, us or anybody else by driving with small margins at that time. You're driving to feed back to the team the limitations of the car and you should not be finding those limitations by clipping a barrier and missing the rest of practice on that day."

Rightly or wrongly, I've gained a reputation for always giving drivers a bollocking. I think the number of times I've given drivers a hard time is actually not that many. But I'm a fairly direct person by nature and usually I hope people are fairly direct with me. If they think that I make a mess of something, I prefer to have them tell me that than seethe in resentment and say nothing.

MH One time I remember you doing that was in 1995 when I was doing a book with the team, a fly-on-the-wall thing. At Suzuka, you had words with Damon. When he came out the back of the garage, his face was the colour of that white piece of paper there. I asked, "What did Patrick say?" He said, "I can't tell you." Even allowing for Damon being secretive, I could tell it wasn't good! They had a bad weekend, both him and DC.

PH Yes, I remember that! We've had years where the capability of the team has been massively damaged by the drivers being too interested in what their team-mate is doing. That was very much the case with Juan-Pablo Montoya and Ralf Schumacher, in that the only thing they were interested in was beating each other. Quite honestly, that was seriously damaging and, to some extent, was a participatory thing in us not winning the 2003 World Championship. When we got to Monza with three races to go, we were eight points in the lead of the Constructors' Championship and one point behind in the Drivers' Championship with the slope of our development going upwards.

Fundamentally, the main reason we didn't win the championship was poor starts, but contributing to it was a terrible relationship between the two drivers. When the driver puts more weight behind his dislike of the other driver than the furtherance of the team, that's incredibly self-indulgent and counter-productive. Quite honestly, going forward, we really don't want to employ drivers who are like that.

MH Which drivers of the many you've had was a great team player? Jonesy?

PH Alan wasn't really interested in his team-mate or the furtherance of his team-mate, but he was a good team man. We've had some very good people. Keke Rosberg had a very limited but good time with us. We got on very well with Keke. He pretty much just turned up at the races but, when he did that, he was on it. When he was out there, he was giving 100 per cent, no question about it. But I don't think Keke ever felt that he was in any way either responsible for, or participatory in, the development of the team or even necessarily the developmental direction of the car.

But he was fantastic in the car. I've seldom come across anybody who could drive a qualifying lap every lap of the race if he needed to. He was a very exciting driver. With his outstanding win in 1982, when he won at Dijon, his car was never pointing in the same direction. He was driving it as if it was a rally car, every lap of the race. There are very few drivers who can do that and yet Keke wasn't necessarily one of the fittest drivers. And he smoked as well!

MH Nelson Piquet?

PH Nelson was great. He could be evil with his team-mate, particularly if he was called Nigel Mansell, but he was a great team player. When he won his F3 championship in 1978, he was heavily involved in running that team. Nelson would know the names of all his mechanics. He knew when their birthdays were and it wasn't just false, he was very much into 'his' men that were around him in the team. If you had a wet day's testing with nothing happening on the track, Nelson could keep the team entertained with jokes from 9 o'clock in the morning till you went home in the evening. He was very funny, but not a good guy to have as an enemy, I'd say.

MH Where would Alain Prost figure in all this? He was only with you for a year. It's almost easy to forget he won the championship with you.

PH That's very true. Alain was a bit enigmatic for us. I'm sure he wasn't like that at McLaren, but he'd had this experience of feeling he'd been pushed out of McLaren by

Ayrton Senna. So, he came to us and won the 1993 World Championship, but it was almost like he came and he went. He walked in this door and he walked out the other door and we never really knew him. He and his engineer, David Brown, worked closely together but I'm not sure that even David Brown knew him. We didn't really get to know the personality of Alain Prost.

MH Where did Nigel fit into all of this? How would you categorise him?

PH First of all, you've got to look at the statistics. Nigel won 31 grands prix and 29 of them he won in Williams cars. Okay, in 1992 he had a great car and he could have won a hell of a lot more. I think there was a bit of a myth in that people liked to categorise Nigel in the Graham Hill mould, as if he was the gritty trier but didn't have the skill of Ayrton Senna and Alain Prost.

I think anybody who worked close to Nigel would realise that not only was he extremely brave but he had a very high level of skill as well. He was gritty but he was not overcoming a lack of skill. In order to keep himself calm in the car, he talked very slowly to his engineer, which might have given the wrong impression because he knew what to do, he knew what to tell us about the car to get it the way he needed it so that he could drive it very quickly.

Out of the car he could be quite a difficult character. If you weren't for him, his view was you were against him. So if there was anybody in the garage that talked to Riccardo Patrese and treated Riccardo equally with Nigel, then Nigel's attitude was, that guy must be an enemy because he's on Riccardo's side as well as mine. But then Juan-Pablo Montoya was very much the same in character.

So yes, there was some baggage that came with Nigel. But, when he walked into the garage, everybody knew The Man was there. They knew if he was in the car, he was on it, every moment, wet or dry. That makes a team jump to attention. Everybody's on it as well. So Nigel was really good for us.

Okay, sorry, the board meeting calls. I've got to go. Thanks for lunch.

MH It's been great fun Patrick. Many thanks.

At lunch with **Alan Jones**

"To say they weren't ready for me to win is an understatement – they didn't even have an Australian national anthem! A drunk played 'Happy Birthday' on a trumpet, but it still sounded good to me."

It's a long way in every sense from fish and chips and a mug of tea on a cross-channel ferry to sitting in a fashionable restaurant in Melbourne. A lot has happened to Alan Jones since our encounter between Zeebrugge and Dover; every mile of racing on his way to the 1980 World Championship and beyond being worth a story told in that direct Aussie style.

Jones was a treat to work with back then, and time will not have threatened the entertainment value of a lunch with the first of many world champions at Williams. We snatched a couple of hours between activities leading up to the 2012 Australian Grand Prix, choosing the popular restaurant at the Crown Hotel. We had to get permission to have the photographs taken. With everyone happy and the formal boxes ticked, we got down to some good, honest chat.

Maurice Hamilton This place is a bit different from where we had our first formal interview sometime in 1978 or 1979 at your house in Ealing, west London.

Alan Jones Was it a reasonably small house on a corner, semi-detached?

MH That's the one. You were just starting to come right after struggling to make ends meet. This was before, or just after, you signed for Frank. You'd been running a boarding house before that, which worked out well for you, didn't it?

AJ It did. I had to figure out something that would give me an income but also give me freedom from reasonably early in the morning for the rest of the day. So if I wanted to pursue a drive, or if I wanted to go down to Goodwood and do testing for March, or something like that, then I could do it. The deal was I would get up and cook the breakfast from about 6.30am until about 8.30am, and then I was out of there.

MH How on earth did you come across a place like that?

AJ Ah, well, people used to wonder why a married couple wanted to buy a six-bedroom house. I told them I came from a very wealthy family in Australia and when the family came to visit, they all came and everybody insisted on their own bedroom, so what could I do?

As soon as I got the house, we went straight down to the army disposal store and bought all these double bunks, sleeping four or six in each room and charging them, I think in those days it was five quid a night. For that, they'd get bed and breakfast.

MH There must have been a constant flow of Australians coming through?

AJ Yes, basically it was a backpackers' place. In 1975, there hadn't been too much money forthcoming. I didn't know what I was doing from one year to the next. I really appreciate to this day what Harry Stiller did. He was a wealthy guy who used to race and I drove his Formula Atlantic, winning a support race to the F1 curtain-raiser at Brands Hatch. Then Harry rang me up and said, "I've got you a Formula One drive. I want you to go up to Easton Neston."

This was Lord Hesketh's place. I went around the back where they were preparing the F1 cars and, you know, I thought I'd died and gone to heaven. It was immaculate. I had a fitting in the car and it's, "Do you want this altered? Do you want that?" and I'm thinking, "How good is this?" I did the non-championship race at Silverstone, got seventh and beat some reasonable names. Then I did a Grand Prix or two.

MH Your very first was the Spanish Grand Prix on the fabulous Montjuich Park circuit. But it was quite a tense weekend for your debut, wasn't it? There was a drivers' strike and then an accident when a car flew over the barrier.

AJ There was all this talk about not racing because the barriers weren't safe, and then maybe the cars would be impounded if we didn't. I hadn't been in F1 that long and I just said, "I don't know about you blokes but I want to race." It went ahead and then, as you say, quite tragically that accident happened.

I loved that track, it was great. I'll never forget staying in a typical continental hotel, it was square with a big air shaft in the middle. All the windows from the toilets and what have you opened onto this central thing. I was about one or two floors above Mario Andretti, and all I could hear was his missus saying, "Mario, Mario, I've got diarrhoea." She obviously had no idea her voice was carrying the whole way through the hotel!

MH So, what happened to that Hesketh drive?

AJ At one point, Lord Hesketh was talking about running a two-car team; he got a bit excited, and so did I. Then I got a phone call from Harry saying, "I'm going to America." And he was gone. So I thought, "Bloody hell, what's going to happen now?"

John Surtees asked me for a test drive at Goodwood. John wanted to sign me and he said, "I'm going to South Africa, I'd like you to do some miles down there." I went to the airport and in the lounge, Surtees says, "Oh, before we hop on the aeroplane, sign this." I said I'd like time to have a read of it. To which John replied something along the lines of, "Well, I can't be taking you all the way to South Africa and spending this money, so I want some sort of commitment."

So I thought, "Oh bugger it, I'll sign anything." He said he'd reserved two seats in economy but the one in the middle would be empty. We get on board and there was a lady sitting between us. John blows up! The cabin crew say, "Well sir! If we could, we would, but the plane's full."

During the flight, I started speaking to this lady and he's nudging me, saying to be careful because she could be a spy. I mean, what would anyone want to pinch from Surtees at that point in time? We get to Kyalami and I was there for seven days and did about seven laps because Brett Lunger, who'd paid for a drive, made sure that he got looked after.

MH But you did get to race the Surtees in the non-championship races at Brands Hatch and Silverstone. I remember that because of all the fuss over the BBC showing a car covered in Durex sponsorship.

AJ That's right. I finished second at Brands, right up James Hunt's backside and the BBC had no alternative but to film us because we were in the leading bunch. Bloody ridiculous, the fuss they made. Now they'd give you a knighthood! I mean, they're handing them out free!

Anyway, in a nutshell, John was a difficult man to drive for, and I don't think I'm the only driver to say that. It got to the point where I basically said, "Look, if this is the only way I can do F1, I'd rather not do it."

MH Is this when you disappeared to the States for a while and had a go at Indycar?

AJ Yeah, I drove one of Bill Simpson's McLarens. We went out to Ontario Motor Speedway and I've never worn a pair of overalls for so long and done so little in all my life. Like an aeroplane would fly over and they'd stop practice because of the shadow. I didn't like it at all. Teddy Yip had helped set this up and I said to Teddy, "Look, I don't want to do this." So Teddy says, "All right, come on, we'll go to Las Vegas for three days."

"I was throwing in a hand grenade and walking away"

MH As you do!

AJ I went back to Australia and I thought, "I hate Indycar racing, I'm out of F1, what now?" And then poor Tom Pryce got killed in Kyalami.

MH In the Shadow during the 1977 South African GP. Absolutely horrendous.

AJ Jackie Oliver called and asked if I'd take Tom's place. I told him I had a bit of a contractual issue with Surtees, and Jackie said he'd deal with that. Tony Southgate joined the team and modified the car. It was still very heavy, but we were getting better and better results.

MH And the rest! You actually won in Austria.

AJ Didn't expect to because I qualified 16th, but then it started to rain a bit and the track was damp. Of course, because the old girl was that soft and heavy, it probably had the best wet set-up of anybody. I came through the field. James was leading and he broke down. I ended up not only winning, but I also beat Niki Lauda, which didn't go down that well in Austria.

But to say that they weren't ready for me to win is a bit of an understatement because they didn't even have an Australian national anthem. A drunk played 'Happy Birthday' on a trumpet, but it still sounded good to me. I remember thinking, "I don't care what happens now, I've won a grand prix."

MH Did it make much difference? This was August. Did anyone want to talk about the 1978 season?

AJ Luca di Montezemolo rang up and asked if I'd like to come and have a talk about driving a Ferrari. I thought, "Hello! I'm only human." So when he said we'd have to keep it fairly secret, I knew that meant Ferrari were talking to other drivers and they didn't want anyone to know.

I flew into Milan and the Italian idea of keeping a secret was to have a bloke, wearing pale blue overalls with 'Ferrari' emblazoned all over them, standing there holding up a sign saying 'Jones'. And he had a Ferrari parked out the front which was a Tipo prototype of some sort!

I physically signed a contract and they said, "Look, we'll level with you. We're trying to get Mr Mario Andretti. If we can't get him, you're our boy." Okay, no problem. In those days, you used to be able to get *Autosport* a day early if you went to a station such as Charing Cross or somewhere. I went there on a Wednesday night and read that Andretti had signed for Lotus. I thought, "Yes! You beauty!"

I rang them up and asked when would they like me to come down. There was silence for about three minutes, which I thought was a bit ominous. Then they said, "You know we told you we wanted a North American driver? Well, we've signed Mr Gilles Villeneuve." When I asked what should I do with the contract, they said, in a nice way, to put it where the sun don't shine.

MH When did Frank Williams come into the picture? You must have been talking to him at this stage?

AJ Yeah I had, but, obviously, with Ferrari showing interest, I had been stalling. So, this happens and I call Frank and say "Look, Frank, I've been giving a lot of thought to your offer..."

I went to the factory, met Patrick and saw the FW06. It was a really purposeful, neat little car. And I was really impressed with Patrick. I was even more impressed with 'Saudia' on the rear wing because they were the flavour of the month. Cut a long story short, I did a deal with Frank but I didn't realise we went to the first two GPs on his credit card. He hadn't quite signed Saudia! But we qualified eighth in Brazil and then, at Long Beach, I was dicing with Carlos Reutemann for the lead.

MH And the front wing collapsed.

AJ It did but, actually, it wasn't all that noticeable. The thing that really buggered me was an electrical problem. It was intermittently cutting out, and the silly part about it was, Reutemann spun towards the end even though he eventually won.

It's ifs and buts, I know, but if I could have stayed close to him, the chances are I might have won. A lot of Saudis were there for that race and I think that's what really helped to seal the deal. We finished off 1978 with a second place at Watkins Glen.

MH Speaking of Watkins Glen, wasn't that where you had a major suspension or wheel-related failure?

Montreal 1980: Jones and the FW07 were the class of the field

AJ It was a central peg. I was going through a fairly quick corner and the bloody thing broke and sent me into a big spin down the road. Luckily, I didn't hit anything. A marshal came up and handed me the bit that broke. So when they drove me back to the pits, I just threw it at Patrick.

MH He remembers that very well because he told me the story during our lunch for *F1 Racing* magazine a year ago.

AJ They needed to get some more made or have some better heat treatment. Of course, being typical American, none of the engineering shops wanted to do it in case it broke and we sued them. But Charlie Crichton-Stuart, Williams's sponsorship co-ordinator, smooth-talked someone into doing it.

MH The point is, Patrick remembers that you took his word that the job would be done. Your trust in him was absolute. You arrive the next morning, he said, "It's all right," and you get straight into the car.

AJ Patrick was a down-to-earth genuine engineer and we had such a strong rapport. If he said to me it was okay, then, as far as I was concerned, that was okay. If you don't have trust with your engineer, what can you do?

MH The teams are too big now for that kind of personal rapport.

AJ Yeah, now they'd all be marching in with their barristers and lap-tops. I wouldn't enjoy racing now because you have to do too much out of the cockpit. I mean, all these bloody media things; you can't say this, you can't say that. You can't say this circuit's shit because it's in Germany and Mercedes might get upset. It's like a political speech every time.

On the other hand, some things are a lot easier now. If you're testing these days you would have cell phones, cable TV and all that sort of stuff. But, back in the day, you'd go down to the hotel foyer and you had to tell the receptionist which country you wanted to ring up. You'd have to give them a bit of paper, then you'd wait to be told it's booth number 3 and you'd go in there to make your call.

MH And there was nothing to do in the room because the TV, if you had one, was rubbish.

AJ Exactly. I don't speak any other languages and you're sitting in your room watching some bloke babble incomprehensibly and you're thinking, "What time's dinner? I've got another hour to wait." We used to test at Paul Ricard in late November, early December, just when it was getting a bit cold. You couldn't get on the track until about 10 o'clock until it had dried up a little and, of course, it would get dark at 4pm. So, as soon as it got dark, my job was over. I'd hop in the car and drive to whatever that village was on the top of the mountains. You'd get there at 5.15pm. Dinner was at 9 o'clock. So what do you do for three-and-three-quarter hours? You can only walk around the village so many times. It was all those sort of things that used to get me down a little bit, but, saying that, they were good fun days

MH Things have changed in so many ways. Look at 1979, your car, FW07, didn't appear until a few races into the season. It sat in the pit-lane at Long Beach, didn't race and people were taking pictures of it.

AJ We were going to Ontario Motor Speedway to test it. I did about four or five laps and now that we had proper downforce, I just couldn't believe the grip this car had. I came straight in and said, "Bloody hell! No wonder Andretti and Lotus are winning everything." So we had grip, but we also had unreliability. The first race we led was at Zolder in Belgium. I was pulling away and we had electrical problems again. It took us a few races to sort out those niggling little reliability issues.

MH I was covering that race for *The Guardian*. I remember we were catching the ferry back to the UK on the Monday and who should be getting on but you, in a big flash Merc.

AJ The 6.9 V8?

MH That's the one; silver it was. Very impressive. You came on board with your leather brief case, which in those days was de rigueur, and you sat in the café with us with your tray of fish and chips and a mug of tea!

So, I'm scratching my head, wondering what to write as a follow-up story for Tuesday's newspaper. You suss this and you feed me, as if it's a passing comment, a story about how Williams better pull their socks up because this car's so bloody unreliable and the team's going nowhere. I mean, it's dynamite! I'm trying to look nonchalant and

"I remember dancing in the shower: 'I am the champion!'"

can't wait to get to the nearest pay phone once we reach Dover. It was a headline the next day. But you knew the team would react in a positive way.

AJ It's called, throwing in the hand grenade and walking away.

MH Yeah, you passed me the hand grenade and I threw it! So, now you had reliability and then came Silverstone and a huge step forward in performance. You were on pole and I suppose it must be one of your great regrets that your car broke even though Clay Regazzoni went on to win.

AJ Absolutely. I would have loved to have given Frank his first win. I was pulling away and then a weld cracked and let all the water out.

MH Shame that the car came out so late because you went on to win four races. But you won the championship the following year in Canada. Two things I remember at Montreal: one was the garages being located down the far end of the rowing lake.

AJ And you had to walk up next to the lake to get to the pits.

MH Correct. Do you remember what you did on race day?

AJ Went by boat or something?

MH No, you put on your overalls and helmet and marched along the towpath. All on your own. It was an extraordinary sight. We used a picture in *Autocourse*.

AJ I was probably trying to scare the shit out of Nelson Piquet.

MH I'd say you succeeded one way or the other because you both started from the front row and he ended up in the wall at the first corner.

AJ And they stopped the race because there was shit all over the track. I could have continued because only my engine cover had come off, but that was it.

MH And Nelson had to take the spare Brabham with a special engine and it blew up. You became champion. Do you remember much about the celebration afterwards? It was in the Bonaventure Hotel, I think.

AJ It was good. I went back to the hotel and I remember dancing round in the shower going "I am the champion!" By the time we went down to the ballroom, Mansour Ojjeh, the owner of team sponsor and investor TAG, had about 40 photographs which he'd blown up and framed with non-reflective glass and hung around the walls. We had a band, and it was full on.

Mansour made a Lear jet available to me because the next race was Watkins Glen, a week later. He said, "Go wherever you want." So Charlie Chrichton-Stuart and I jumped in and went down to New York. Then we flew to Watkins Glen and ended up trying to play a few games of golf before the US Grand Prix weekend got started. None of this having to go off and please sponsors stuff.

MH So, 12 months later, you've retired. I was talking to Frank about this the other day and he said that he had begun to get the feeling you were ready to go. You were talking about Australia more and more. Do you reckon that was the case at Monza in September 1981 when you said you would quit?

AJ Absolutely! I read somewhere that Frank said he didn't think I did it on purpose, he just thought I was inconsiderate. And he's right, because I didn't even think about it.

MH What was the attraction?

AJ I had a farm and I wanted to live here. I told Frank I wanted to knock it on the head. After the final race in Las Vegas, which I won, he asked me to test the six-wheeler in England. I said, "I don't want to go back; I just want to go home." Frank thought that if I drove the six-wheeler, I'd get all enthusiastic. We were staying at that motel near Donington and I remember getting up in the morning and it was that icy I had to boil the kettle and pour it over the lock on my Jaguar. There was no central locking in those days, so the bloody thing wouldn't unlock. I'm thinking, "Bugger this, I'm off." After the test was over, I drove to Heathrow in the drizzle, hopped on a Qantas jet and, within about 15 or 20 minutes we'd gone through the cloud base into bright sunshine and I had a cold Fosters in my hand. I thought, 'This is me'.

MH Life back in Australia didn't quite work out as planned. You made a brief appearance in an Arrows in 1983, but the comeback with Haas Lola was more serious. That looked promising on paper - the car, the engine, the team, sponsorship from Beatrice.

Alan Jones wins the Canadian GP on his way to the 1980 world title

AJ I liken it to somebody going out and buying the best possible ingredients you can get for a cake, then the cook stuffing it up. And I won't tell you who the cook was.

MH I can guess. Did he have a headset, one foot on the wheel, telling you how to set the car up?

AJ Exactly! Teddy Mayer, commonly known as 'The Weaner'. That deal came about because Carl Haas used to eat in this restaurant in Chicago and that's how he met James Dutt, the chairman of Beatrice. I had driven for Carl in CanAm in 1978 and, next to Frank, Carl is the best bloke I've ever driven for. Charlie Crichton-Stuart called, saying Carl wanted me to drive the Lola. I said, "I'm sort of out of it, mentally and physically." So Charlie said, "I've been told to offer you X, but I can go to Y. Why don't I come out for a week, we'll go to Y straight away and then I'll have a week with you having a bit of fun out in the boat? I can call them and say, 'He's nearly there. Give me another day or two'."

I threw myself in the gym, lost some weight and took it seriously. There was supposed to be a Ford engine but, when I got there, we had the Brian Hart engine, which I always thought was a boy trying to do a man's job. We had one retirement after another.

They said, "Go back to Australia over the off season but be prepared to come back as we've got a full test in California for the new Cosworth engine. Come March and the Cosworth still wasn't ready. We started 1986 with the Hart again. The car itself wasn't too bad, but the Cosworth engine, when it arrived, was just gutless. We were 15 or 20km/h slower down the straight at Monza than the Ferraris.

MH One of the most appalling moments must have been testing at Paul Ricard when Elio de Angelis had his fatal accident after his Brabham flew over the barrier.

AJ As he went through the chicane, the rear wing collapsed and sent him over the fence. I had just come out of the pits to start a run. I saw bits of Fibreglass all over the place and I looked to the right and there was a plume of smoke coming from the other side of the Armco.

I jumped out of the car, ran over and the bloody thing was upside down with his arm hanging out, wiggling. I couldn't do anything; I couldn't lift the car. The bloody fire marshals were probably off having lunch or something. The poor bugger died of suffocation because the heat had burnt up all the oxygen. It was a minute or more before enough people arrived to turn the car over. Absolutely terrible.

MH You mentioned Carl Haas. I've another memory of Montreal in 1980. You're out to win the championship and on race morning Carl's going round the front of the Williams, touching it all over. Your mechanic, Wayne Eckersley, was not happy.

AJ Carl was blessing the car, as he did at every race. I said, "Wayne, get out of the way. It worked for me in 1978." I used to sort of poke fun at it, but you look at the races that guy's won, the reliability factor of his cars. I wasn't going to stop him, that's for sure. He could have touched my head. I think he might have!

MH And then look what happened. As you said, there's a collision in the race, and your car's fine!

AJ Exactly!

MH If you're talking about people who have influenced your life in one way or another, when I came to see you in Ealing you told me about your dad and how close you'd been. You went around with him when he was racing. Is that how it got into your blood?

AJ Yeah. Absolutely. I remember as a kid going to all the different races with him. I often wonder how other people got into racing because, for me, it was a natural progression. He was the first Australian to ever win a Grand Prix outside of Australia. I just grew up in that environment.

MH It was very sad because he was very young when he died, wasn't he?

AJ Yeah, he was 50. It seems young now, I can tell you!

MH He was living with you in England, wasn't he? And you won an F3 race not long after he died.

AJ Yes, he came over and he'd had a stroke. I'd signed to drive the works GRD F3 car and I won the race at Silverstone the week after he died. We put the wreath in the coffin.

MH You've seen racing from every aspect: your dad as a racer, then you raced and became champion, and then you were involved in running the Australian team in A1GP. You were very much into that, weren't you?

AJ I was. But I knew it was destined for failure as soon as South Africa got involved. Had they been able to make the planned race on the Gold Coast in Australia, that would have set them up because they were going to get quite a considerable amount of money. Then Emerson Fittipaldi had done a good deal to go to Brazil. Had they been able to do those two races, I reckon they would have been all right.

But, typical South Africans, they're in it for 0.3 of a second and then couldn't be told anything. They had John Surtees, Emerson, myself and Niki Lauda, but they wouldn't listen to anybody. They had a cast of thousands; you'd see them all going down the car park and the girls would be hopping into their own hire cars rather than sharing. And that was just one small thing. Totally ridiculous. Such a shame.

MH Did you enjoy being team principal? Were you able to use the experience you'd had and not interfere with your drivers?

AJ Absolutely. I used to give the drivers encouragement when I could, but I would never abuse them if I thought they were doing the wrong thing. Frank was very good at that. He used to get the very best out of me, and it wasn't because of threats. I would never try and get back into the cockpit via the driver, which I think a lot of ex-drivers try and do.

The thing I found with A1GP, I used to call it the America's Cup on asphalt, was nation against nation, country against country appealed to a lot of people who might not otherwise have been interested in motor racing. That really worked.

And the racing itself was good because the cars slid and locked up under braking. They had some good drivers from time to time. People like Nico Hülkenberg, who really showed his skill.

MH Speaking of which, we'd better get back to Albert Park and see how Nico and the rest of them are getting on.

AJ I suppose we'd better. I'll give you a lift in my ISF, I'm an ambassador for Lexus.

MH So, you're still driving nice cars.

AJ Yeah, but no fish and chips. Thanks! That was good.

At lunch with **Charlie Whiting**

"The biggest weapon in our arsenal is deterrent. Making a mistake is one thing, but if there seems to be a deliberate attempt at cheating, the consequences will be significant."

Charlie Whiting is motor sport's poacher-turned-gamekeeper. A former mechanic who helped put F1 cars together, Charlie is the race director who now makes sure they start safely and run exactly as they should from a technical and sporting point of view.

Although instantly recognisable at the race track, Whiting maintains a low profile off it. But it seemed a shame not to tap into his vast experience while having lunch around the corner from his office in Monte Carlo. Even before the first course at Maison du Caviar in December 2011, we were off and running at Las Vegas in 1981.

Maurice Hamilton I hate to remind you of this, Charlie, but it was 30 years ago last October when Nelson Piquet won the championship in your car.

Charlie Whiting It's a dreadful thought. Not Nelson winning, of course! But it doesn't seem like 30 years.

MH I was covering the race in Vegas that weekend and I clearly remember you standing on the pit wall to see if Nelson was going to make it to the end of the last lap. I wrote that your face lived up to your name; you were as white as a sheet.

CW That day in Vegas is still quite vivid. It wasn't an easy race. Nelson was hanging on in fifth place with a one point lead in the championship. He was completely finished. Even Jonesy [*Alan Jones*], who was leading the race, had his head hanging out of the car.

MH The whole season was coming down to this one race and you could lose it within another lap or two because his lap times had gone right off and someone was catching him. And what a weird place to hold a race, in effect a car park at the back of Caesar's Palace Hotel.

CW It was a pretty appalling track, even by the standards of 1981, never mind today. The actual layout was defined by a load of concrete blocks. You could just see the heads of drivers zigzagging above the concrete. The bit that amused me was staying in the Flamingo Hilton Hotel, which was opposite Caesar's Palace. Beside the light switch in the room, there was a little note which said, "Conserve energy, turn your light out before you leave in the room." You'd look out the window, and all you could see for miles in every direction were millions and millions of lights!

MH How did you get to being in Las Vegas as a mechanic for the Brabham F1 team?

CW I lived in West Kingsdown, a little village close to Brands Hatch. Dad was a farmer, and my brother, Nick, was interested in cars. He started his own little garage at the age of about 17. He was quite enterprising. I was well into cars and followed F1 as best I could in those days because you struggled to find anything in the newspapers. When the British Grand Prix - actually it was called the European Grand Prix - came to Brands for the first time in 1964, I dutifully sneaked over the fence, as you do, and watched that race. That was it for me; I just wanted to be involved in F1.

My brother started doing a little bit of autocross and rallycross in 1968. I helped him prepare his cars; I was about 14 at the time. I learned an awful lot from Nick. After I finished school, I just wanted to work on cars but my mum wouldn't let me; she said you need an education. I did five years at a Polytechnic and came away with a Higher National Diploma in mechanical engineering. Then, much to my Mum's disgust, I worked in a garage. I continued doing Nick's cars for him.

MH Thundersaloons, wasn't it?

CW Yes, he used to race these Ford Escorts with big engines. They were brilliant cars. Then, in 1976, Nick did a deal with John Webb at Brands Hatch to run Davina Galica in an old Surtees TS16 F1 car. We ran that in 1976 and a TS19 in 1977 and, at the end of that year, I went off to work in F1.

MH So what happened? Did you get a call from someone, or was there an advert?

CW Davina got a drive in F1 at Hesketh. That didn't last very long. She didn't qualify and then I think we ran Eddie Cheever for one race, Derek Daly for one race. After the Belgian Grand Prix, Hesketh folded. Beaky Sims, who was the team manager, told me Herbie Blash, then team manager at Brabham, was looking for someone. I went for a chat. They wanted a number three mechanic on the T-car, and I was that man.

MH So, that was right at the bottom of the pile?

CW Yes. That was in 1978 with the Brabham BT46 and the flat-12 Alfa engine. It was a lovely car – we won a few races with that. In 1979, I was put onto Niki Lauda's car, which was now a BT48 with the V12 engine. Not a very good car.

MH It pumped out a lot of oil, I seem to remember.

CW Among other things. In the latter part of 1979, Bernie Ecclestone, then owner of Brabham, decided to get rid of the Alfas. We built the BT49, a wonderful little car with a DFV in it, very easy to work on. I remember testing at Mallory Park and Thruxton and it was stupendously quick. Nelson Piquet, who had replaced John Watson, loved it.

I'd built this BT49 for Niki for the Canadian Grand Prix. He went out, did one practice session and he came back in and said the rev-counter wasn't working. I fixed that, ready for the next session. Where was Niki? His bag and helmet were on the pit counter. But he'd gone, retired! I didn't see him again for about five years!

In 1980, I was the number one mechanic on Nelson's car; we came close to winning the championship that year. He won his first race in Long Beach, but then Alan Jones took Nelson off at the first corner in Canada, the penultimate round, and we took the restart in his T-car, which was allowed in 1980. Nelson was disappearing in the lead and the engine blew up after about half distance.

MH What was the story with the engine in that car? Was it a qualifying engine that shouldn't have been there? Can you remember?

CW That's what I understood. I think we'd got a fairly special engine from Cosworth for qualifying, I wasn't involved deeply in the engines in those days. It was a different engine and the decision was taken not to change it on Saturday night, but suddenly we had to use it and it didn't last the race.

MH Today, with all the checks and procedures and so on, that sort of thing would never happen, would it? The engine would be changed as a matter of routine.

CW Absolutely. It wouldn't be an issue.

MH What are your memories of working with Gordon Murray? In those days he was a way-out character, wasn't he? He was such a funky guy.

Whiting became poacher turned gamekeeper after Brabham

CW He still is to a certain extent. He was brilliant to work with. The guy was a legend. He just re-wrote the rule book on so many things. David North was another excellent chap. There were only two of them working in the drawing office at that time. That was it! It was a fun, relaxed atmosphere, which was something that Gordon always tried to foster. I was talking to Jonathan Wheatley, now race team manager at Red Bull, recently and I said, "You guys always look like you're having fun." He said because he used to work at Benetton and they used to play loud music, it was actually modelled on Brabham. They wanted to be the new Brabham. And that's been carried into Red Bull.

MH Of course, you were helped a lot by having Nelson there as well. He would have embraced that sort of atmosphere.

CW It worked perfectly, particularly with Nelson, as you say, being that sort of character. The amazing thing is, Nelson is exactly the same now. His sense of fun just knows no bounds really.

MH What sort of tricks did he play on you? I've heard stories about him doing things to the washer bottle of your hire car, or if you hit the brakes, the horn would come on or something bizarre would happen in your car.

CW Yeah, all of that! One of his favourites was, and obviously we got wise to it, sitting on the grid in the car and saying, "I think there's something wrong. Is the fuel leaking?" Panic! "Oh my God, what's that? The race is about to start." Then we discovered it was piss. He couldn't be bothered to get out for a pee. And he sat there watching us going mental, loving every minute of it of course!

MH I'll bet Riccardo Patrese would never have done anything like that.

CW No way. Such a nice guy. In 1981, I was made chief mechanic until 1985 and then I was promoted to race engineer on Riccardo's car.

MH But the team was starting to slide downhill by then.

CW Bernie was finding too much of a conflict of interest between the FIA, or FISA, as it was then, and the teams, so he gave up. He offered to keep me on, doing whatever he could find for me. It was his idea that I could perhaps work for the FISA. Having been on one side of the fence, perhaps I'd be good at catching the buggers from the other side! That's how it all started. When Max Mosley became FIA president at the end of 1991, he promoted me to technical delegate. My next milestone was 1996 when I was given the job of starting the races. In 1997, I became race director.

MH So, given your background, you knew exactly how it all works, how the mechanics work, how the designers work, how the drivers think. But, as you gradually worked your way up, did you feel it becoming an onerous responsibility?

CW I came in at ground level. As things evolved we had a few big issues arising in the early 1990s with fuel, for example, and then active suspension. We had some quite big fights on our hands. Then it became far more complicated, so I had to get a few experts. In 1994, there was the traction control saga, then the whole business with Ayrton at Imola and all the subsequent changes that were needed. We needed to get more and more specialised in a number of fields to try and keep pace with the technology.

MH But that's very hard for you, because you're dealing with some of the best brains in the world and it's just you guys. You must have to get up very early in the morning to stay ahead.

CW The biggest weapon in our arsenal is deterrent. Making a mistake is one thing, but if there seems to be a deliberate attempt at cheating, the consequences could be significant, as we saw with the Toyota rally car which meant two years out of business.

MH But these guys are going to work right up to the edge of the regulations, aren't they? So, when they come to you with a proposal, I know you don't pass judgement, but what can you do?

CW We give them our opinion. They'll come to us with a scheme and say, what do you think about that? We'll say, yeah, that should be okay. Strictly speaking, I can't say whether it is or not. Ultimately, it's up to the stewards. But if there is an interpretation needed, we can offer a view which, 99 times out of 100, turns out to be definitive.

MH So there must be times when you see something coming through and you think, "That's clever. They're right. It's within the regulations"?

"The Schumi and Villeneuve clash, Jerez 1997, was a racing incident"

CW The double diffuser was exactly that. We thought it was legal; it was quite a clever loop hole. If we see a so-called loop hole, we will always try and close it, we will try and think of an argument to stop it. But it's quite difficult to actually stop it because the rules are the rules. However, whatever interpretation we try and put on it, it's sometimes not quite enough. More difficult, though, is to see where it might lead. Without being an aerodynamicist, you're unlikely to know.

MH You've got to be a jack-of-all-trades in many ways. You've got to know a bit about aerodynamics, a bit about all sorts.

CW You don't need to know too much about aerodynamics as such. Bodywork rules are normally about dimensions, that sort of thing. I've not got any great interest in what flow patterns there are or what all these vortices look like or what they do because if it complies with the rules, then that's fair enough. The difficulty we have is knowing how far they can go. If you say "yes" to a little slot here, what's to stop them from doing something that goes round and round and then ducts the air through somewhere that we just wouldn't think of. Nor, in fairness, would they in the beginning! But that's how things tend to snowball and we get caught out sometimes.

MH There is a lot of money at stake for the teams. They must get quite passionate about it if you rule against them. Sometimes you must think the world hates you. How do you cope with that?

CW It's very difficult sometimes when you feel a bit sorry for someone having developed something and you say "No". They try and pull the wool over your eyes, of course, but you have to try and see through it. I'm not suggesting for one second that I manage that every time, but it can be quite difficult to be able to see exactly why they want to do something; why it's absolutely necessary to have a certain thing on the car.

MH So you think, 'What's the motive here? They're up to something, what the hell is it?'

CW You almost have to assume they're up to something.

MH They are! But that's the name of the game, isn't it? This is the business we're in. It's a deeply competitive game at all levels, particularly yours.

CW Unbelievably so. And just as much on the sporting side. We've only talked about technical matters thus far, but it's equally competitive, possibly more competitive, on the sporting side in the races. All sorts of comments and accusations fly around when, say, a driver cuts a chicane. Did he gain an advantage? They say, "We're sure he did this. We're sure he did that." You check, and, no, he didn't! We're forever checking things and very often they don't turn out to be true.

MH At least there's no arguing about DRS, the wing's open or it's not. What are your thoughts on DRS after one season? I know it's been a work in progress and you've been learning as you go.

CW I think I'm a bit biased because I consider it as my baby. I think it works exceptionally well. There were a few places where it didn't work well enough - Melbourne was one, purely because the straight wasn't long enough. What we want to do is make it so that the driver still has to work hard; we don't want to make it easy. In China, we could have had it over the whole straight but it would have been really tedious. We've got to try and make it a little bit better.

There are a lot of things to consider when you actually analyse it; things like the comparative speed of the cars at the beginning of the sector. You need to see if the guy would have passed anyway, without DRS. You also have the differences between the efficiency of the DRS on one car compared to another. Obviously, as always, the whole set-up of a car is a compromise, and some teams go towards the slightly more optimum qualifying performance. If you're a team expecting to qualify at the front, you might do something different to a team that knows they're going to qualify at the back.

So we've got to look at all those factors. You can't say DRS didn't work there, because it may have worked for some but not others, because of how the team have set up DRS and the car. Overall, I think it's been a success. It got everybody talking and provided a lot more overtaking. It did result in more accidents, but that's going to happen; when guys try to overtake they sometimes hit each other. If it hadn't been that close, then they wouldn't have hit each other, that's obvious. I don't think it's anything that's been remotely dangerous.

MH Have the drivers had to realign their judgment in a way?

Whiting carries out an inspection at Yeongam in South Korea

CW The most refreshing thing about 2011 is that it was clear drivers haven't forgotten how to race. In fact, it was quite clear they love it. You could be forgiven for thinking they'd forgotten how to do it because it used to be much more difficult.

MH On the subject of racing, can you clarify the change regarding the number of moves a driver can now make?

CW You saw Michael and Lewis in Monza, where Michael would go into Ascari, move left to defend his position, Lewis would go to the right, then Michael, coming up to the corner, would move back to the right to take his line. It's been an unwritten rule that you should leave room for the car to your right, if you're going to move back.

So, you could say, "Once you've moved, you can't move back." But, if a driver did move to the left and then moved slightly right, there'd be someone who'd say, "He moved twice!" So you've got to leave enough space for one to pass if he can, and equally importantly, if a driver moves back in front of another one and that car is a bit late on brakes, you've got potential for nose-to-wheel contact and flying cars. I think Michael was right on the limit. Now we've made it a written rule; it hasn't really changed anything.

MH You must have heard all the excuses by now.

CW "I didn't see him!" They always say that.

MH I sympathise with that a little because you surely can't see much from the cockpit these days. There are blind spots with the head protection and the little mirrors.

CW I dispute that because the mirrors have got bigger and bigger over the years; they are chunky great things. You look at how small they used to be. If you can't see out of these mirrors, you should put them in a better place. It's just a standard excuse. He must have known the other driver was there or thereabouts. Anyway, they've got peripheral vision; if you haven't, then there's actually something wrong with your eyes.

MH Talking about seeing everything, how did you feel when first asked to start a race? There must be so much to take on board.

CW When Max asked me, I said I'd love to do it. I was very nervous before the first one, which was Melbourne in 1996 when Martin Brundle had that big shunt on the first lap. In those days, we stopped the race rather than use the safety car. So I had to start the race twice!

I'm not suggesting that I'm not nervous now, because it's a moment of high tension for everyone and there are lots of things to think about. You have to programme the lights; you've got to know exactly what to do within a split second if something happens. There are so many different scenarios; there's hardly a race goes by when something comes up that you haven't seen before. You have to be aware of exactly what's going on. I don't know how many races I've started now, it must be over 250, but it's definitely not routine. You still get an adrenalin rush.

MH I was at Monza in 1978 when we had the terrible accident that Ronnie Peterson was involved in – the press tribune was then in the main grandstand, directly behind the starter's rostrum. In those days, they would get a local bloke to drop the national flag. And this guy was clearly intimidated by Gilles Villeneuve in the Ferrari, sitting on the front row, looking up at the starter and blipping the throttle. He drops the flag and, of course, the back half of the field haven't reached their grid slots. Those guys, most of them, see the flag fall and floor the throttle while still moving forward. No wonder there was chaos where the big wide track hit the bottleneck before the first chicane.

CW It's unthinkable now that that could happen. They come onto the grid and they have their routines so perfectly worked out; they know exactly how long they're going to have to wait, how hot the car has to be when they get there and they're forever doing clutch bites and burn outs, it's so precise. But obviously things do go wrong, although cars don't stall on the grids nearly as much these days.

The drivers at the front know if they streak away and then have to sit on the grid for a minute-and-a-half, it's their own silly fault. So now they get their tyre temperatures right and burn outs done and normally 45 seconds is the longest they have to wait.

MH During 'Spygate' and all that, there was this 'FIA means Ferrari International Assistance' stuff. How did you feel when people said the FIA were favouring Ferrari? What can you do to show you really are neutral?

CW I don't know what more we can do. I think if anyone has got that in their brain, then there is no shifting it, frankly. I can say, hand on heart, that has never been the case, nor will it ever be. I know it's not, so I'm perfectly comfortable with that. It's

When the starter got it wrong, Peterson died: Monza 1978

completely ludicrous, but I can see why people might sometimes put three things together and say it means the FIA is biased towards Ferrari. But we never went out of our way to do anything special for Ferrari, or anybody else. We've tried to be as even-handed as possible. And if we're not, then I think the whole thing would collapse. The trust would disappear. We have to make sure we do our best to maintain that trust.

MH There is also this thought that Max might have been on the phone dictating what to do when there was an incident or something controversial.

CW Again, I can say hand on heart that has never happened; never during a race and never during any stewards' enquiry. The closest I've seen Max come to saying anything was after Jerez 1997 when Michael Schumacher drove into the side of Jacques Villeneuve's Williams as they disputed the final round of the championship. Max was in the control tower, not in the stewards' room or race control, and he said to the chief steward something along the lines of, "So, a small investigation now?" And the steward said, "No, it was a racing incident." Max left it at that. It had been a question, not an instruction. And nothing did happen at that race.

MH Was Max good to work with?

CW Very much. A very good decision maker; very clear about which direction to go. He understood racing and he was very good technically as well.

MH When you go to the races, you're always there before most of us. I've seen you walking around the track. In Abu Dhabi, on Thursday afternoon, I saw you standing on your own, down at the last corner, looking up the straight.

CW Final inspection is on a Thursday; it's a traditional thing more than anything else. Most of the work has already been done; I'll have been round the track on the Wednesday. It's good to have a final look and remind yourself of the detail. In Abu Dhabi, I was probably looking at the pit entry line; we'd made a couple of changes to the last two corners with additional artificial grass. You check things such as kerbs and bollards on corners once it's all done. You check places where drivers might try to cut chicanes and decide what deterrents you need to put in place to make it slower if they try a short-cut.

MH What about Korea in 2010, for example? By the time you got there, it was done and only then could you see the effect of the walls being too close at the final corners, and people were saying, "For Christ's sake, what were they thinking of allowing this?"

CW Exactly. Generally speaking, it doesn't happen very much. I've usually got an answer for most of the questions that emerge because it is detailed work. There is an awful lot of work even before I visit a circuit. I went to Delhi six times to make sure there was no repetition of Korea. I only went twice before the 2010 Korean event, I should have gone an extra once or twice. Not that it would have made that much difference because the work was so late, it wasn't really finished. In 2011, it was a lot better.

MH You must be working 24-7. Do you get a holiday?

CW I do.

MH But you must be working in the winter with the sporting and technical regs, that's masses of pages.

CW It is, but you don't rewrite the whole thing every year! You're just adjusting them. I chair all the technical and sporting working group meetings. That's when we decide the new rules and discuss ways of doing things. That keeps me well up to speed with everything.

MH Do you enjoy it?

CW Definitely. I still enjoy the racing. Okay, you're not there to sit and actually enjoy the racing, the two primary objectives are to make sure it's done fairly and safely, but it doesn't stop you appreciating it. Sometimes you get wrapped up in various things and you can't actually see what's happening from the racing point of view. We have all sorts of systems and people who alert us as to what's going on at various parts of the circuit. We've got a very good information flow.

MH Do you have camera angles for virtually everything?

CW That's a bit hit-and-miss sometimes because we have to rely on the host broadcaster. What we've got are CCTV cameras, about 30 of them around the track; pictures of every bit of track that we can adjust and zoom. We've got four or five pit cameras of our own covering the entry and exit and so on; 10 on-board cameras at all times; we won't always have the right one on the right car at the right time, but the chances are you'll get what you need.

In 2011, we started what we call the Race Incident System. Using GPS, which we have on all the cars, this system knows what an incident is. So, if the safety car is out and the system sees two cars pass, it will flag up 'possible overtaking under safety car'. It will then automatically find every image there is of the two cars involved. This saves you having to trawl though the cameras to find the incidents. If we decide there is an incident then the whole thing is sent to the stewards' room and they will have everything. All the images will be ready to go. In the past, I would call the stewards and say, "I think this car overtook that one behind the safety car on lap 32," and they would then have to check every camera on that lap and try to find the incident.

MH Has it been good having an ex-F1 driver on board?

CW Yes. Very good. It has improved the credibility of some decisions although, of course, not everyone will agree with everything they say. There will always be differences of opinion.

MH I think it's funny, for instance, that Jonesy should be on the panel when he squeezed Nelson at the start in Montreal in 1980. But that's why it works, he's been there and done it, so to speak.

CW A bit like me, really! Which reminds me, I've got a technical meeting in a few minutes, so I have to go. Thanks for lunch.

MH No problem, Charlie. Thanks for the chat. See you in another pitlane somewhere!